EU Sovereignty and Direct Taxation of Businesses

EU Sovereignty and Direct Taxation of Businesses

François Barreau

Formerly Institute for Austrian and International Tax Law, Vienna University of Economics and Business, Vienna, Austria

Edward Elgar PUBLISHING

Cheltenham, UK • Northampton, MA, USA

Published by

Edward Elgar Publishing Limited
The Lypiatts
15 Lansdown Road
Cheltenham
Glos GL50 2JA
UK

Edward Elgar Publishing, Inc.
William Pratt House
9 Dewey Court
Northampton
Massachusetts 01060
USA

Authorised representative in the EU for GPSR queries only: Easy Access System Europe – Mustamäe tee 50, 10621 Tallinn, Estonia, gpsr.requests@easproject.com

A catalogue record for this book is available from the British Library

Library of Congress Control Number: 2026934128

This book is available electronically in the **Elgar**online
Law subject collection
https://doi.org/10.4337/9781035383696

MIX
Paper | Supporting responsible forestry
FSC® C014540

ISBN 978 1 0353 8368 9 (cased)
ISBN 978 1 0353 8369 6 (eBook)
ISBN 978 1 0353 8370 2 (ePub)

Printed and bound in the UK by Short Run Press Ltd, Exeter EX2 7LW

Contents

1. Introduction to *EU Sovereignty and Direct Taxation of Businesses*

1.1 ON THE EUROPEAN INTEGRATION PROCESS IN THE FIELD OF DIRECT TAXATION OF BUSINESSES

This book highlights an inconsistency in the European integration process. Since the original creation of the European Union (EU) by the Treaty of Rome,[1] the Member States have constantly kept their taxing powers in the field of direct taxation like if they were exclusive powers. As such, the EU, to this day, does not have any direct taxing power in this field and cannot put in place its own tax policy. The EU does not have a direct competence in the field of direct taxation and can act only under its general and shared competence for the internal market. Also, at the EU level, the attribution of the power to decide on a policy follows the attribution of the competence.[2]

[1] Treaty establishing the European Economic Community [1957] 294 UNTS 3

[2] There are two aspects. The first is that the attribution of competence designates also the attribution of the power to decide of the related tax policy. As such, the non-attribution of a direct competence to the EU lets both remain in the hands of the Member States. The second aspect is the legal consequence of this approach. Technically, unanimity voting in article 115 TFEU blocks any idea of a European tax policy as, even if there is a possibility to legislate at the EU level, the power of decision remains in the hands of the Member States. It is a political choice to attribute such competences and write such dispositions with such requirements, but technical dispositions must be in adequation with their entire legal context and so with the legal system they are meant to apply. This idea of coherence between the entire system and the technical dispositions to make it effective must be kept in mind when the concept of legitimacy as well as the articulation between the concept of shared sovereignty and the attribution of competences between the EU and the Member States are explained. Thus, as a shortcut, as is demonstrated in the book, concerning the field of direct taxation of businesses, the concept of sovereignty must manifest itself through the notion of tax policy and it is under this notion of tax policy (power to decide) that the competences (or powers) can then be exercised

Thus, the consequence of the current repartition of competences between the EU and the Member States in the field of direct taxation is that, due to their having direct competence while the EU only has a general, and so indirect, competence, the Member States kept the power to decide in terms of direct tax policy as a national prerogative. Any legislative instrument of secondary law that is enacted at the EU level in this field is voted unanimously through article 115 of the treaty on the Functioning of the European Union (TFEU),[3] which is a general provision not specific to the direct tax field. Therefore, such legislation remains a tax policy prerogative of the Member States. At the EU level, such prerogative can undermine the EU integration process. Yet, the initial choice of attribution of competences was a political choice. However, the EU is based on objectives,[4] and especially on the objective of achieving the internal market (article 26 TFEU). Even if, politically, it was created with an objective of pacification of Europe,[5] the main original objective written in the Treaty of Rome is the creation of an internal market without borders. Such objective is supposed to be economically achieved especially through the fundamental freedoms (article 26 TFEU).[6]

Hence, on this basis, the Court of Justice of the European Union (CJEU) rendered its first decision in the field of direct taxation at the end of the 1980s.[7] Similarly, the first directives in the same field were enacted at the beginning of the 1990s.[8] CJEU decisions in the field of direct taxation are now extremely numerous while secondary law remains scarce because the Member States protect their competence in this field.[9] Yet, interactions between the EU order and the Member States' orders are logical and unavoidable as the internal

---

3 Consolidated Version of the Treaty on the Functioning of the European Union [2012] OJ C326/47

4 P Pescatore, *Le Droit de l'Intégration* (Bruylant 2005) 41: EU law is dynamic, based on objectives

5 R Schuman, 'Declaration of 9 May 1950' <www.robert-schuman.eu/en/declaration-of-9-may-195> accessed 19 November 2025

6 Article 26(1) TFEU is the objective of achieving the internal market and article 26(2) TFEU enumerates the different fundamental freedoms in relation to it

7 Case 270/83 *Commission v France* [1986] ECR 273

8 See Council Directive 90/435/EEC of 23 July 1990 on the common system of taxation applicable in the case of parent companies and subsidiaries of different Member States [1990] OJ L225/6; Council Directive 90/434/EEC on the common system of taxation applicable to mergers, divisions, transfers of assets and exchanges of shares concerning companies of different Member States [1990] OJ L225/1

9 Member States, as such, protect their tax sovereignty: see A Maitrot de la Motte, *Souveraineté Fiscale et Construction Communautaire: Recherche sur les Impôts Directs* (Bibliothèque de Science Financière, tome 44, LGDJ 2005)

market is integrated within the Member States' orders.[10] However, an inconsistency exists to the detriment of the internal market when the protection of their direct competence by the Member States prevents the EU from achieving its own objectives and so its very reason of existence. Indeed, disparities exist between the Member States in the field of direct taxation, as illustrated by the case law of the CJEU.[11] They are the consequence of the reserved powers and so of the national tax policies of the Member States in this field. Moreover, such attribution of powers (or of competences) creates excessive disparities to the detriment of the internal market, which are known as distortions.[12] Such excessive disparities must be eliminated for the EU to achieve and preserve the internal market. Thus it is mainly through negative integration that the EU has the possibility to do it when it is possible,[13] and so on a case-by-case analysis with an a posteriori approach, through the application of the fundamental freedoms and of the State aid rules by the CJEU.[14] Then, positive integration, through the enactment of directives, could help to prevent such distortions, as there would be an a priori approach.[15] The CJEU would be cleared of many cases on very specific points, which also necessitate recurrent punctual modifications of the Member States' domestic laws when there is an infringement of EU law. However, due to unanimity voting and the reluctance of the Member States, few directives exist in the field of direct taxation to protect or enhance the internal market. Yet, the abundance of the CJEU cases and the existence of several directives prove that there are inherent interactions between the internal market and the field of direct taxation. The two cannot be separated. As such, to solve this issue, it is demonstrated that the EU has the legitimacy to attain taxing powers, coming alongside an adequate power

---

10 Case 6/64 *Costa v ENEL* [1964] ECR 585: the EU is a different order but integrated to the orders of the Member States

11 See eg S Douma, 'The Three Ds of Direct Tax Jurisdiction: Disparity, Discrimination and Double Taxation' (2006) 46 [11] European Taxation 524. Disparities between the Member States are not in the field of EU law because they are not in its attributed competences: it is further explained in pt 3, ch 6

12 See eg Joined Cases C-106/09 P and C-107/09 P *Commission v Gibraltar* [2011] I-11113; S Douma, 'The Three Ds of Direct Tax Jurisdiction: Disparity, Discrimination and Double Taxation' (2006) 46 [11] European Taxation 524: it is further explained in pt 3, ch 6

13 There are harmful disparities that are outside the competence of the EU and the CJEU uses inadequate means to eliminate some of them to protect the internal market: see pt 3, ch 6

14 See pt 3, ch 6

15 Through positive integration, any harmful disparity can be prevented as long as a consensus is reached among the Member States: for more details, see pt 3, ch 7

of decision, in the field of direct taxation, and especially in the field of direct taxation of businesses.

Indeed, there is an inconsistency between the current repartition of competences between the EU and the Member States and the European integration process as expressed by its main objective of achieving the internal market. This inconsistency is the result of the current interactions between the direct competence of the Member States in the field of direct taxation and the EU objective of achieving the internal market. Thus, this inconsistency is the result of the overprotected tax policies of the Member States, in contrast with their involvement towards the internal market by signing the EU treaties,[16] in the field of direct taxation. It is mainly expressed through the legal procedure of unanimity voting written at article 115 TFEU. Moreover, there is a focus on the direct taxation of businesses. As a matter of fact, as the EU is based on objectives, the European integration process follows a step-by-step approach.[17] Considering this, as the economic market was the first internal market to exist in the Treaty of Rome,[18] the same step-by-step approach should be applied to the field of direct taxation, with an initial focus on businesses and not on individuals. Business taxation is inherently connected to the internal market.[19]

Thus, it is demonstrated that the EU has the legitimacy to attain taxing powers in the field of direct taxation of businesses through an analysis based on the concept of sovereignty. In a first step, the concept of sovereignty is explored to determine its intrinsic meaning and inherent criteria. Then, in a second step, such concept is applied to the European context. As such, a theory of shared sovereignty is provided for the EU. Finally, in a third step, the theory of shared sovereignty is applied in the field of direct taxation of businesses. It is demonstrated that the concept of tax sovereignty, often invoked to protect the direct competence of the Member States in the field of direct taxation,[20]

---

16 There is an assumption here that the Member States have an interest to participate in the EU and to have an internal market. Thus, with this book, the objective is not to question the EU's existence but to restore coherence in terms of legitimacy within the internal market, especially in the field of direct taxation of businesses.

17 M Blanquet, *Droit Général de l'Union Européenne* (Sirey 2018) 2: a functionalist approach as envisaged in the Schuman Declaration of 9 May 1950.

18 It is through the treaty of Maastricht in 1992, so after 1958 and the initial Treaty of Rome, that the European Communities became the EU, with a political dimension: see pt 2, ch 4, para 4.2.1.1 on the evolution of the EU and pt 3, ch 7, para 7.2.1.1 on the focus on businesses

19 See pt 3, ch 7, para 7.2.1.1

20 See eg A Maitrot de la Motte, *Souveraineté Fiscale et Construction Communautaire: Recherche sur les Impôts Directs* (Bibliothèque de Science

is a material concept, which does not amount to a concept of sovereignty. It is only the association of two powers – the competence to tax as the power to enact the tax law and the power to tax as the power to levy taxes – which form an autonomy. Thus, the EU has the legitimacy to attain a competence to tax under its general competence for the internal market. With this competence, it also has the legitimacy to get a power to decide in its field of competence. Such power to decide means a power in terms of direct tax policy. Therefore, such power in terms of direct tax policy should be conjointly exercised with the Member States. Then, concerning the power to tax, in the current European institutional framework, the EU does not have the democratic legitimacy to levy tax-based own resources.

Providing for a theory of shared sovereignty must help to strengthen the foundations of the EU integration process seen through the prism of legitimacy. Thus, the application of this theory to the field of direct taxation of businesses is a choice. The choice has been made to analyse the repartition of taxing powers in the field of direct taxation between the EU and the Member States from a theoretical and an institutional point of view. As such, the theory of shared sovereignty of the EU that is proposed can also be applied to fields other than that of direct taxation of businesses. However, here, the initial statement remains the inconsistency between the Member States' orders and the EU order in the field of direct taxation of businesses. Getting into the general theory of EU law has been found to be the most pertinent way to get into the general theory of European tax law as, if the general theory of EU law can be applied to different fields of competence, the general theory of European tax law is rooted in the general theory of EU law. Also, this approach offers the possibility to deepen until the tiniest point of origin of European tax law and so of EU law. As such, the purpose is to be as objective as possible by not relying on too many levels of intermediary conceptualizations that could pull away the conclusion from the reality of the relations between the EU and the Member States.

Finally, it must be highlighted that the wording 'shared sovereignty' might be used in different contexts. However, here, through the proposed definition of sovereignty, it is an independent concept of sovereignty that is proposed. The objective is to explore the deepest meaning of the concept of sovereignty. Thus, the idea of shared sovereignty as the consequence of the repartition of different sovereign competences between the EU and the Member States is rejected here. What is explained is the process of apparition of sovereignty, where competences follow the authority of the sovereign. Going the other way around is not possible. Having a sovereign attribute can be an indication of who

Financière, tome 44, LGDJ 2005)

is the sovereign in the facts, but the use of this attribute cannot define the sovereign in terms of legitimacy. Thus, such relation must be applied to the field of direct taxation of businesses: in terms of legitimacy, the tax policy and so the power to decide depends on sovereignty and not on the use of the competence. As such, when the EU has the legitimacy to be sovereign in a field it should have the competence in relation to it, independently of the technical attribution of the competence, which should have followed the coherent assumption that the sovereign must have the technical means to exercise its sovereignty. However, in the facts, incoherences can exist when it comes to such attribution of competences. Concerning the EU, inconsistency came about over the course of the European integration process. Thus, it is important to highlight that the concept of legitimacy is the point of reference. Legitimacy is the guiding principle of the whole demonstration.

1.2 ON LEGITIMACY AS THE DRIVING PRINCIPLE

Concerning the methodology, it must be emphasized that it is a legal demonstration. Indeed, deepening the analysis into the concept of sovereignty, and so the general theory of the State, as well as into the EU integration process necessitates approaching neighbouring fields that play a role in such topic, such as political philosophy or political science.[21] However, the basis remains the observation of the EU evolution from a legal and so an institutional point of view.[22] It is the European order that is observed in its relations with the Member States' orders.

Thus, the concept of legitimacy, as the driving force of the demonstration, must be explained. Indeed, there are many ways to understand this concept. It can be defined differently depending on the field of competence of an author and depending on its context.[23] For instance, Max Weber identifies three forms of legitimacy: traditional legitimacy, where the power is accepted based on customs and habits; charismatic legitimacy, based on ideas and personal charisma of a leader; and rational or legal legitimacy, based on an institutional

---

21 See O Beaud, *La Puissance de l'Etat* (PUF 1994): here, law does not work alone, and it is necessary to take into account such neighbouring fields

22 As said by Beaud, taking proper account of the facts is the basis for the validity of a theory: O Beaud, *La Puissance de l'Etat* (PUF 1994) 449. Thus, even if legally transposed, the source of the work is an empirical observation of the relations between the EU and the Member States

23 See PG Stillman, 'The Concept of Legitimacy' (1974) 7 [1] Polity 33; JHH Weiler, 'Europe in Crisis – On "Political Messianism", "Legitimacy" and the "Rule of Law"' [2012] Singapore Journal of Legal Studies 248

system with rules and procedures.[24] Weiler must also be mentioned for the different types of legitimacy he proposed for the EU.[25] For him, there are two basic genres and also three kinds of forms of legitimacy. The two basic genres are normative legitimacy and social legitimacy. Normative legitimacy is supposed to be objective even if there might be different ideological views behind it.[26] It is about 'legitimate governance'[27] and its vocabulary is 'moral, ethical, and […] informed by political theory'.[28] On the other side, social legitimacy is empirical.[29] It is subjective and related to social attitudes.[30] It evaluates the 'acceptance of the political regime'.[31] Then, according to Weiler, the three different forms of legitimacy are:

- 'Process (or input) legitimacy', which – in the current circumstance can be, with some simplification – synonymized with democracy. It is easier put in the negative: to the extent that the European mode of governance departs from the habits and practices of 'democracy' as understood in the Member States, its 'legitimacy', in this case both 'normative' and 'social', will be compromised.
- 'Result (or output) legitimacy', which – again simplifying somewhat – would be all modern versions of 'bread' and 'circuses'. As long as the Union delivers the 'goods' – prosperity, stability, security – it will enjoy a 'legitimacy' that derives from a subtle combination of success per se, success in realizing its objectives and contentment with those results. There is no better way to legitimize a war than to win it. This variant of 'legitimacy' is part of the very ethos of the European Commission ("Commission").
- 'Telos legitimacy' or 'political messianism', whereby 'legitimacy' is gained neither by 'process' nor 'output' but by promise – the promise of an attractive "Promised Land".[32]

---

24 See M Bovens and others, 'Institutional Legitimacy in Open Societies' (Institutions for Open Societies – Think Paper Series 2, Utrecht University 2020) 4

25 Weiler wrote extensively on European integration both from a political and from a legal point of view: see JHH Weiler, 'Europe in Crisis – On "Political Messianism", "Legitimacy" and the "Rule of Law"' [2012] Singapore Journal of Legal Studies 248–68

26 JHH Weiler, 'Europe in Crisis – On "Political Messianism", "Legitimacy" and the "Rule of Law"' [2012] Singapore Journal of Legal Studies 248

27 ibid

28 ibid

29 ibid

30 ibid

31 ibid

32 ibid 250

Thus, the different forms of legitimacy as evoked by Weiler are deeply linked with the concept of democracy and of rule of law, so in relation with the idea of democratic deficit of the EU.[33] However, the analysis of the concepts of sovereignty and tax sovereignty must be done through all of their facets and not only from a democratic perspective, even if the democratic aspect remains decisive. Moreover, the process of empirical analysis of the EU must entail all the aspects that can come into play. Yet, the analysis remains a legal analysis of the EU as institution, and it consequently obeys a logic of system.[34] This is why, in order to define legitimacy here, a pure theory of the concept such as the Weberian theory must be used.[35] Therefore, a theory from Stillman is proposed to understand the point of view that is taken here concerning the concept of legitimacy within a legal and political system.[36]

Still, other authors must be mentioned to make the comparison with Stillman's approach. For example, Max Weber writes:

> Submission to an order is almost always determined by a variety of motives [...] So far as it is not derived merely from fear or from motives of expedience, a willingness to submit to an order [...] always in some sense implies a belief in the legitimate authority of the source imposing it.[37]

Other authors think that legitimacy works inversely with violence within a political system.[38] Thus, legitimacy is different from legality and lies in men's ideas.[39] It is through legitimacy that a political order flourishes.[40] Consequently, given the importance of the concept of legitimacy, several authors give their own definitions of the term. Friedrich defines it with human feelings as a basis: 'whether a given rulership is believed to be based on good title by most men subject to it.'[41] Then, for Polin, legitimacy of rulership can only be total when it

---

33 ibid 251–55

34 How the EU responds to this logic of system is seen throughout this work

35 Indeed, with the concept of sovereignty, in addition to its legal side, aspects of political philosophy and political science must not be neglected. Consequently, a philosophical definition of the term can be used indifferently in each domain contrarily to a definition already tainted with one of them

36 PG Stillman, 'The Concept of Legitimacy' (1974) 7 [1] Polity 32–56

37 M Weber, *The Theory of Social and Economic Organization* (T. Parsons ed., 1964) 132

38 TR Gurr, *Why Men Rebel* (Routledge 1970) 185

39 PG Stillman, 'The Concept of Legitimacy' (1974) 7 [1] Polity 33–34

40 ibid 32–56

41 CJ Friedrich, *Man and His Government: An Empirical Theory of Politics* (New York: Mc Graw-Hill 1963) 234

is viewed as being so by other governments[42] and, for Burke, legitimacy comes with time through tradition or prescription: 'prescription is the most solid of all titles.'[43] Also, for Kelsen as a legal positivist, legitimacy only means validity for a system of laws.[44] Finally, Stillman proposes this definition: 'a government is legitimate if and only if the results of governmental output are compatible with the value pattern of the society.'[45] For him, the 'value pattern of the society' is 'the generalized criteria of desirability, the standards for evaluation, the normative priorities, for the society'.[46] In other words, it is, according to a given society, the objectives defined by the context of such society. Stillman gives the example of Athens, which esteemed the 'arts of war' but less so than 'the fine arts'.[47] In addition, the 'value pattern' does not have to be conscious; it is the 'character of the society'.[48] Then, 'governmental output' must be taken in a broad sense.[49] It includes the promulgation of laws as well as any action that has an effect on the society.[50] Only the result, and not the intention, must be taken into account.[51] For instance, Stillman explains that 'surely Lyndon Johnson did not wish what transpired in Vietnam',[52] but that only the result is 'central to legitimacy'.[53] Thus, 'the results of governmental output must be "compatible with" the value pattern of society'.[54] This compatibility must ensure the 'maintenance and continuation of the society, by preventing value schizophrenia, value contradictions, and self-destruction'.[55] Furthermore, the coherence must be preserved at all levels of the society, including minorities and individuals but also the international system.[56] Also, for Stillman, with such definition there is objectivity, as legitimacy does not rely on the feelings

---

42 R Polin, 'Analyse Philosophique de l'Idée de Légitimité' in P. Bastid and others (eds.), *L'Idée de Légitimité* (PUF 1967) 22 and 28

43 As quoted in CJ Friedrich, *Man and His Government: An Empirical Theory of Politics* (New York: Mc Graw-Hill 1963) 235 footnote 5

44 H Kelsen, *General Theory of Law and State* (Cambridge, Massachusetts: Harvard University Press 1949) 115–22

45 PG Stillman, 'The Concept of Legitimacy' (1974) 7 [1] Polity 39

46 ibid 40

47 ibid

48 ibid

49 ibid

50 ibid

51 ibid 41

52 ibid

53 ibid

54 ibid

55 ibid

56 ibid

of the people; each system is specific with its own 'value pattern'.[57] As such, legitimacy 'varies along a continuum'[58] and even a revolution can have its own legitimacy.[59] The latter would be a revolution that 'overthrows a government whose future output results have a high probability of being illegitimate'[60] while the next government is supposed to be a better government.[61] In the same vein, legitimacy could not exist when the value pattern of the society is too chaotic.[62] This could be the result of overly strong oppositions between different portions of the society or because of a chaotic system in itself.[63]

Hence, Stillman's definition of the concept of legitimacy is the inherent reason why such definition must be used as the driving principle. Other definitions from political philosophy are not sufficient in themselves to explain the self-construction of the system, knowing that the EU is based on objectives and engaged in a permanent process towards their achievement. Similarly, Kelsen's positivist view defines a system once it has already been defined, without taking its context and its origin into account.[64] Such view could not include the concept of sovereignty as a founding concept with origins rooted in law as well as in political philosophy. Stillman's definition of legitimacy asks for compatibility between a system as defined through its value pattern and the actions of this system through governmental outputs such as the enactment of law. Here, it corresponds to the consistency between the EU as legal system and its actions or potential of action in the field of direct taxation of businesses. Thus, as an inconsistency has been observed, the issue to solve is whether the EU must act as a legal system in the field of direct taxation of businesses and, logically following, whether it has the adequate means to do it. Consequently, the EU is analysed as a legal system through the concept of sovereignty in order to define its value pattern, especially through the objective of achieving the internal market. Then, once inconsistencies have been identified, it is demonstrated that the EU must get the adequate means in order to restore its legitimacy in terms of governmental outputs. Consequently, it is demonstrated that the EU must get the adequate taxing powers, according to its value pattern, to solve inconsistencies and so a lack of coherence between the objective of having an internal market and the concrete realization of such internal market from the perspective of the field of direct taxation of businesses. The objective is to pro-

57 ibid 42
58 ibid 43
59 ibid 44
60 ibid
61 ibid
62 ibid 43
63 ibid
64 See pt 1, ch 3, para 3.2.1.1

vide for coherence in the relations between the European level and the Member State level in the field of direct taxation of businesses within the system that encompasses both levels for the sustainability and so the competitivity of the internal market, the latter being a concern for both levels.

1.3 STRUCTURE

There are three parts to this book. In Part I, Chapter 2 determines the inherent criteria of the concept of sovereignty and Chapter 3 gives the definition and the methodology of the concept. In Part II, Chapter 4 demonstrates the political sovereignty of the EU and Chapter 5, taking into account also the concept of democratic sovereignty, explains the theory of shared sovereignty whereby the EU and the Member States constitute one unique sovereign system. In Part III, Chapter 6 looks at the concept of tax sovereignty alongside the concept of sovereignty and explains that, in terms of legitimacy, the EU does not have the adequate means to achieve its sovereign objectives in the field of direct taxation. Chapter 7 applies the theory of shared sovereignty to the current state of play in the field of direct taxation of businesses in the relations between the EU and the Member States. Leads to restore coherence between the two levels are proposed.

PART I

About the Concept of Sovereignty

2. The origins of the concept of sovereignty

2.1 INTRODUCTION

There can be different conceptions of the concept of sovereignty. Thus, it is necessary to frame the main criteria that persist in the different conceptions. It is these criteria that must determine what sovereignty means and who can be sovereign in the modern world.

To initiate the debate, a first distinction must be made between conception and concept. As said by Prokhovnik, 'sovereignty is a robust concept with many conceptualizations'.[1] She means that history and sovereignty are both involved in the different theorizations of the concept of sovereignty.[2] Through history, many different theories of sovereignty with a small 't' have been elaborated. It is not an evolution of one concept but always different conceptions of the same one. However, some criteria come back regularly in the theories of the different authors. Even if it is a subjective domain,[3] through all these subjective opinions it is possible to approach a Theory of sovereignty with a big 'T', which is the concept of sovereignty. Through the history of the concept of sovereignty, among its different conceptions can be found sufficiently distinct and ultimate criteria in order to define the content of the concept of sovereignty.

The method applied to the concept of sovereignty can be compared to some of the main scientific methods as theorized in the philosophy of science. In a first step, it seems hardly possible to be objective when trying to define the concept of sovereignty; there is always an element of subjectivity depending on the origin and the context of the author. Therefore, instead of trying to objectivize

[1] R Prokhovnik, *Sovereignty: History and Theory* (Imprint Academy 2008) 1

[2] ibid

[3] D Baranger, 'The Apparition of Sovereignty' in H Kalmo and Q Skinner (eds), *Sovereignty in Fragments – The Past, Present and Future of a Contested Concept* (Cambridge University Press 2010) 53

subjectivity, it is aimed at defining a 'situated knowledge'[4] as conceptualized by Haraway in 1988.[5] She proposes this idea of situated knowledge against the dominant conception of scientific objectivity and its opposite conception, which is relativity.[6] Scientific objectivity means that the scientist can see everything and relativism that all theories (understood as opinions) are equivalent.[7] With a situated knowledge, the position of the author can be questioned and, by defining the concept, there is a better chance to reach real objectivity, or at least to come closer to it.[8] Also, against relativism, some positions are closer than others to objectivity.[9] Thus, to define a better position, the scientific method of 'experimentum crucis'[10] (crossed experimentation) is appropriate. Initially conceptualized by Francis Bacon in his 'Novum Organum'[11] as an 'instantia crucis'[12] (present being crossed), crossed experimentation is experimentation that allows the determination of whether one hypothesis or a theory is more accurate than other theories accepted by the scientific community.[13] In such a way, trying to remain as close as possible of objectivity, the most sound and coherent criteria of the concept of sovereignty have been found.

Then, a second distinction must be made between political sovereignty and legal sovereignty. Once again, according to Prokhovnik, legal sovereignty is the legal supremacy and the law-making power, and political sovereignty is the legitimate power to rule on the other.[14] The distinction can be confused depending on the different conceptions of different authors through history. For instance, authors such as Bodin or Hobbes propose conceptions of a legal sovereignty, which is then confused with political sovereignty. On the other side, with Rousseau, both are strictly delimited but it is more complex to define who is the true political sovereign (the people or the ruler). Here, it is criteria

---

4 D Haraway, 'Situated Knowledges: The Science Question in Feminism and the Privilege of Partial Perspective' (1988) 14 [3] Feminist Studies 575–99

5 ibid

6 ibid

7 ibid

8 ibid

9 ibid

10 Expression created by Robert Hooke, and used notably by Isaac Newton: JA Lohne, 'Experimentum Crucis' (1968) 23 [2] Notes and Records of the Royal Society of London 169–99

11 F Bacon, *Novum Organum Scientiarum* (1620)

12 ibid

13 JA Lohne, 'Experimentum Crucis' (1968) 23 [2] Notes and Records of the Royal Society of London 169-199

14 R Prokhovnik, *Sovereignty: History and Theory* (Imprint Academy 2008) 3

of political sovereignty (the real and definitive sovereign) that must be found and given.

Therefore, analyses are provided of the first theorist of sovereignty (Bodin) and of the situation before him and then of the main authors who developed different conceptions of the concept after him, in the State and the Federation. It is demonstrated that there can be political variations between the different authors, but these fit around common features and persistent criteria.

2.2 BODIN AND 'THE SIX BOOKS OF THE REPUBLIC': THEORIZING SOVEREIGNTY

2.2.1 Sovereignty before Bodin

2.2.1.1 The Ancients

Jean Bodin was one of the first scholars to theorize a conception of sovereignty. In 'The Six Books of the Republic'[15] he analyses ancient conceptions of the State using the concept of sovereignty.[16] However, without having been extracted from its political context, this concept found its first expression and so its first criteria long before Bodin.

Plato is the first thinker to be mentioned. His theories evolved throughout his life. There are two important steps in his dialogues on the concept of sovereignty. The first one is the philosopher-king.[17] The political power must be exercised by the experts who know the good.[18] Only true philosophers can have the political knowledge.[19] They should rule over the citizens. This dominant idea[20] that the authority should lie in the hands of the philosopher can be found in his central work, *The Republic*,[21] among others.[22] With Plato, moral perfection is always the objective.[23] Even the organization of the city must have the ultimate good as objective[24] and it can be obtained only by being

---

[15] J Bodin, *Les Six Livres de la Républiqu*e (1576)

[16] ibid

[17] Z Hitz, 'Plato on the Sovereignty of Law' in RK Balot (ed), *A Companion to Greek and Roman Political Thought* (Blackwell Publishing 2009) 367

[18] ibid

[19] ibid 368

[20] ibid 367

[21] Plato, *The Republic* (around 375 BC)

[22] Z Hitz, 'Plato on the Sovereignty of Law' in RK Balot (ed), *A Companion to Greek and Roman Political Thought* (Blackwell Publishing 2009) 367

[23] ibid

[24] ibid

virtuous. However, in subsequent dialogues, such as *The Statesman*,[25] and also in his final work, *The Laws*,[26] Plato tries to define and find a practical application of his conception. His criticism of democracy in *The Republic* seems to be essentially philosophical and without any practical application. In *The Statesman* he begins to define political power and how it is different from the arts of rhetoric or judging.[27] The true statesman knows what to use and when to use it in order to produce virtue in the city.[28] This perfect knowledge is described by Plato through the age of Cronus,[29] a mythic past when gods governed humans.[30] However, when human beings are in charge of the city, this political ideal seems almost impossible to reach, even for Plato.[31] This is why he proposes an alternative in order to come as close as possible to this ideal: the sovereignty of the law.[32]

In *The Statesman*, regimes are desirable when the king rules according to the laws (even if they are still the second-best form of organization behind the philosopher-king/expert ruler).[33] A lawful regime is a regime where the law has the ultimate authority.[34] Thus, there is a distinction between a lawless regime and a lawful regime. Both regimes have laws and a sovereign. However, in a lawless regime, the ruler does not change the law for the ultimate good but for private interests.[35] It is a tyrant who is the sovereign. In a lawful regime, the ruler seeks the ultimate good through the political knowledge and changes the laws accordingly.[36] To rule according to the law is a rule of reason

---

25 Plato, *The Statesman* (around 360 BC)

26 Plato, *The Laws* (around 356 BC)

27 See eg Z Hitz, 'Plato on the Sovereignty of Law' in RK Balot (ed), *A Companion to Greek and Roman Political Thought* (Blackwell Publishing 2009)

28 ibid 368

29 Plato, *The Statesman* 275c; Plato, *The Laws* 713e

30 Z Hitz, 'Plato on the Sovereignty of Law' in RK Balot (ed), *A Companion to Greek and Roman Political Thought* (Blackwell Publishing 2009) 369

31 Plato, *The Statesman* 292e1–2; Z Hitz, 'Plato on the Sovereignty of Law' in RK Balot (ed), *A Companion to Greek and Roman Political Thought* (Blackwell Publishing 2009) 369

32 See eg Z Hitz, 'Plato on the Sovereignty of Law' in RK Balot (ed), *A Companion to Greek and Roman Political Thought* (Blackwell Publishing 2009)

33 See M Peixoto, 'On the Limits of Law and the Sovereignty of the Wise. Conjectures about the Primacy of Law in Plato's Statesman' in BB Lopez and TM Robinson (eds), *Plato's Statesman Revisited* (De Gruyter 2019) 260

34 ibid 262

35 C Horn, 'What Makes a Law Good? Plato on Legal Theory in the Statesman' (2021) [Special Issue] Filosofický časopis 89

36 M Peixoto, 'On the Limits of Law and the Sovereignty of the Wise. Conjectures about the Primacy of Law in Plato's Statesman' in BB Lopez and TM

where the virtue is the central preoccupation of the city.[37] The main distinction is that, in a lawless regime, the ruler is sovereign because it does not obey the law (which is made for the ultimate good).[38] It has the ultimate authority. In a lawful regime, the ruler is restricted by the law and obeys it because it contains the rules dictated by political knowledge.[39] The law has the ultimate authority and is sovereign.[40] It is only when it is appropriate, due to the political knowledge, that the ruler may adapt some laws, in accordance with the law itself.

Aristotle also considered the welfare of the people but he took a more practical approach. He did not give a theory of the State as, at that time, philosophers did not distinguish between the government and the State. However, he gave a first theory of democracy, which embodied his conception of sovereignty. This conception can be found in his *Politics*, especially at Book 3, chapter 11.[41]

For Aristotle, there is also a sovereignty of the law.[42] However, he questions its origin and who makes it.[43] This also questions who has the power. The person who can make the law is the person who has the power and the control. In oligarchies and monarchies, the office-holders have the control and the power,[44] and they can make the law in an unaccountable way. In Aristotle's democracy, these office-holders are controlled by the majority[45] and the law is ultimately the expression of the will of the people.[46] In the fifth century BC, not everyone was eligible to be elected to the role of magistrate.[47] The ancient conception of democracy is different from the modern one. There was a strong hierarchy and only some elites were able to be in charge of the

---

Robinson (eds), *Plato's Statesman Revisited* (De Gruyter 2019) 262

37 ibid

38 C Horn, 'What Makes a Law Good? Plato on Legal Theory in the Statesman' (2021) [Special Issue] Filosofický časopis 100

39 M Peixoto, 'On the Limits of Law and the Sovereignty of the Wise. Conjectures about the Primacy of Law in Plato's Statesman' in BB Lopez and TM Robinson (eds), *Plato's Statesman Revisited* (De Gruyter 2019) 262

40 See Z Hitz, 'Plato on the Sovereignty of Law' in RK Balot (ed), *A Companion to Greek and Roman Political Thought* (Blackwell Publishing 2009)

41 Aristotle, *The Politics* (4th century BC)

42 M Lane, 'Popular Sovereignty as Control of Office-Holders: Aristotle on Greek Democracy' in R Bourke and Q Skinner (eds), *Popular Sovereignty in Historical Perspective* (Cambridge University Press 2016) 53

43 ibid

44 ibid 54

45 Aristotle, *The Politics*, 1281b23–4

46 M Lane, 'Popular Sovereignty as Control of Office-Holders: Aristotle on Greek Democracy' in R Bourke and Q Skinner (eds), *Popular Sovereignty in Historical Perspective* (Cambridge University Press 2016) 67

47 ibid 58

city.[48] Nevertheless, the majority had the power to elect the magistrates and it had control over them.[49] Aristotle employs the Greek word *kurios*[50] which involves the notion of mastery or control[51] and which, as a noun, means 'lord' or 'master'.[52] Bodin recognizes that this was an expression of the concept of sovereignty even if he thinks that Aristotle failed to give a full definition of the term.[53]

Hence, for Aristotle, the constitution is the expression of the will of the person holding the *kurios*.[54] This might be the office-holders but, in his time in Athens, it was the majority of the people.[55] Aristotle gave an initial conception of democracy and the early stages in order to determine the criteria of the concept of sovereignty.

Plato concedes that, in fact, the sovereign is the ultimate authority. Aristotle recognizes that sovereignty belongs to the ultimate and so supreme authority but, in addition, emphasizes that the concept of sovereignty is a concept of control or power, in a less idealistic reflection.

Finally, Cicero must be mentioned for his political theory. He did not bring new philosophical conceptions, as Plato and Aristotle did, but, by essentially compiling older thoughts,[56] he defined the Roman organization in order to lay the first stones of a political theory for the State. In Cicero's democracy,[57] the people also initially have sovereignty. The State is the constitution of the whole people[58] and individuals are socially bound by nature.[59] In order to follow the

---

48 ibid 57

49 ibid 60

50 ibid 55

51 ibid

52 ibid

53 ibid 68

54 ibid 71

55 ibid 60

56 F Celik and K Sahin, 'Determining the Sovereignty on the Ground of State-Citizen Relations in Cicero and Bodin's Works' (2014) 2 [3&4] Review of History and Political Science 46; see also V Arena, 'Popular Sovereignty in the Late Roman Republic: Cicero and the Will of the People' in R Bourke and Q Skinner (eds), *Popular Sovereignty in Historical Perspective* (Cambridge University Press 2016) 73

57 V Arena, 'Popular Sovereignty in the Late Roman Republic: Cicero and the Will of the People' in R Bourke and Q Skinner (eds), *Popular Sovereignty in Historical Perspective* (Cambridge University Press 2016) 73

58 ibid 74

59 F Celik, K Sahin, 'Determining the Sovereignty on the Ground of State-Citizen Relations in Cicero and Bodin's Works' (2014) 2 [3&4] Review of History and Political Science 47

common good, the citizens live for the State.[60] This is part of the Stoician vision of Cicero.[61] The citizen has more duties towards the State than the State has responsibilities towards the citizen (there is a prioritization of the duties of the citizen).[62] Thus, the latter must be virtuous and there is a formal delegation of sovereignty from the people to the authority, which is needed in order to maintain the prosperity of the State. This authority can be the magistrates[63] in the senate, as in *De Re Publica*,[64] or the *optimates*[65] (a political tendency of that time that would favour the aristocracy by opposition to the people) as in *De Legibus*.[66] In the first case, the citizens entrust the senators, and in the second case, there is a quasi-alienation of the powers of the people.[67] It seems that, in practice, the difference might not be that important as, for Cicero and his Stoician philosophy, the most important point is that the people need an exterior power in order to bring them justice.[68] This is where the State has a role to play and why, logically, because it brings them freedom and equality, the citizens have important duties towards the State. Nevertheless, it must be remembered that, even if the people need an authority commanding them, the foundation is still a popular sovereignty. Cicero's Republic is a mixed regime where the people have free will. This will, because of the transcendental purpose that is the Stoician common good, is alienated to the authority, which is necessary to govern the people.[69]

As such, what is important to take from Cicero's conception is that he made Rome a legal organization with a State and a government. The people had the *jus imperium* (understood as the original power to command) while the Roman

---

60 ibid 49

61 ibid 48

62 ibid 49

63 V Arena, 'Popular Sovereignty in the Late Roman Republic: Cicero and the Will of the People' in R Bourke and Q Skinner (eds), *Popular Sovereignty in Historical Perspective* (Cambridge University Press 2016) 84

64 Cicero, *De Re Publica* (54 BC)

65 V Arena, 'Popular Sovereignty in the Late Roman Republic: Cicero and the Will of the People' in R Bourke and Q Skinner (eds), *Popular Sovereignty in Historical Perspective* (Cambridge University Press 2016) 87

66 Cicero, *De Legibus* (52 BC)

67 V Arena, 'Popular Sovereignty in the Late Roman Republic: Cicero and the Will of the People' in R Bourke and Q Skinner (eds), *Popular Sovereignty in Historical Perspective* (Cambridge University Press 2016) 83

68 F Celik and K Sahin, 'Determining the Sovereignty on the Ground of State-Citizen Relations in Cicero and Bodin's Works' (2014) 2 [3&4] Review of History and Political Science 48

69 ibid 49

government had the *summa potestas* (understood as the sum of powers and so the competence to effectively govern and so exercise the powers).

2.2.1.2 Marsilius, the Church and sovereignty

Marsilius of Padua lived during the decades between 1280 and 1350. During this period, at the beginning of the 14th century, there was a conflict between Louis the Bavarian and Pope John XXII.[70] Louis the Bavarian, emperor of the Holy Roman Germanic Empire, did not recognize the Pope's powers over him.[71] According to him, his powers came directly from God and all the Pope had to do was to crown him.[72] The Pope excommunicated the Emperor because he did not recognize his higher authority.

Marsilius took the side of the Emperor and developed his own conception of popular sovereignty.[73] His anti-papal arguments are made in his *Defensor Pacis*.[74] For him, the government and the State exist in order to render possible a higher life.[75] His ideas are based on the 'human law-giver'.[76] Ultimately, it is the people who are the human law-giver.[77] They have the ultimate authority to make the law, and all right and all power come from it.[78] The whole people knows its needs and must choose itself a ruler.[79] Then, after the election, the people delegates the power to the ruler, who must govern in accordance with the objective of a higher life. For Marsilius, the best regime is an elective monarchy.[80] However, his conception could work also in a hereditary monarchy

70 S Ferente, 'Popolo and Law: Late Medieval Sovereignty in Marsilius and the Jurists' in R Bourke and Q Skinner (eds), *Popular Sovereignty in Historical Perspective* (Cambridge University Press 2016) 106

71 ibid

72 ibid

73 ibid

74 Marsilius of Padua, *Defensor Pacis* (1324)

75 See eg Marsilius of Padua, *Defensor Pacis* (1324) Discourse I, ch IV; S Ferente, 'Popolo and Law: Late Medieval Sovereignty in Marsilius and the Jurists' in R Bourke and Q Skinner (eds), *Popular Sovereignty in Historical Perspective* (Cambridge University Press 2016) 106

76 S Ferente, 'Popolo and Law: Late Medieval Sovereignty in Marsilius and the Jurists' in R Bourke and Q Skinner (eds), *Popular Sovereignty in Historical Perspective* (Cambridge University Press 2016) 99

77 Marsilius of Padua, *Defensor Pacis* (1324) Discourse I, ch XII.3

78 S Ferente, 'Popolo and Law: Late Medieval Sovereignty in Marsilius and the Jurists' in R Bourke and Q Skinner (eds), *Popular Sovereignty in Historical Perspective* (Cambridge University Press 2016) 99

79 ibid 98

80 ibid

or an aristocracy, for example,[81] and many Italian cities were based on this imaginary model at that time.[82]

This model can be considered imaginary because the 'whole people' was not the real people but a part of the people.[83] This part was constituted by the citizens and could even be constituted of only some great electors (aristocracy).[84] Moreover, Marsilius developed a defence of the Emperor but it does not seem that he wanted to theorize the empire. In later books (*Defensor Minor*,[85] *De Translatione Imperii*[86]) he wrote on the relation between the empire and the cities, but it seems that his first objective was a radical condemnation of the Pope's position. For him, the Pope's claims were the main reason for worldly discord.[87] The spiritual power of the clergy should be restricted to religious instruction[88] and he subjected this power to the authority of the Emperor.[89] The Emperor, the successor of Constantine, has a temporal and a spiritual power.[90] The issue was that the Pope could not accept the higher authority of the Emperor of the Holy Roman Germanic Empire.

The advance represented by Marsilius's thought lies in the fact that he distinctly formulated the idea that sovereignty is the supreme authority of the people residing in the people itself and that the ruler is a delegate of the community as well as subject to its supremacy. However, at that time it was still an imaginary conception, and Marsilius is considered as a precursor for the

---

81 S Ferente, 'Popolo and Law: Late Medieval Sovereignty in Marsilius and the Jurists' in R Bourke and Q Skinner (eds), *Popular Sovereignty in Historical Perspective* (Cambridge University Press 2016) 98

82 ibid 99

83 ibid 100

84 ibid

85 Marsilius of Padua, *Defensor Minor* (1342)

86 Marsilius of Padua, *Tractatus de Translatione Imperii* (supposedly 1342)

87 See eg S Ferente, 'Popolo and Law: Late Medieval Sovereignty in Marsilius and the Jurists' in R Bourke and Q Skinner (eds), *Popular Sovereignty in Historical Perspective* (Cambridge University Press 2016) 106: Pope John XXII considered as 'heretical and guilty of *crimen laesae maiestatis*' (crime of lèse-majesté)

88 See eg Marsilius of Padua, *Defensor Pacis* (1324) Discourse I, ch VI; S Ferente, 'Popolo and Law: Late Medieval Sovereignty in Marsilius and the Jurists' in R Bourke and Q Skinner (eds), *Popular Sovereignty in Historical Perspective* (Cambridge University Press 2016) 98

89 S Ferente, 'Popolo and Law: Late Medieval Sovereignty in Marsilius and the Jurists' in R Bourke and Q Skinner (eds), *Popular Sovereignty in Historical Perspective* (Cambridge University Press 2016) 106

90 ibid

theories of Rousseau, Locke and even Bodin,[91] even if his approach was not based on reality and not a conceptualization of the State in itself.

Thus, as a conclusion on the Ancients, Plato, Aristotle, Cicero and Marsilius showed that the concept of sovereignty existed before Bodin. They all presented their own conceptions of the best organization of the society. However, this organization always had a virtuous or spiritual objective. The recognition of the necessity of a supreme authority was a means to serve a moral goal. With Bodin, natural law still had a crucial role to play. Nevertheless, he considered all the different kinds of government he could know and he compared them. Then, he gave his own definition of the concept of sovereignty and he isolated its inherent criteria that still persist in modern theories. In doing so, he wrote a political theory of the State and compiled the preceding ideas. His work is the basis for all modern theories of sovereignty.

2.2.2 Sovereignty for Bodin

2.2.2.1 The sovereign

Jean Bodin was born in 1529 or 1530 and died in 1596. His most famous work is *The Six Books of the Republic*, published in 1576.[92] With this book he was one of the first theorists to give a comprehensive view of the concept of sovereignty.[93] He analysed many political systems and many writings from Antiquity to his day and, through comparison, proposed his own definition of the concept of sovereignty. This definition is characterized by criteria which persisted through time as the inherent criteria of the concept of sovereignty above his own conception of such concept. Indeed, Bodin, when theorizing the concept, had the objective to strengthen the power of the king in a feudal system. During the Middle Ages, under the king, there were many different political and religious powers that the king had to deal with and still respect.[94] However, while Bodin is consequently now famously known as the theorist of the absolute monarchy, this view is not exactly true as even the king's sover-

---

91 ibid

92 J Bodin, *Les Six Livres de la République* (1576)

93 M Lane, 'Popular Sovereignty as Control of Office-Holders: Aristotle on Greek Democracy' in R Bourke and Q Skinner (eds), *Popular Sovereignty in Historical Perspective* (Cambridge University Press 2016) 53

94 See eg V Hugo, *Notre-Dame de Paris* (1831) Book X ch IV and Book X ch V: even if only an historical novel, it is an accurate description of the maze that was the feudal system in the Middle Ages. Even in Paris, the residence of the king, the latter had to respect the local authorities which could be religious, civil or military. Some of these authorities were only limited to two streets and each of them had power on the citizen.

eignty remains limited in his theory. Also, even if monarchy is the best system for him, it is not the only possible system in his theory.

Therefore, as a first step, it must be emphasized that sovereignty is considered necessary by Bodin. In chapter II of Book I on the family,[95] he makes a comparison between the household and sovereignty.[96] Using the metaphor of the ship of Theseus, he explains that it is the union of the people under the sovereignty of a lordship that makes the city.[97] Thus, the ship can continuously be repaired but when one of its essential elements (such as the bow or the keel) is missing, it is not a ship any more.[98] It is the same with sovereignty.[99] Without it, there is no more Republic and the people is scattered.[100] The unity of the household with its head is reproduced in public life by the Republic (the State) and this unity is reached through sovereignty.[101] From this first insight on Bodin's thoughts, it can be understood that sovereignty cannot be divided because it personalizes the necessary unity for the State to exist. As such, it is the authority (meaning sovereignty) that will lead the legal system as a body politic to its existence.

That being said, the main chapter on sovereignty is chapter VIII of Book I. As the Republic is 'the rightful government of several households with sovereign power',[102] it is necessary to define what this power is. 'Sovereignty is the absolute and perpetual power of a Republic':[103] this is how the chapter begins. As such, this power is perpetual. It is the distinction between the sovereign power and the delegated power. Somebody who has a limited power in time is not the sovereign but got the power by delegation.[104] On this, there is no distinction between a general and a corporal. This is the origin of the distinction between the sovereign State and the government. The only limitation to the criterion of the perpetual aspect of sovereignty is revolution, when the whole political organization changes.[105] Then, likewise, as sovereignty cannot be limited in time, its power is unlimited.[106] There is nothing greater except

---

95 J Bodin, *Les Six Livres de la République* (1576) Book I ch II
96 ibid
97 ibid
98 ibid
99 ibid
100 ibid
101 ibid
102 J Bodin, *Les Six Livres de la République* (1576) Book I ch VIII
103 ibid
104 ibid
105 On this aspect, see Pt 1, ch 3. It is argued that only the political shape can change but that the concept of sovereignty is persistent
106 J Bodin, *Les Six Livres de la République* (1576) Book I ch VIII

for God.[107] The sovereign is not accountable to anybody except God[108] and cannot be subject to anything except the law of God.[109] If it was, it would only have a delegated power and it would not hold the sovereign power.[110] In this regard, the sovereign power can only be absolute and, consequently, it cannot be bound by any law from its predecessor or even from itself.[111] If the sovereign was bound by a law, even from itself, it would not be sovereign anymore. This is the supremacy of sovereignty. The sovereign authority must be supreme or is not sovereign. However, absolute power as defined by Bodin is not a tyrannical power in a platonic sense. There are limits that are symbolized by the law of God and natural law. The sovereign power, so the king for Bodin in his time (depending on the kind of political organization, it could be the people, the constitution, and so on), must respect natural law and rule fairly according to God.[112] In this respect, there are limits to absolute sovereignty and the king could have to nonetheless respect some laws of his predecessors if they are made in accordance with natural law.[113] Consequently, sovereignty for Bodin is a supreme, absolute and perpetual authority that embodies the unity of the body politic, but this organization of the body politic through sovereignty still respects the natural order, which is a higher order and which is personalized/symbolized by God.

Finally, after giving his own definition of sovereignty by observing and analysing political systems and modes of government worldwide, Bodin defines the modes of organization that are possible according to sovereignty and offers his preference.[114] Only three kinds of republics are possible: monarchy, aristocracy and democracy.[115] Monarchy is when only one person has sovereignty, aristocracy when a smaller part of the people has it and democracy when the full people or most of the people as one body has it.[116] Only these three kinds of republics have legitimacy but they cannot be mixed because the mode of presentation of the sovereignty is different in each of them.[117] Sovereignty is unity and cannot be mixed. This is why Bodin is famously known as the theorist of the absolute monarchy because, in Book VI chapter IV, he explains that

---

107 ibid
108 ibid
109 ibid
110 ibid
111 ibid
112 ibid
113 ibid
114 J Bodin, *Les Six Livres de la République* (1576) Book II ch I
115 ibid
116 ibid
117 ibid

the best mode of organization is monarchy. Democracy is the most laudable kind of republic, where the public good is shared and where there is equality, but this mode of organization could never be preserved and never worked in practice.[118] Similarly, monarchy is considered better than aristocracy because there is only one sovereign and not several people considered as one.[119] Thus, Bodin sometimes creates a confusion between formal sovereignty and material sovereignty[120] because he does not believe in one sovereign being conceptually united, which would be the people or the aristocrats. He prefers the sovereignty of one real person because it will command alone over a multitude, which is most able to take bad decisions: 'in aristocratic and popular States the soundest part is vanquished by the biggest part: and in a monarchy the opposite.'[121]

As a conclusion, Bodin defined what sovereignty is through what can be considered its inherent criteria: being a supreme, perpetual and absolute authority. This personalizes the unity of the republic/the State. Moreover, he made the important distinction between the government and the true sovereign through the idea of delegation of powers. However, the distinction between formal sovereignty and material sovereignty is blurred in his theory. This must be enlightened through the notion of marks of sovereignty.

2.2.2.2 The law: act of sovereignty

For Bodin, the power to make the law is the main mark of sovereignty.[122] To this main mark, he adds:

- the power to make war and peace;
- the power to put in place the main office-holders;
- the power to judge in last resort; and
- the power to condemn to death or pardon a convict.[123]

If somebody tries to usurp one of the marks, he is worthy of death.[124]

The marks of sovereignty can be considered as the powers that are inherent to sovereignty. They are not the criteria in order to define the concept but, when sovereignty must manifest itself, it does it through its own powers (or,

118 J Bodin, *Les Six Livres de la République* (1576) Book VI ch IV

119 J Bodin, *Les Six Livres de la République* (1576) Book VI ch IV

120 About the concept of material sovereignty, see the next paragraph, and for its application in tax law, see Pt 3, ch 6, para 6.1

121 J Bodin, *Les Six Livres de la République* (1576) Book VI ch IV

122 J Bodin, *Les Six Livres de la République* (1576) Book I ch X

123 ibid

124 ibid

more rightly, competences) which are the marks of sovereignty. These marks are the materialization of the concept of sovereignty in the visible/real world. Their accumulation is what corresponds to the material sovereignty.[125] While formal sovereignty is the concept of sovereignty in itself, material sovereignty is the total of the powers/marks that are inherent to the concept. Thus, there is an important distinction because even if the idea of the marks is that they belong only to the sovereign, they are not the sovereign in itself. On this particular point, Bodin sometimes creates confusion.[126] The marks cannot be separated from the Prince. Bodin justifies the indivisibility of sovereignty through this affirmation but the marks are still different from the Prince and there is still an important distinction. In the end, only the sovereign in itself is supreme (ultimate authority) and not the marks, because they need the sovereign to use them. Consequently, the sovereign is above the marks and they do not correspond to the concept of sovereignty. The marks, even if inherently bound to the sovereign, are just the manifestation of the concept and not the concept in itself. The expression 'material sovereignty' is used here in order to define this particularity.

Finally, Bodin says himself that all the marks of sovereignty can be resumed in the ultimate mark of making the law.[127] All the other marks are the consequence of this first one. They manifest themselves through the law. Indeed, sovereignty institutes the State and once there is a political organization to create the civil society, the law is the means of expression of the authority within the legal sphere. The law is the materialization of the legal order as a concept.

Thus, through Bodin, it is demonstrated that there are intrinsic criteria of a concept of sovereignty. The latter can be conceptualized differently according to the possibilities permitted by the different political organizations that are possible within the general definitions of the monarchy, the democracy and the aristocracy.

125 See Pt 1, ch 3, para 3.2.2 and Pt 3, ch 6, para 6.1

126 J Bodin, *Les Six Livres de la République* (1576) Book II ch I

127 ibid

2.3 THE EVOLUTION IN THE DIFFERENT CONCEPTIONS OF SOVEREIGNTY

2.3.1 The Evolution in the State

2.3.1.1 Following Bodin: Grotius, Hobbes, the social contract and absolute sovereignty

Bodin's criteria of sovereignty persisted through time and were even strengthened by new conceptions arising due to the political contexts subsequent theorists were living in. Thus, while Bodin remains the most important theorist on sovereignty due to his analysis of all of the different systems in his knowledge, his successors were deeply anchored in their own political contexts. As such, Hugo Grotius (1583–1645) is the first theorist of the social contract. While the Ancients analysed sovereignty by considering only the State, modern thought takes the perspective of the individuals for its analysis and this begins with Grotius.[128] For him, human beings are reasonable and all humanity should be able to live in a state of nature as a universal community under natural law.[129] However, corruption forced them to unite themselves in civil societies.[130] It is only through civil societies that individuals can organize themselves. Therefore, the State is a union of freemen in order to enjoy the law and for the sake of common welfare.[131] Indeed, according to Grotius, individual freedom is different from political freedom and individuals can still be free even if governed by an absolute political regime.[132] Grotius has a legal view of sovereignty. It is indifferent that sovereignty is exercised in a monarchy, an aristocracy or a democracy; it cannot be divided and the ruler is defined as having the power to make the law.[133] When, by social instinct, individuals promise to form the civil society, such promises are inviolable and civil rights are derived from them.[134] It is a promise to obey the majority or to any man.[135] Due to this original and inviolable will, the ruler has an absolute right to govern except if it violates the initial promise.[136] However, what is important to highlight with Grotius is that he is the main theorist of the concept of sovereignty in international law. For him, there is no right of the strongest and,

---

128 FEM Bullowa, *The History of the Theory of Sovereignty* (1895) 31
129 H Grotius, *De Iure Belli ac Pacis* (1625) prolegomena
130 ibid
131 ibid
132 FEM Bullowa, *The History of the Theory of Sovereignty* (1895) 31
133 ibid
134 ibid
135 ibid
136 ibid

as the whole of humanity cannot initially form only one universal society, the different civil societies have to learn to live peacefully together. He gives strict reasons for a just war (defence, inevitability) but States must limit themselves in their international relations.[137] The will of each nation through each individual must be respected and there are international norms that must regulate the relations between the States. His writings served as a basis for the organization of international law and for the definition of the external sovereignty as freedom and independence.[138] However, his successors developed the theory of the social contract, in particular, from an internal point of view.

One such successor is Thomas Hobbes, who was born in 1588 and died in 1679. He lived during the troubled times that preceded the English revolution of 1688. These times were the civil wars of Charles I, which Hobbes experienced and then studied[139] to give birth to *The Leviathan*,[140] first published in 1651. It is in this book, the impact of which was felt only after his death, that Hobbes explains his theory of absolute sovereignty based on popular sovereignty. He was one of the first philosophers, following Grotius, to give a theory of the social contract, where for him the starting point is the famous motto *homo homini lupus*[141] (man is wolf to man).

For Hobbes, and it is similar for Bodin,[142] the government (or here the person who governs the people) is the State (the expression of the unity of sovereignty) and so it embodies the idea of sovereignty as being the sovereign.[143] Hobbes accepts Bodin's conception of sovereignty and so follows the principal criteria. However, his own construction of the society is based on a fictitious contract.[144] Thus, the locution *homo homini lupus* is meant to describe the state of nature according to Hobbes. Men are by nature equal and the state of nature is defined by their appetite for 'competition, diffidence and glory'.[145] It is a state of war which leads men to seek each other's destruction. In this kind of state of nature, there is no place for the notions of right and wrong or justice and injustice.[146] There is no common power and no law.[147] The different appetites

---

137 H Grotius, *De Iure Belli ac Pacis* (1625)

138 On external sovereignty, see Pt 1, ch 3, para 3.2.1

139 FEM Bullowa, *The History of the Theory of Sovereignty* (1895) 32

140 T Hobbes, *The Leviathan* (1651)

141 This quote is not in *The Leviathan* but it can be found in *De Cive* from Hobbes. The locution in itself dates back to the Antiquity.

142 See in this chapter, para 3.2.2.1

143 FEM Bullowa, *The History of the Theory of Sovereignty* (1895) 32

144 ibid

145 T Hobbes, *The Leviathan*, (1651) ch XV

146 FEM Bullowa, *The History of the Theory of Sovereignty* (1895) 33

147 ibid

and passions of men also give them fear of one another. They still seek and have a desire for a more commodious life where there is peace.[148] It can be said that it is in the end the fear of fear (of being destroyed) that will lead to the social contract: despite their great passions and their love for freedom and dominion,[149] men will restrain themselves in exchange for peace,[150] which is here security. The only way to do it is through the creation of a power able to overawe them all:[151]

> The only way to erect a common power among men, is to confer all their power and strength upon one man or upon one assembly of men that may reduce all their wills into one will; which is as much as to say to appoint one man or assembly of men to bear their persons, and every one to own or acknowledge himself to be the author of whatsoever he that so bears their persons shall act or cause to be acted in those things which concern the common peace and safety, and therein to submit their will, everyone to his will, and their judgment to his judgment. This is more than consent or concord, it is a real unity of them all in one and the same person, made by a covenant of every man, in such manner as if every man should say to every man: I authorize and give up my right of governing myself to this man or to this assembly, on the condition, that thou give up thy right to him, and authorize all his actions in lie manner. This done, the multitude so united in one person is called the Commonwealth. This is the generation of that great 'Leviathan' or rather to speak more reverently of that mortal god to which we owe, under the immortal God, our peace and defence.[152] [...] And he that carrieth this person is called Sovereign, and said to have sovereign power, and everyone besides is his subjects.[153]

This is Hobbes' social contract, where he combines a popular will with an absolute sovereignty. The state of nature is a state of war and, to reach peace, men give up their freedom to an absolute sovereign who will restrain them through law. Furthermore, this 'single sovereign authority created by this transference by all individuals of their barren common right to everything in the state of nature, is most absolute and irresponsible, and his power is irrevocable'.[154] The social contract is definitive and here can be found the same criteria that Bodin used in order to strengthen the position of the absolute monarch: a supreme and perpetual absolute authority which embodies the State as its unity.

However, there are also some subtleties and some limits in Hobbes' theory of absolute sovereignty. First, it is not a direct contract between the sovereign

---

148 ibid
149 ibid 34
150 ibid
151 ibid
152 T Hobbes, *The Leviathan* (1651) ch XVII
153 ibid
154 FEM Bullowa, *The History of the Theory of Sovereignty* (1895) 35

and its people, but between all the different people themselves through general will.[155] Indeed, in the state of nature there is no sovereign to contract with, only individuals who can reach a consensus which would become law through the contract. The consequence is that the sovereign cannot commit injustice but only iniquity, and he cannot be deprived of power or punished.[156] There is nobody (except God) over the sovereign power. This theory is a theory of absolute sovereignty and not of popular rights. It means this is a negative social contract[157] where, at the beginning of society, men accept constraints for peace and so the creation of such society. Hence, to better explain the whys and wherefores of this social contract, the limits to the absoluteness of Hobbes' sovereign should be evoked.

First, the sovereign is judge of all opinions on what could lead or not lead to peace. Men's actions are the result of their opinions. Thus, the sovereign authority has been created to establish peace and so to provide for the way forward. The State (so the sovereign) is the absolute sovereign on earth and represents God; it is chief in everything. In this sense, even if human error is always possible (iniquity), the sovereign cannot be unjust, both for representing God but also because every subject is author of every act the sovereign does.[158] However, its justice is also its limit, and it is the consequence of natural law.

Therefore, second, even if the sovereign can command men's actions, it cannot command their conscience[159] and it is a consequence of natural law. There are rights of conscience of the individuals that the sovereign cannot violate.[160] These rights cannot be surrendered by any contract. For instance, 'no man can be bound to kill himself, to abstain from self-preservation, or to accuse himself'.[161] The power of the sovereign lasts as long as it is protecting the people. Actually, the sovereign is limited by the exact reason that made it the sovereign and that created the State: peace. However, besides these natural rights, people are free to do as they want in every field where there is no law.[162] Hobbes provided for a theory of legal sovereignty where, outside the direct consequences of the social contract, the law defines everything that can be done or not. It is the means of the sovereign as authority. The sovereign is the sole legislator[163] and the motivation of the people to obey the sovereign is the

155 ibid
156 ibid
157 ibid 36
158 ibid
159 ibid
160 ibid
161 ibid
162 ibid
163 ibid 37

sanction of the imperative norm. It is a practical view for Hobbes, as looking for peace could and should be the only motivation in his social contract.

Finally, on Hobbes' conception of sovereignty, similar to Grotius' conception, it must be highlighted that he used the same criteria as Bodin in order to define sovereignty as a supreme and absolute authority in the single State, underlying that absoluteness still has limits – natural law, at that time – and is an absoluteness within the sphere of the legal system/civil society (the State).

2.3.1.2 Rousseau and the general will

During the century following the deaths of Hugo Grotius and Thomas Hobbes, Jean-Jacques Rousseau was born (1712–1778). Native to Geneva in Switzerland, he spent his life as a 'world citizen' and moved from place to place regularly due to the disturbing nature of his ideas, for the time.[164] One of the most important is his conception of the concept of sovereignty, which is, similar to Grotius and Hobbes, based on the idea of the social contract but also, similar to the Ancients such as Aristotle, on a true popular sovereignty. His theory is important because his idea of the general will is one of the bases of modern democracy. He also follows the criteria developed by Bodin. However, as a political philosopher, his conception remains a theory and, even if as a consequence of his environment and of his life in the political context of his time, his proposal could not be fully put into practice either in his time or in ours.

The Social Contract[165] was published in 1762. This is where Rousseau develops his conception of popular sovereignty based on the general will. Like Grotius and Hobbes, he begins with the situation of the man in the state of nature:

> In considering man as he must have come from the hands of nature; I behold an animal less strong than some, less active than others, but upon the whole, an organism having the advantage of them all. I behold him appeasing his hunger under an oak, slaking his thirst in the first brook, finding a bed at the foot of the same tree that furnished his repast, and there you have all his cravings satisfied.[166]

Still, in contrast to Hobbes, Rousseau's natural man is a 'noble savage, solitary, unconventional and unconstrained'.[167] This glorious natural man is then supposed to renounce his natural freedom, which is an unlimited right to everything that can tempt him, in order to attain moral freedom through the society

---

[164] R Prokhovnik, *Sovereignty: History and Theory* (Imprint Academy 2008) 67

[165] JJ Rousseau, *Du Contrat Social* (1762)

[166] This initial statement must however be found in JJ Rousseau, *Discours sur l'Origine et les Fondements de l'Inégalité parmi les Hommes* (1755) 52

[167] FEM Bullowa, *The History of the Theory of Sovereignty* (1895) 46

and so through the general will.[168] This non-natural condition of a citizen with social freedom limited by the general will must bring to Rousseau's savage man his own protection and the one of his own goods. In the state of nature, there is force as physical power and there is no morality that can result from it: 'if it is necessary to obey by force, there can be no necessity to obey from duty.'[169] Naturally, all men are equal and there is no natural authority of one over the others. Similarly, for Rousseau, power is not a means in order to control right; the only lawful authority can be found only in a mutual convention.[170] Without the social contract, 'I recognize nothing belonging to another but what is useless to myself, and I owe nothing to him to whom I had promised nothing'.[171] In the civil society based on the social contract, everyone protects himself and his goods by himself, but only through the strength of the community under a form of association.[172] The general will symbolizes this association of all men creating civil society in order to reach a moral freedom which is materially protection of oneself and of property. That can be done only as a whole and not individually. In social freedom, there are limitations that can be understood as the protection of property and of all citizens individually. Rousseau's social contract creates a common and sovereign power but still leaves every contracting individual free as he was in the state of nature and owing obedience only to himself.[173] It is a self-limitation, which is morally necessary. This paradox is the consequence of the total alienation of all the contracting parties and their rights to the association: 'everybody giving oneself to everybody is giving oneself to nobody.'[174] Every individual gives his person and power 'into a common stock under the direction of the general will'[175] and 'each member is an inseparable part of the whole'.[176] The moral collective body that is created is a unity and if an individual refuses to obey the general will, he can be forced to do so by the whole body.[177] 'He is forced to be free.'[178] In this conception, 'sovereignty is the universally compulsive

168 ibid

169 ibid

170 And this is where Rousseau proves that he is first a moral philosopher of the Enlightment. His idea rests on a moral objective and not on an imperative norm.

171 FEM Bullowa, *The History of the Theory of Sovereignty* (1895) 47

172 ibid

173 ibid

174 JJ Rousseau, *Du Contrat Social* (1762) Book I ch VI

175 FEM Bullowa, *The History of the Theory of Sovereignty* (1895) 47

176 ibid

177 ibid 48

178 JJ Rousseau, *Du Contrat Social* (1762) Book I ch VII

power of the State directed by the general will'.[179] Thus, the general will is not a compilation of individual wills focused on private interests, but one common interest which unites the individuals.[180] Consequently, the sovereign power is the exercise of the general will. It is the latter that cannot be alienated or divided. Rousseau takes Bodin's criteria of an absolute supreme authority and applies it to the general will. For Rousseau, the power can be transmitted or divided, but not the general will.[181] The latter is the true sovereign for him: it is the supreme and absolute authority in the society and it cannot even be represented.[182] Also, similarly to his predecessors, the general will is limited. In this situation it is limited by itself because it is already a moral conception of sovereignty and it can be compared to natural law. By nature, the interests of the general will cannot be contrary to those of the multitude: 'the sovereign, being composed of those elements which make up the multitude, can have no interest contrary to theirs, and by its nature so long as it exists must be everything that it ought to be.'[183]

Subsequently, also for Rousseau, the law is an act of sovereignty: 'it rests upon the social contract, and in submission to it each subject obeys only his own will.'[184] Rousseau's conception of sovereignty is a democratic conception. Hence, as a final point on his theory, it can be highlighted that, through the law – so, practically – the general will becomes the will of the majority over the minority.[185] The minority desires and accepts the will of the majority because it first concluded the social contract: 'the law becomes such because the majority desire it specifically and the minority compendiously, since they in common with the whole body of citizens desire the maintenance of the principle of majority rule.'[186]

Finally, it must be understood that Rousseau's conception is a theorization of sovereignty as it was or at least should have been in the ancient Greek cities: direct democracy.[187] However, he is aware that there are practical impossibilities to restore such political organization. The size of the modern States in his time is one possible example.[188] Moreover, even in his theory, when men leave the state of nature, it is because of a moral impulsion. How could

179 FEM Bullowa, *The History of the Theory of Sovereignty* (1895) 48
180 ibid
181 ibid
182 Rousseau supports direct democracy.
183 FEM Bullowa, *The History of the Theory of Sovereignty* (1895) 48
184 JJ Rousseau, *Du Contrat Social* (1762) Book II ch IV and VI
185 FEM Bullowa, *The History of the Theory of Sovereignty* (1895) 49
186 JJ Rousseau, *Du Contrat Social* (1762) Book IV ch II
187 ibid 49
188 ibid

they all have this in reality? Nevertheless, still following and keeping Bodin's criteria, Rousseau applied them to popular sovereignty, where, paradoxically, the sovereign is the consequence of (meaning created by) its own subjects. The distinction with Hobbes is that Rousseau's popular sovereignty is not a moment with an absolute sovereign distinguished from its subjects. Rousseau's popular sovereignty must persist through time and the subjects must remain their own sovereign. Such conception is one of the seeds of modern constitutional States.

2.3.2 The Evolution in the Federation

2.3.2.1 The American Federation

Bodin's criteria of sovereignty were established in the unitary State and became problematic when they had to be applied in a different political organization such as a federation. Two main examples can be considered to understand whether Bodin's criteria correspond to the shape of the State he was living in or if they are irreducible characteristics of the concept of sovereignty: the American Federation and the German Federation (the continental theory).

The USA organized itself around the Constitution of 1787[189] and its form of association was originally based on individual communities which all had autonomously sovereign prerogatives.[190] In the federal model of the USA, there is an idea of balance or consensus through a compromise between the autonomy of the different communities (former colonies) and the necessity of a union as a whole. Consequently, there is a double level of organization: at the local level and at the federal or central level. When the 13 original colonies organized themselves as a union through the Constitution of 1787, they had to decide how they wanted to shape it. In other words, it was a question of sovereignty as to whether the supreme authority should be initially local or central and as to how to organize the competences between the two levels. The theorization of this organization of sovereignty between two levels was of great importance for the young State that was the USA during the 19th century. It was the opposition between the defenders of particularism (sovereignty of the local States) and the nationalistic spirit (sovereignty at the federal level).[191] Nonetheless, as early as 1787, theoretical disputes rather based themselves on the possibility or otherwise of dividing sovereignty.[192]

---

189 US Constitution (1787)

190 CE Merriam Jr, *History of the Theory of Sovereignty since Rousseau* (Columbia University Studies in the Social Sciences ed, 1900) 82

191 ibid 83

192 ibid 84

Hence, the idea of the divisibility of sovereignty can be rooted in the US courts[193] and especially the case *Chisholm v Georgia*[194] (1793): 'the United States are sovereign as to all the powers of government actually surrendered. Each State in the Union is sovereign as to all powers reserved.'[195] It is the idea of dividing sovereignty and powers between the States and the union. James Madison is one of the most important American theorists of this conception of sovereignty.[196] For him, the American government was sui generis and unique in its construction.[197] It is an example of adaptability to possible new difficulties and evolutions,[198] and the divisibility of sovereignty would be the evident consequence of the historical construction of the USA: 'it is difficult to argue intelligibly concerning the compound system of government in the United States without admitting the divisibility of sovereignty.'[199] '[A]bstract and technical modes of expounding and designating its character' should be abandoned.[200] Then, incidentally, de Tocqueville, in *Democracy in America* (1835),[201] followed the same idea. He thinks that the idea of a divided sovereignty was accepted in the USA in spite of acknowledged important difficulties.[202] He says that 'the rules of logic were broken'[203] and that 'the principle of the independence of the States triumphed in the formation of the Senate and that of the sovereignty of the Nation in the composition of the House of Representatives'.[204] For him, two concurrent sovereignties on the same territory is a reality, but one still specific to the USA.[205]

On the other side, Calhoun is one of the main representatives of the opposite view, which is the particularistic position.[206] This view was mainly shared by the leaders of the Southern movement: the idea of a divided sovereignty was contrary to the possibility of secession by diminishing the sovereignty of the local

193 ibid 85

194 *Chisholm v Georgia* [1793] 2 US 419

195 ibid

196 CE Merriam Jr, *History of the Theory of Sovereignty since Rousseau* (Columbia University Studies in the Social Sciences ed, 1900) 85

197 ibid

198 ibid

199 J Madison, *The Writings*, vol IV (1787) 61

200 ibid 394

201 A de Tocqueville, *Democracy in America* (1835)

202 CE Merriam Jr, *History of the Theory of Sovereignty since Rousseau* (Columbia University Studies in the Social Sciences ed, 1900) 85

203 A de Tocqueville, *Democracy in America,* vol I (1835) ch VIII

204 ibid

205 CE Merriam Jr, *History of the Theory of Sovereignty since Rousseau* (Columbia University Studies in the Social Sciences ed, 1900) 86

206 ibid 87

States.[207] Calhoun starts with the 13 sovereignties of the Confederation.[208] For him, they never abandoned their 'inherent quality as independent States'.[209] Consequently, they are still sovereign and the divisibility of sovereignty is an inherent impossibility: sovereignty is an 'entire thing; to divide it is to destroy it'.[210] 'It is the supreme power in a State, and we might just as well speak of half a square, or half a triangle, as of half a sovereignty.'[211] Half-measures are not possible. However, practically, he makes a distinction between sovereignty in itself and the powers attributed to it, the latter being able to be divided.[212]

In the end, the compromise of divided sovereignty was rejected by both the nationalist and the particularistic positions.[213] The nationalists finally 'began to distinguish between sovereignty in the narrower sense, that is to say governmental sovereignty, which is capable of division, and sovereignty in the broader sense, the ultimate sovereignty which is indivisible and which rests with the people'.[214] The inherent difficulty at that time for the American theorists was the practical application of sovereignty by the government, which must be distinguished from the real political sovereignty which takes an abstract form through the State,[215] especially in a democracy with a popular sovereignty. Finally, as observed by Merriam, the final point on these debates was scientifically formulated by JW Burgess in 'Political Science and Comparative Constitutional Law' (1892): sovereignty is the 'original, absolute, unlimited, universal power over the individual subject and over all associations of subjects'.[216] Indeed, 'the State cannot be conceived without sovereignty: i.e., without unlimited power over its subjects; that is its very essence'.[217]

Finally on the American federation, it can be observed that most debates on a divided sovereignty found their roots in practical and social observations due to the will to share powers and preserve freedom. However, these legitimate expectations do not put into question the origin of the concept of sovereignty: it corresponds to the abstract construction of the State, which necessitates itself

---

207 ibid
208 ibid
209 ibid
210 JC Calhoun, *A Disquisition on Government* (1851) 146
211 JC Calhoun, *Against the Force Bill* (1833)
212 CE Merriam Jr, *History of the Theory of Sovereignty since Rousseau* (Columbia University Studies in the Social Sciences ed, 1900) 88
213 ibid 93
214 ibid
215 ibid 94
216 JW Burgess, *Political Science and Comparative Constitutional Law*, vol I (1892) 52
217 ibid 56

its own supreme authority. Then, powers can be delegated. These debates did not place in question Bodin's criteria and the USA considers itself a State, even if federal, with its own unity. Its internal organization of the competences (the powers of the different governments) only takes place in a second step.

2.3.2.2 The German Federation

During the 19th century, many questions arose around the progressive construction of the German Federation. As with the American Federation, one of these questions was to find a conception of sovereignty which could fit into a State with two levels (a Federation). However, the debates were more theoretical.[218] While the American thinkers focused intensively and mostly on whether or not to divide the supreme authority, the German theorists used the distinction between external sovereignty (international independence) and internal sovereignty (absolute supreme authority within the State) to explain sovereignty in a Federation.[219]

Thus, during the 19th century, there was first a German Confederation composed of 40 States and dating back to 1815.[220] As a Confederation, the sovereignty of the local States was preserved. Attempts at a stronger union succeeded only after the war of 1866, with the North German Confederation composed of 22 States in 1867 and then the German Empire under the constitution of 1871.[221] Incentives for the strongest union had the same impacts as in the USA. Debates and new conceptions of sovereignty arose to justify the new political objectives.

In 1853, Georg Waitz proposed a new theory based on external sovereignty and so on independence.[222] In a *Bundesstaat* (federal State), some political functions must be the charge of the individual States and others that of the association.[223] Both have a different sphere of operation and each one, within its own sphere, is independent in the exercise of its own power.[224] Indeed, according to Waitz, even if the sovereignty of the local States is limited in a Federation, 'only the extent, not the content of the sovereignty is limited, and this for the one as well for the other'.[225] That is to say that the sovereignty of all local States

---

218 CE Merriam Jr, *History of the Theory of Sovereignty since Rousseau* (Columbia University Studies in the Social Sciences ed, 1900) 95

219 See pt, 1, ch 2 on external and internal sovereignty

220 CE Merriam Jr, *History of the Theory of Sovereignty since Rousseau* (Columbia University Studies in the Social Sciences ed, 1900) 95

221 ibid 96

222 ibid

223 ibid

224 ibid

225 G Waitz, *Grundzüge der Politik* (1862) 166

is extensively limited but still preserved in its intensity.[226] 'The sovereignty is to be considered qualitatively rather than quantitatively.'[227] Consequently, both the local State and the central State can be fully sovereign in their own spheres by being independent of control in such spheres.[228] There may be two sovereigns in the State 'if we understand by this two independent political powers, each supreme in its own particular sphere'.[229] Sovereignty is independence in a certain sphere and can be shared by many.[230]

This theory remained dominant for some time, as it was able to conciliate the will for unity while preserving the identity and independence of the local States.[231] Then, after the formation of the German Empire, another conception took the lead. This is the idea of *Kompetenz-Kompetenz* (competence of the competence).[232] For Meyer, for instance, when there is a constitutional power that can take away the individual powers of the local States, these States 'are no longer sovereign'.[233] Only the constituent power is sovereign. Similarly, Haenel argues for 'the "Kompetenz-Kompetenz" as the characteristic feature of the notion of sovereignty'.[234] Within the State, the powers are limited and only the sovereign can operate at will. The sovereign State, however, has nothing above it that can limit it. This would be the essential mark of sovereignty: 'in this legal power of the State over its competence lies the first requisite of self-sufficiency, the kernel of its sovereignty.'[235] The sovereignty of a State is the 'legal self-determination of its jurisdiction'.[236] 'Lack of a legal superior constitutes sovereignty'[237] and Haenel found that the true sovereign is the Empire.[238] It is on exactly the same basis that Laband rejected Waitz's idea of

---

226 CE Merriam Jr, *History of the Theory of Sovereignty since Rousseau* (Columbia University Studies in the Social Sciences ed, 1900) 97

227 ibid 96

228 ibid 97

229 ibid

230 ibid

231 ibid

232 ibid 99

233 G Meyer, *Staatsrechtliche Erörterungen über die Deutsche Reichverfassung* (1872) 6

234 CE Merriam Jr, *History of the Theory of Sovereignty since Rousseau* (Columbia University Studies in the Social Sciences ed, 1900) 99, by reference to: A Haenel, *Studien zum Deutschen Staatsrechte* (1873) Pt I and A Haenel, *Studien zum Deutschen Staatsrechte* (1888) Pt II

235 A Haenel, *Studien zum Deutschen Staatsrechte* (1873) Pt I, 149

236 CE Merriam Jr, *History of the Theory of Sovereignty since Rousseau* (Columbia University Studies in the Social Sciences ed, 1900) 99

237 ibid

238 ibid

double-sovereignty: States are sovereign or they are not. There is no possibility of a 'half, divided, diminished, dependent or relative sovereignty'.[239]

Georg Jellinek, an Austrian publicist, then slightly modified the criterion of the power of self-determining its legal competence for the State. He observed, for instance, the situation of Turkey over Bulgaria[240] at the end of the 19th century and found that 'neither the superior nor the subordinate power (State) has the right to change the limits of its legal competence with reference to the other'.[241] Also, there were similar situations in the relations between Hungary, Croatia and Slavonia at that time.[242] Thus, Jellinek proposed a different criterion and emphasized the manner in which a State can be legally bound.[243] He changed the positive criterion of a power of self-determination of its own jurisdiction to a negative criterion, which is not able to be bound except by its own will.[244] It is the true international independence that qualifies the sovereignty of the State. With the German Empire, it is this last conception of the concept of sovereignty that became dominant, and only the federal State remained sovereign.[245]

Nonetheless, sovereignty has always been understood by its theorists as the personification of the State. Even if authors such as Jellinek or Laband kept the criteria of indivisible sovereignty defined by Bodin, the German context had to conciliate the sovereignty of the federal State with the non-sovereignty of the local States knowing that, in the German view, local States must be understood as real States and not as mere communities or regions. This is why such authors still accepted the idea of non-sovereign States.[246] They did not refuse the concept of sovereignty as it can be defined through its own criteria but the new international context that was arising, especially after the treaty of Westphalia, highlighted serious theoretical questions on its application and preservation. This is especially true at the international level, where the limitation of the States' powers due to their cohabitation and so due to the conclusion of international treaties was, for many publicists, incompatible

239 CE Merriam Jr, *History of the Theory of Sovereignty since Rousseau* (Columbia University Studies in the Social Sciences ed, 1900) 100, by reference to: P Laband, *Das Staatsrecht des Deutschen Reiches* (2nd edn, 1894) 15
240 CE Merriam Jr, *History of the Theory of Sovereignty since Rousseau* (Columbia University Studies in the Social Sciences ed, 1900) 100
241 ibid
242 ibid
243 ibid
244 ibid
245 ibid 102
246 ibid 107

with the absoluteness of sovereignty,[247] even if this view is not accurate. It is through such conceptions of the local States that ideas of divided sovereignty still persist, even if they are incompatible with the concept of sovereignty in itself. Such conceptions were an accommodation with the political context of the moment. Thus, what is important to underline is that the idea of dividing sovereignty must be considered as the consequence of the difficulty to apprehend the modern legal and political context for the States. However, the inherent criteria of the concept of sovereignty cannot be changed only due to a new context, because it would then become a new concept with a new definition. Sovereignty would not be sovereignty any more.

2.4 CONCLUSION

The inherent criteria of the concept of sovereignty as defined by Bodin have persisted over time. This shows that sovereignty always has been present in a way or another in the theory of the State and that, when a conceptualization tries to eliminate one criterion or change it, it is because of the evolution of the historical context and not of the concept of sovereignty as such. Indeed, the way the State is organized can evolve and change but the inherent elements of the concept of sovereignty must persist for a State to remain a State. Thus, the evolution of the State cannot change the concept of sovereignty because it is the impulsion that creates the State and the necessary element of its unity. Even in a Federation, unity is necessary. There cannot be one people organized as one civil society without unity. Therefore, it must be demonstrated that it is the concept of sovereignty that organizes the society and so the State as legal system, and not the other way around.[248] The concept of sovereignty organizes the legal system; the strict form of the State as such (as usually conceived) is not one of the essential elements of its definition. When the State personifies the concept of sovereignty, it is as a legal system.[249]

Also, in past theories it is possible to find some confusion between legal sovereignty and political sovereignty. This confusion can be found in Bodin and Hobbes because they define an absolute ruler, which is not the people. In a non-democratic State, the Prince makes the law and is the sovereign. There is no distinction between legal sovereignty and political sovereignty. However, in a democratic State there is a distinction between the people as the political sovereign and the delegated law-maker (government) as the legal sovereign

247 ibid
248 See pt 1, ch 3
249 ibid

and, when it comes to the concept of sovereignty, it is the political sovereign that must be found.

Finally, the distinction between a monarchy or an aristocracy and a democracy is a distinction with direct democracy. Nowadays, most modern democracies are constitutional democracies and the political sovereign, in such political organization, is the constitution, which is originally elaborated by the people as the constituent power.[250]

[250] The implications of constituent sovereignty are explained in Pt 2, ch 5, para 5.2. There is a distinction between political sovereignty and constituent sovereignty even if they work together and shape the same legal system. Political sovereignty is inherent to all political organizations while constituent sovereignty gives the shape of the constitutional State to such organization

3. The concept of sovereignty: modern perspectives

3.1 INTRODUCTION

The concept of sovereignty can be understood in many different ways, but these ways are only different perceptions of the essence of the concept. Thus, these perceptions lead to different conceptions. However, variations are mainly observed in the political organizations conceptualized by the different authors around the concept of sovereignty. Consequently, it has been observed that sovereignty's essential criteria, or more accurately attributes, persist over time.

Hence, the essential attributes of the two faces of sovereignty must be defined to avoid any misunderstanding about the concept. These attributes try to be as universal as possible and they are also defined in order to avoid any language issues. The universality of the concept amidst a diversity of conceptions has been demonstrated. Then, the concept must be defined beyond language differences. Indeed, for instance, when the English word 'jurisdiction' implies the territorial application of sovereignty, the German word *Staatsgewalt* is a reference to the public power of the State as sovereign. The definition given of the very essential attributes of sovereignty tries to reach its essence and not only explore some of its apparent facets depending on the language used. Coming back to the word 'jurisdiction', for instance, territorial sovereignty is involved in the fact that the State is the personification of sovereignty as a legal system[1] and that a territory is necessary to the apparition of the State. This word has

[1] It must be emphasized that the State personifies the concept of sovereignty as a legal system that organizes the society around it. However, the State as such (the form of the State) has not been proved as being one of the essential elements of the concept of sovereignty or of its modes of apparition. Therefore, even if, through this chapter, the concept of sovereignty is defined through its current mode of apparition, which is the State, the necessary personification of the concept of sovereignty through a legal system that organizes the society does not seem to require the form of the State. As such, it should be understood that the concept of sovereignty can self-manifest through other forms of legal systems as long as its definition through its essential criteria is respected

its own application and utility but it is not the most pertinent one in order to define the concept.

This leads to a second aspect. When sovereignty is defined, specificities of the concept appear alongside the methodology used to find sovereignty today thanks to its essential attributes. The main idea is that sovereignty exists and is not created. It appears through its marks but it is the necessary authority in a given legal order. Nowadays, possible arguments on the disappearance of sovereignty are facilitated by the increasing importance of international organizations and of the international legal order. However, even the use of wording such as 'disappearance' is ambiguous. It participates in the modes of presentation of sovereignty. Disappearance involves existence and complexification does not mean death. It is argued that sovereignty does not disappear but must be found. It is one of the aspects of the general theory of the State where the line between facts and law is blurred because it participates in the creation of the legal sphere.

Thus, to define the concept and to give a specific methodology for its application, the starting point must be the theories of the two main authors who wrote on the concept during the 20th century. Kelsen extensively wrote on the concept in the perspective of international law[2] and Carré de Malberg defined it in public law.[3] Their theories are still the basis for the definition of external and internal sovereignties. They must help to define the essential attributes of the concept but also to demonstrate that, when it comes to the essence of sovereignty and so to the creation of the State, even pure positivist theories cannot avoid the necessity of the visible world (facts) to define the legal order (law). Finally, explaining the definition and the methodology of the concept of sovereignty must help to apprehend the contemporaneous impact of international organizations such as the EU on sovereignty beyond the pure content of the law by also considering its context.

3.2 TWO SIDES OF THE SAME COIN

3.2.1 External Sovereignty

3.2.1.1 Kelsen and international sovereignty

External sovereignty concerns the relation between the State and its international environment. Kelsen and Carré de Malberg are among the main writers

[2] H Kelsen, 'Sovereignty and International Law' (1960) 48 [4] The Georgetown Law Journal 627–40

[3] R Carré de Malberg, *Contribution à la Théorie Générale de l'Etat*, vol 1 (Sirey 1920); R Carré de Malberg, *Contribution à la Théorie Générale de l'Etat,* vol 2 (Sirey 1922)

who wrote on sovereignty during the 20th century. Their theories are still used to define the concept. While Carré de Malberg gave a general definition of the term but focused essentially on its internal aspect, Kelsen explained his views on sovereignty in international law according to his positivist views.[4] His theory is an unavoidable starting point to define external sovereignty in the modern context.

In Kelsen's theory, sovereignty is derived from the Latin *superanus*[5] (superior). Sovereignty is the supreme power of the State, which must be understood as the legal order. When a legal order has this supreme authority, it is sovereign. It can become problematic in the interactions between the State and international law because it means there are two legal orders: the national legal order and the international legal order.[6] In order to explain which of them can be the true sovereign, Kelsen begins with the distinction between monist and dualist States.[7] In the dualistic theory, the national legal order and the international legal order are independent and simultaneously valid. In the monistic view, both orders form a unity. This unity can be performed in two ways: either international law derives its validity from national law, which is consequently superior, or national law derives its validity from international law, which would be inversely superior. The former is the primacy of national law, and the latter is the primacy of international law.[8]

For Kelsen, the dualistic theory is not concerned by the sovereignty issue because of the logic of norms.[9] Two facts cannot 'be' and 'not be' at the same time. This is the principle of contradiction. Similarly, even if a norm is not true or false but valid or not, two 'statements describing norms'[10] cannot be 'ought to be' statements and 'ought not to be' statements at the same time. Therefore, the two systems cannot be simultaneously valid, and the sovereignty issue does not even come into play.

Then, in the monistic theory, which is the only possible theory, there are two possibilities.[11] First, when there is primacy of national law, it presupposes the sovereignty of one national legal order over international law. The national legal order recognizes international law and, consequently, the latter becomes part of the first-mentioned order. The sovereignty of the national legal order is

---

4 H Kelsen, 'Sovereignty and International Law' (1960) 48 [4] The Georgetown Law Journal 627–40

5 ibid 627

6 ibid 628

7 ibid 629

8 ibid

9 ibid 630

10 ibid 629

11 ibid 630

established but it is a presupposition. The science of law does not confirm this point of view. It is the assumption that the national legal order is the supreme normative order, and that international law derives its validity from it. Kelsen assumes that, when the view of the primacy of national law is taken, only one national legal order is sovereign. Only this order can be the starting point of the theory, even if it can relate to any State. Then, once international law is recognized, the State can also recognize other national legal orders through international law. However, only one national legal order is supreme and so sovereign in this view. Second, when there is primacy of international law, the validity of a national legal order comes from the international principle of efficacy. This principle determines the reason for and the sphere of validity of national law. According to Kelsen, this international norm says:

> The government of a community existent within a certain firmly circumscribed place, if it exercises effective control over the members of this community and is independent of other governments of analogous communities, is to be regarded as the legitimate government, and the community under this government as a State in the sense of international law.[12]

If the criteria of this international principle are fulfilled, a national legal order exists. However, this national legal order would be a partial legal order among many others, being part of a universal legal order, which is international law. In this sense, only the international legal order is sovereign.

Finally, in Kelsen's opinion, the two monistic theories could be compared to a subjectivistic and an objectivistic world view.[13] The subjectivistic world view is the primacy of national law, where the world is seen from 'one's own sovereign ego in order to comprehend the external world'.[14] This means that the external world is not truly external but part of the internal world of the ego. Both the international legal order and the other national legal orders are part of this conception. It is a kind of solipsism.[15] Everything exists through the ego of the first State, which can be the only sovereign. On the other hand, the objectivistic world view is the primacy of international law. It is the real external world, which comprehends everyone's ego as integral parts of the world. There are equal partial legal orders that are parts of a total: the international legal order.

Hence, it must be emphasized that, in Kelsen's view and for the science of law, the two approaches are equal and possible. The science of law does not

---

12 ibid 631

13 ibid 638

14 ibid

15 ibid

come into the realm of political science or sociology and does not argue for one system over the other.[16]

Thus, Kelsen's theory gives interesting perspectives on the meaning of sovereignty in international law. The first element is independence. In the monistic theory, from the perspective of the primacy of international law, the sovereign international legal order gives legitimacy to the creation of independent partial legal orders and is independent itself by being the unique international legal order. Similarly, when the perspective of the primacy of national law prevails, it is to the detriment of the independence of the other national legal orders. Only one State is sovereign because the other States cannot be independent from its perspective. External sovereignty is about independence as the result of supreme authority; this can be demonstrated from Kelsen's theory.

Then, the method used to discover, or not, independence is the theory of recognition, which is a major tool in international law. Kelsen does not investigate this theory, and it is one factor in order to demonstrate that his theory does not apply to reality. His legal theory is strictly based on a theoretical and legal conception. It tries to find confirmation in facts. However, facts can be the basis in order to define a legal theory, but they never have to fit into a legal conception. For Kelsen, according to the science of law, there are two possibilities to define sovereignty in international law. Both are equal and monistic views. A dualistic view is not possible. One could correlate these two monistic views with a subjectivistic world view and an objectivistic world view. One could argue that it is hardly possible to have an objectivistic point of view in such a matter and that the only possibility is to try to reach objectivity from its own subjectivity. However, here, Kelsen's theory is only denounced through the paradox between sovereignty and the science of law as conceptualized by him. This paradox as such is illustrated by the theory of recognition.

When Kelsen begins to explain his theory, he uses a definition of the term sovereignty: *superanus* being supreme power. Then, he defines who can be the sovereign between the national legal order and the international legal order depending on each different view. The paradox is that the definition of sovereignty (supreme power) that is used as the basis is not a norm but a fact. Furthermore, recognition means discovering something that exists and not creating something through law. The consequence is that the line between facts and law is thinner that could be admitted, especially when it comes to sovereignty. When Kelsen explains that the international legal order could be sovereign, he does not mention that international law finds its roots and has

16 ibid

been created through the national laws of the States.[17] This is true for both the monistic and the dualistic theories. Kelsen's theory does not consider the factual and national origins of the international legal order. He proposes a theory that can be true at one moment but that is not justified by the whole history of the context.

Thus, a modern definition of external sovereignty must be proposed. Such definition must also be based on independence as a quality of the State. Then, it must also be demonstrated that sovereignty, as a concept of political law, appears and is not created.

3.2.1.2 Independence as a quality

Carré de Malberg, in his definition, gives three different meanings to the term sovereignty:

> Originally, it is the supreme character of a full independent power and especially of the Power of the State. Then, it is the amount of the powers included in the power of the State, being a synonym to this last expression. Finally, it designates the supreme holder, in the State, of the power of the State; here sovereignty is identified with the power of the body.[18]

Combacau, in his main article on the international sovereignty of the State,[19] discards the last two meanings and concentrates on the original signification. The definition does not say what sovereignty is but designates the traditional uses associated to this term.[20] For Combacau, the definition can be true only in relation with a social fact: in law, there are no things but only names of things, and so it depends on what practice calls sovereignty.[21] As a matter of fact, in international law as well as in national law, sovereignty cannot be separated from the State. To determine what sovereignty means in international law, it is necessary to begin with a definition of the State. As such, as a legal basis, the 1933 Montevideo Convention gives this definition. 'The State as a person of international law should possess the following qualifications: (a) a permanent

---

17 See D Grimm, *Sovereignty: The Origin and Future of a Political and Legal Concept* (Columbia University Press 2015) 82: a State is needed to apply international law

18 R Carré de Malberg, *Contribution à la Théorie Générale de l'Etat,* vol 1 (Sirey 1920) 79 (Author's translation)

19 J Combacau, 'Pas une Puissance, une Liberté : la Souveraineté Internationale de l'Etat' (1993) [67] Pouvoirs 47–58

20 ibid 48

21 ibid

population; (b) a defined territory; (c) government; and (d) a capacity to enter into relations with other States.'[22]

According to Distefano, 'the emergence of a State is fundamentally a historical fact'.[23] The original construction of the State does not depend on international law: 'there is no standardized process of statehood.'[24] Consequently, the three first criteria are outside the scope of the investigation of the legal definition of sovereignty in international law.[25] The territory and the population are inherent attributes of the State as a fact. They participate in its factual construction. The State will be able to be recognized according to international law in a second step. Similarly, the government is an organ of the State, and a government change does not affect its continuity.[26] In this sense, the State is in a higher position compared to the government and only the State can have supremacy, not the government. This aspect is about the internal sovereignty of the State. Consequently, only the last criterion, namely the capacity to enter into relations with other States, gives a legal perspective on the sovereignty of the State in international law, and, according to the arbitrator Max Huber in the *Island of Palmas* case: 'sovereignty in the relations between States signifies independence. Independence in regard to a portion of the globe is the right to exercise therein, to the exclusion of any other State, the functions of a State.'[27]

For Combacau, the international sovereignty of the State is not a power but a quality of the power.[28] In the definition of Carré de Malberg, the power of the State corresponds to the public power. It is its internal sovereignty. On the other side, full independence is the quality of this power in international law: external sovereignty. This external sovereignty is the negative aspect of the term. Combacau defines it as a freedom.[29] Internal sovereignty is the supreme

---

22 Montevideo Convention on the Rights and Duties of the States (1933) art 1

23 G Distefano, *Fundamentals of Public International Law: A Sketch of the International Legal Order* (M Fitzmaurice and S Singer eds, Queen Mary Studies in International Law, Brill Nijhoff 2019) 75

24 ibid

25 See eg D Grimm, *Sovereignty: The Origin and Future of a Political and Legal Concept* (Columbia University Press 2015) 82: a State is needed to apply international law.

26 G Distefano, *Fundamentals of Public International Law: A Sketch of the International Legal Order* (M Fitzmaurice and S Singer eds, Queen Mary Studies in International Law, Brill Nijhoff 2019) 117: Principle of State continuity consecrated in the 1831 London Protocol relating to the newly born Kingdom of Belgium ('States survive their Government').

27 *Island of Palmas Case (United States v the Netherlands)* [1928] 2 RIAA 829

28 J Combacau, 'Pas une Puissance, une Liberté: la Souveraineté Internationale de l'Etat' (1993) [67] Pouvoirs 49

29 ibid 51

power of the State, containing all of its different and specific powers. External sovereignty is the supremacy of this power: there is no higher authority.[30] The consequence is that the full independence of the States, understood as a freedom, is strictly negative.[31] When a State acts at the international level and concludes a treaty, it is through its internal sovereignty, using its public power, and not through external sovereignty, which is only a quality of this power. There is a logical consequence to this construction of sovereignty as a concept. As external sovereignty is a quality of (internal) sovereignty, the origin of the concept in international law must be found in internal law. The State is prior to international law. Many internationalists share this view.[32] The origin of international law is the States and this is why, at least when it comes to sovereignty, the theory of recognition is the fundamental aspect of international law.

Thus, the theory of recognition is one of the tools of international law to give legal status to a State and for it to leave the state of nature in order to form a civil society. In a first step, when a State wants to leave the state of nature, it recognizes rules regulating the natural actions of its subjects.[33] The State gains an autonomy, which is inherently self-limited by the law.[34] It is similar to Hobbes' social contract.[35] Law is a social construction and it is in this sense that sovereignty must be understood: the institution of the legal freedom of the State which is different from the natural freedom of the human beings not constituted as subjects within the empire of sovereignty.[36] This is the paradox of the obedient sovereign,[37] which limits itself through law. Then, only in a second step, once the State does not consider itself as a fact but as a legal entity, can it exist on an international level and be assessed on this level. This is confirmed by the *Lotus* case[38] from the International Court of The Hague: in the beginning was the internal law as the freedom of the State to act unilaterally,

---

30 ibid 50

31 ibid

32 See eg G Distefano, *Fundamentals of Public International Law: A Sketch of the International Legal Order* (M Fitzmaurice and S Singer eds, Queen Mary Studies in International Law, Brill Nijhoff 2019) 75; J Combacau, 'Pas une Puissance, une Liberté: la Souveraineté Internationale de l'Etat' (1993) [67] Pouvoirs 53; A Pellet, *Le Droit International à l'Aube du XXIème siècle* (Cours Fondamental 1997) 55

33 J Combacau, 'Pas une Puissance, une Liberté: la Souveraineté Internationale de l'Etat' (1993) [67] Pouvoirs 51

34 ibid

35 See Pt 1, ch 2, para 2.3.1.1

36 J Combacau, 'Pas une Puissance, une Liberté: la Souveraineté Internationale de l'Etat' (1993) [67] Pouvoirs 51

37 ibid

38 *Lotus case (France v Turkey)* [1927] S A PCIJ 10

until it renounced its freedom in order to become a subject of international law, but as a sovereign.[39] The State, in order to live with its peers, will limit its freedom (independence), but it is a self-limitation. Even if it limits its powers, it remains a free sovereign. This is also why international law can only be second behind internal law. However, States, as peers and creating international law, defined the necessary criteria for a factual State to be recognized (Montevideo Convention). Indeed, if a State wants to legally exist at the international level, it must be recognized by its peers. International law, in the end, is the sum of all the self-limitations of the different States recognizing each other.

For Distefano, recognition is

> [a] juristic act, that is to say, a unilateral legal transaction aimed at creating rights and obligations for one or more subjects of the law in a specified legal order. A legal transaction is an expression of will to which the legal order ascribes the power of engendering such effects of law. A juristic act can either be conventional (a contract presupposing two or more subjects of the law) or unilateral (i.e. one will is expressed).[40]

In international law, there are two theories of recognition to consider a State as a legal person. The first theory is the declaratory theory: the State always existed, and the recognizing State takes this situation into account from the recognizing moment.[41] It is a confirmation of the status. The second theory is the constitutive theory, where the recognizing act of the recognizing State gives a legal status to the recognized State.[42] It is a creation of the status. The second theory is not coherent with the concept of sovereignty. The State is a fact before being a legal person. The different criteria, which are a population, a territory and a government, together create the State, which will acquire on its own its legal status to leave the state of nature. It is only in a second step that this new State will have the opportunity to confirm its legal status to its peers. The other States cannot create its legal status because it already exists on the internal level: it is the internal side of the sovereignty. The consequence is that, if the new State has internal sovereignty, it also has an external sovereignty, and the other States can only recognize it on a declaratory basis. On the other side, if it is ultimately considered internationally that this new State is not a State, it is because it does not fulfil the necessary criteria and because

39 J Combacau, 'Pas une Puissance, une Liberté: la Souveraineté Internationale de l'Etat' (1993) [67] Pouvoirs 53

40 G Distefano, *Fundamentals of Public International Law: A Sketch of the International Legal Order* (M Fitzmaurice and S Singer eds, Queen Mary Studies in International Law, Brill Nijhoff 2019) 165

41 ibid 167

42 ibid 166

it is not a true sovereign. Nonetheless, in any case, the sovereign status of a State does not depend on the will of another State because if it does, the new State could not be sovereign. This is the situation Kelsen evoked in his theory on the international sovereignty: it is the subjectivistic world view. However, it is demonstrated that it is not coherent with the reality of the apparition of the State. Facts precede law and the other States can only declare that they recognize the new State.[43] The latter must preserve its freedom. Without it, it is not a sovereign State and so not a State at all.

Furthermore, as a consequence of the preexistence of the State, one inherent attribute of the State that is recognized in international law is 'immediacy'.[44] The fourth criterion of the Montevideo Convention (a capacity to enter into relations with other States) is a consequence of this attribute: a State can conclude treaties because it is a State and, consequently, it has direct access to the international legal life.[45] This aspect is a consequence of the inherent internal sovereignty of the State because it involves a positive action (the conclusion of a treaty). External sovereignty is the inherent quality of this capacity to conclude treaties because if it is a capacity, it is a free capacity to act. If there was no freedom it would not be a capacity but merely a possibility and it would not depend on free will.

Thus, to resume, the international sovereignty of a State is characterized by its independence. It is the external side of sovereignty and Combacau perfectly defines it as a freedom. This side of sovereignty is a quality of its internal side, which is its public power. Furthermore, as it is a freedom, it is a negative quality. This means that it characterizes the supremacy of the sovereignty: there is no higher authority and no possibility to limit it. The only limitations endured by a sovereign State that can be observed on the international scene are self-limitations, and so voluntary limitations that do not restrict the freedom of the State. These limitations, as positive actions such as treaty conclusion, are carried out through the internal sovereignty of the State. The external sovereignty can be seen as a protection of the State's sovereignty on the international scene when it treats with its peers. Finally, it is important to underline that the State must previously exist in the facts to be able to get a legal status afterwards, and that it can only be recognized on a declaratory basis by the other States.

---

43 Arbitration Commission of the Conference on Yugoslavia (1991) opinion 1

44 A Pellet, *Le Droit International à l'Aube du XXIème siècle* (Cours Fondamental 1997) 53

45 ibid

3.2.2 Internal Sovereignty

3.2.2.1 Carré de Malberg and the definition of sovereignty

Carré de Malberg wrote his theory of the State at the beginning of the 20th century.[46] Born in Alsace in 1861, he left his region in 1870 when the Prussians conquered the territory. Then he spent his life analysing the French Third Republic, which was a parliamentary system, through the prism of the French Revolutionary Constitution of 1791.[47] Carré de Malberg considered this constitution, which established national sovereignty in France,[48] as the true original constitution of his country.[49] However, he was not focused only on the French aspects of sovereignty. As a German-speaking Alsatian, he was influenced by, and translated in French, authors such as Jellinek and Laband. Thus, the school of the Isolierung influenced Carré de Malberg in his positivist will to propose a pure theory of the State.[50] His attempt can be considered as a success because, in spite of inherent but minor flaws, his theory is still a pillar of the modern concept of sovereignty, as exemplified by Beaud.[51]

The main theory of Carré de Malberg relies on two elements: the Power of the State and the self-limitation of the State. He also proposes an alternative theory of the construction of the State that he wrote at the very end of his life and that must be mentioned.[52] First, concerning the Power of the State, if it is obvious that the State has a public power, Carré de Malberg prefers to use the expression 'Power of the State' (translation of *Staatsgewalt*), which is for him the founding element of the State.[53] It was only later, at the end of the 20th century, that Beaud would prove that there is no distinction between the Power of the State and its sovereignty.[54] The Alsatian professor writes that the State

---

[46] R Carré de Malberg, *Contribution à la Théorie Générale de l'Etat*, vol 1 (Sirey 1920); R Carré de Malberg, *Contribution à la Théorie Générale de l'Etat*, vol 2 (Sirey 1922)

[47] D Mineur, 'De la Souveraineté Nationale à la Volonté Générale: L'Evolution de Carré de Malberg, du Projet Positiviste au Parti-Pris Démocratique' (2012) [8] Jus Politicum 1

[48] Constitution of France (1791) Title III, art 1

[49] D Mineur, 'De la Souveraineté Nationale à la Volonté Générale: L'Evolution de Carré de Malberg, du Projet Positiviste au Parti-Pris Démocratique' (2012) [8] Jus Politicum 1

[50] ibid

[51] O Beaud, *La Puissance de l'Etat* (PUF 1994) 15

[52] R Carré de Malberg, *La Loi, Expression de la Volonté Générale: Etudes sur le Concept de la Loi dans la Constitution de 1875* (Sirey 1931)

[53] G Guiheux, 'La Théorie Générale de l'Etat de Raymond Carré de Malberg' [1999] Revue Juridique de l'Ouest no spécial 84

[54] O Beaud, *La Puissance de l'Etat* (PUF 1994) 15

holds a power without any other origin than itself and with no other equal power.[55] It is the sovereignty of the State, which is often understood as the *summa potestas*.[56] As already demonstrated, Combacau defines this aspect of sovereignty through the notion of 'supremacy of the Power'.[57] This means that there is one supreme power. It is a stronger expression than *summa potestas*, which only defines a sum of all powers. The original power is the Power of the State and not a sum of underlying powers. When Carré de Malberg first sketches a definition of sovereignty, he is aware of the difficulties of the notion and simply writes that 'sovereignty is the sum of the rights of the active Power, internal or external'.[58] This is a definition of internal sovereignty, which is confused with the Power of the State. At the origin of the State, there is sovereignty. It is the founding principle of the State and its continuity.[59] However, in order to last, it needs to be institutionalized.

As such, the organ theory (on the government bodies) is the explication of the theory of the State, and Carré de Malberg writes: 'the people or bodies who exercise any portion of the public power are, in this exercise, the bodies of the State: the power they hold is the one of the State.'[60] The State, as the collectivity and the place of unity of all its individuals, habilitates people or assemblies to exercise its public power. When an individual or an assembly act by reason of this habilitation, they act as bodies of the State. There is a distinction between the individual and the function exercised in the name of the State.[61] The function is the exercise of the Power of the State in a specific sphere of competence. The Power of the State remains one in the unique person of the State.[62] According to Carré de Malberg, the habilitation is a constitutional vocation: it is defined in the constitution.

---

55 R Carré de Malberg, *Contribution à la Théorie Générale de l'Etat,* vol 1 (Sirey 1920) 70

56 G Guiheux, 'La Théorie Générale de l'Etat de Raymond Carré de Malberg' [1999] Revue Juridique de l'Ouest no spécial 85

57 J Combacau, 'Pas une Puissance, une Liberté: la Souveraineté Internationale de l'Etat' (1993) [67] Pouvoirs 50

58 R Carré de Malberg, *Contribution à la Théorie Générale de l'Etat,* vol 1 (Sirey 1920) 77

59 G Guiheux, 'La Théorie Générale de l'Etat de Raymond Carré de Malberg' [1999] Revue Juridique de l'Ouest no spécial 85

60 R Carré de Malberg, *Contribution à la Théorie Générale de l'Etat*, vol 1 (Sirey 1920) 143

61 G Guiheux, 'La Théorie Générale de l'Etat de Raymond Carré de Malberg' [1999] Revue Juridique de l'Ouest no spécial 86

62 R Carré de Malberg, *Contribution à la Théorie Générale de l'Etat*, vol 2 (Sirey 1922) 27

In a second step, once the Power of the State is established, its self-limitation comes inherently into play. The State self-limits itself through law. Carré de Malberg develops his own theory of the constitutional constitution of the State through the distinction between the original constituent power and the derived constituent power.[63] The State is created by the original constituent power, which is, by nature, unlimited. Once the State is constituted, the constituent power is the derived constituent power, which is the body that can amend the constitution. Yet, the State must have the *Kompetenz-Kompetenz*, which is the constituent sovereignty.[64] This means that the original constituent power cannot remain unlimited because it could impose limits to the constitutional order and the constitution would lose its compulsory nature.[65] In order to avoid this issue, Carré de Malberg uses the idea of national sovereignty.[66] The nation, as the abstract collectivity of the people embodied by the State, is the only sovereign and the only author of the original constitution. This is the principle of sovereignty that can be found in the French Constitution of 1791.[67] All other powers are instituted powers justified by the organ theory.

Moreover, the theory of national sovereignty avoids the pure application of the theory of popular sovereignty. National sovereignty embodies an abstract notion within the State as a person, which is inherently limited.[68] The same is not true of popular sovereignty, which is the direct expression of the will of the people. The latter is a real unlimited original constituent power. In modern democracies, it is common to understand that sovereignty is a popular sovereignty. However, there is the paradox of the sovereign people being obedient to the State personified in a governing body. Troper explains that it is a question of ideology.[69] This means that it relies on a political choice. In a constitutional ideology, the State, through the constitution, is the true sovereign. It is still a

---

63 G Guiheux, 'La Théorie Générale de l'Etat de Raymond Carré de Malberg' [1999] Revue Juridique de l'Ouest no spécial 88

64 ibid

65 ibid

66 D Mineur, 'De la Souveraineté Nationale à la Volonté Générale: L'Evolution de Carré de Malberg, du Projet Positiviste au Parti-Pris Démocratique' (2012) [8] Jus Politicum 3

67 Constitution of France (1791) Title III, art 1

68 G Guiheux, 'La Théorie Générale de l'Etat de Raymond Carré de Malberg' [1999] Revue Juridique de l'Ouest no spécial 88

69 M Troper, 'Souveraineté de l'Etat et Hiérarchie des Normes dans la Jurisprudence Constitutionnelle – En guise d'Introduction: La Théorie Constitutionnelle et le Droit Constitutionnel Positif' (2001) [9] Les Cahiers du Conseil Constitutionnel 98: about the hierarchy of norms, he makes a distinction between two ideologies: one where the people is legislator and one where the people is the original constituent power. The idea is that there are different ways to

democracy where the people have the original constituent power but they put in place the constitution with its fundamental laws and, then, in a second step, the constitution organizes through other laws the political life. The people, as original constituent power, act at one moment. After this moment, they are subjects of the constitutional State. The ideology of national sovereignty is one example of this kind of democracy. On the other side, in a State with the application of the ideology of popular sovereignty, the people, as original constituent power, permanently retains its sovereignty and participates directly in political life. This would be the Greek idea of democracy, where the citizens are involved in the law-making process. Carré de Malberg, at the very end of his life, changed his opinion and advocated for the ideology of popular sovereignty.[70] During the Third Republic (a parliamentary system), the constitution lost its predominance over the law and popular sovereignty became parliamentary sovereignty.[71] The law can be legitimate and valid only as an emanation of the constitution and Carré de Malberg proposed therefore to put in place a constitutionality review. However, this was not enough for him: he wanted direct participation of the citizens in political life.

Finally, nowadays, it is the constitutional ideology of the State that persists, and Carré de Malberg gave internal sovereignty its main characteristic: it is the Power of the State. Furthermore, it must also be highlighted how the positivist theory of the Alsatian professor does not hold in respect of the strict positivist separation between facts and law. Kelsen's international sovereignty theory is not realistic but holds in its concept. Carré de Malberg's theory is different. The French legal theorist uses the notion of national sovereignty, which comes from the French Constitution of 1791. This constitution is based on natural law and the concept of national sovereignty is inspired by natural law.[72] Actually, national sovereignty is a fact.[73] As it is considered as the original constituent power, it cannot be determined by the law in a positivist theory: it exists in the state of nature. There is always a state of nature before the legal society and

legally organize the State within one kind of political organization (being democracy here)

70 R Carré de Malberg, *La Loi, Expression de la Volonté Générale: Etudes sur le Concept de la Loi dans la Constitution de 1875* (Sirey 1931) 216

71 G Guiheux, 'La Théorie Générale de l'Etat de Raymond Carré de Malberg' [1999] Revue Juridique de l'Ouest no spécial 89; D Mineur, 'De la Souveraineté Nationale à la Volonté Générale: L'Evolution de Carré de Malberg, du Projet Positiviste au Parti-Pris Démocratique' (2012) [8] Jus Politicum 2

72 D Mineur, 'De la Souveraineté Nationale à la Volonté Générale: L'Evolution de Carré de Malberg, du Projet Positiviste au Parti-Pris Démocratique' (2012) [8] Jus Politicum 2

73 ibid 6

the original constituent power can only be a fact. Once again, when it comes to sovereignty, social facts cannot be ignored.

3.2.2.2 Absolute supreme authority as a criterion

With the theory of Carré de Malberg in mind, it is possible to analyse the three different meanings he gives to the term sovereignty:

> Originally, it is the supreme character of a full independent power and especially of the Power of the State. Then, it is the amount of the powers included in the power of the State, being a synonym to this last expression. Finally, it designates the supreme holder, in the State, of the power of the State; here sovereignty is identified with the power of the body.[74]

In the first meaning, which is 'the supreme character of a full independent power', the external and internal aspects of sovereignty are understood as two faces of the same coin. Independence, meaning freedom, is external sovereignty and the Power of the State is internal sovereignty. The second meaning is the *summa potestas* or the sum of powers whose equivalence with the Power of the State is assessed. The last meaning is the expression of the organ theory where the sovereignty of the State is exercised by a habilitated body. Only the first two meanings can relate to sovereignty. It is first demonstrated that the Power of the State as its public power is its internal sovereignty and, in a second step, the elements of the substance of the concept must be highlighted.

Even if Carré de Malberg does not confuse both the Power of the State and sovereignty, Beaud explains that they relate to the same content.[75] They have the same characteristics in Carré de Malberg's theory.[76] The possible distinction could be the consequence of the German use of different wordings. In the definition previously quoted, the formal sovereignty (Power of the State) would be the *Staatsouveränität*, the material sovereignty (sum of the powers) the *Staatsgewalt* and the organic sovereignty the *Organsouveränität*.[77] The distinction between the two first terms does not exist in Bodin's theory; it is a German creation in order to distinguish between the sovereignty of the federal State (*Staatsouveränität*) and those of the federated States (*Staatsgewalt*) which have the public power.[78] However, according to Beaud, there is no distinction between the public power of the federated States in the German

---

74 R Carré de Malberg, *Contribution à la Théorie Générale de l'Etat*, vol 1 (Sirey 1920) 79 (Author's translation)

75 O Beaud, *La Puissance de l'Etat* (PUF 1994) 16

76 ibid 15

77 ibid

78 ibid

doctrine and sovereignty in the first sense.[79] This would be an instrumental doctrine in order to justify the German Federation.[80] Sovereignty and the public power have the same characteristics. Distinguishing both terms would empty one of both of its meanings. Furthermore, the second meaning (sum of the powers) must be discarded. Only a formal definition is possible.

Thus, the marks of sovereignty in Bodin's theory must be distinguished from the definition of sovereignty in itself. They can be compared to the functions exercised by the bodies of the State in Carré de Malberg's theory. Both are competences to do something, or powers in a legal sense, as applications of the sovereignty and not sovereignty in itself. Marks of sovereignty or functions of the bodies are, as a whole, the sum of the powers of the State. This is its material sovereignty, which is its competences. This material sovereignty cannot be named sovereignty because it is an emanation of the formal sovereignty: the State, as sovereign, has competences. Only the formal sovereignty, being supreme, can be named sovereignty. In addition, the expression 'sum of powers' implies the fact that there are several enumerated powers to constitute a sum. These powers are inherently limited because only their sum can be assimilated as a full supreme power. Yet, sovereignty cannot be limited in its role as Power of the State and *Kompetenz-Kompetenz*. It is the original competence of all competences as a 'full independent power'.[81]

Thus, the non-limitation of this full independent power must be understood as an expression of the absoluteness of sovereignty. This element of the concept of sovereignty is understood here as indeterminacy. The formal definition of sovereignty involves an indeterminacy of the Power of the State. It is expressed through its public power when publicists insist on the absolute indeterminacy of the missions of the State. If the public power is not indeterminate, there remains room for another power at the same level (or even at a higher level concerning this empty place) and the coexistence with another power would remove from the formal sovereignty its supremacy.[82] It would no longer be the highest authority.

Then, the supreme authority must be understood as the highest legal power and so as the characterization of sovereignty itself. Indeterminacy is an attribute of this highest legal power and, consequently, it is also an attribute and so a characteristic of sovereignty. In a constitutional system such as the modern

---

[79] ibid 16

[80] See Pt 1, ch 2, para 2.3.2.2

[81] R Carré de Malberg, *Contribution à la Théorie Générale de l'Etat*, vol 1 (Sirey 1920) 79

[82] It is emphasized that indeterminacy is a characteristic of the internal sovereignty. On its external face, sovereignty is a freedom. Sovereignty needs absoluteness only on its internal side. On its external side, it needs independence

democracy, the supreme authority is expressed through the law.[83] It is the power to make the law in a given legal order. The constitutional system identifies the constitution to the sovereign as the supreme authority.[84] As already evoked, this kind of democracy is based on the popular sovereignty as original constituent power which institutes the constitution as the fundamental law of the State. It is the constitutional moment. Then, the constitution, as supreme authority, is the institutionalization of the State and delegates to its bodies the power to make the law. The ultimate authority, understood as the highest authority or supreme authority, is the constitution. For example, the German Fundamental Law enacts in its preamble that the German people put in place a constitutional order (a legal order) that binds the legislative power.[85] It does so by virtue of its constituent power.[86] On the other side, the executive power and the judicial power are bound by the law.[87] Furthermore, article 1 institutes fundamental human rights that cannot be violated by any of the powers (legislative, executive and judicial).[88] Here, the people, as original constituent power, institutes the constitution through popular sovereignty. It is the constitutional moment. The constitution becomes the sovereign within the legal order once the state of nature has been left and it receives from the people the power to make the law, which becomes inherently self-limited (the power to make the law is limited by fundamental laws). In such a system, the supreme authority of the constitution over the people and the different instituted powers is a relation organized within a legal order. Therefore, the supreme authority is inherent to the State as sovereign, and indeterminacy is an inherent attribute of this supreme authority.

Finally, the necessity of the factual moment before the organization of the society within a legal order must be addressed. In this process, sovereignty is justified as an inevitable characteristic of the State.

---

83 D Baranger, *Le Droit Constitutionnel* (PUF 2017) 36: since Bodin, the power to make the law is the one and sufficient mark of sovereignty

84 ibid 47

85 German Fundamental (1949) preamble

86 ibid

87 ibid art 20

88 ibid art 1

3.3 THE RECOGNITION OF SOVEREIGNTY

3.3.1 The Concept of Sovereignty and the Blurred Line between Facts and Law

3.3.1.1 The apparition of sovereignty

As said by Combacau, 'in law, there are no things but only names of things'.[89] Baranger deepens this idea and moves beyond some conceptual distinctions that positivism made hard law during the 20th century.[90] The objective is to demonstrate that facts and law are not clearly separated when it comes to sovereignty. Through analysis of the specific wording used in the General Theory of the State, it becomes clear that sovereignty appears. This means that it exists and must only be found. The process is similar to the one that has been used for the Declaration of Human Rights and a parallel can be made.

First, here is a translation of article 3 of the French Declaration of Human and Civic Rights of 1789: 'the principle of any Sovereignty lies primarily in the Nation. No corporate body, no individual may exercise any authority that does not expressly emanate from it.'[91] And here is a translation of the preamble of the German Fundamental Law of 1949:

> Conscious of their responsibility before God and man, inspired by the determination to promote world peace as an equal partner in a united Europe, the German people, in the exercise of their constituent power, have adopted this Basic Law. Germans in the *Länder* of Baden-Württemberg, Bavaria, Berlin, Brandenburg, Bremen, Hamburg, Hesse, Lower Saxony, Mecklenburg-Western Pomerania, North Rhine-Westphalia, Rhineland-Palatinate, Saarland, Saxony, Saxony-Anhalt, Schleswig-Holstein and Thuringia have achieved the unity and freedom of Germany in free self-determination. This Basic Law thus applies to the entire German people.[92]

The English translation of the German Fundamental Law is not accurate. The words 'have adopted' is a translation of *hat sich gegeben*, which should be translated as 'has given itself'. The use of this word and of similar words ('lies'

---

[89] J Combacau, 'Pas une Puissance, une Liberté: la Souveraineté Internationale de l'Etat' (1993) [67] Pouvoirs 48

[90] D Baranger, 'Notes sur l'Apparition de la Souveraineté (et des Droits de l'Homme)' (2012) 4 Annuaire de l'Institut Michel Villey 259–308; see also D Baranger, 'The Apparition of Sovereignty' in H Kalmo and Q Skinner (eds), *Sovereignty in Fragments: The Past, Present and Future of a Contested Concept* (Cambridge University Press 2010) 47–63

[91] French Declaration of Human and Civic Rights (1789) art 3 (Author's translation)

[92] German Fundamental (1949) preamble (Author's translation)

and 'emanate') in the French Declaration illustrate a vocabulary specific to concepts such as sovereignty. Such a vocabulary shows the relation that can exist between law and the visible world (the world of facts).[93] For instance, human rights are declared, not created. Similarly, when sovereignty is given by the people or lies in the nation, it is not constituted by a legislative power. The use of the word 'emanation' is even stronger because it reveals an origin, something that must be looked for.[94] In other words, there is an essence that reveals itself and it does so through indicators or marks. It relates to such kinds of distinctions as title/exercise or essence/marks. These distinctions are used very often in relation with sovereignty.[95] It can be said that the legal language ties itself down to the visible world and, in some specific situations, law is the result of an apparition.[96]

However, this argumentation does not focus on the language used in positive law to demonstrate that facts are still present within. As seen with the English translation of the German Fundamental Law, it would be too approximate to prove anything. The vocabulary used in matters such as sovereignty or human rights is just an indication of the permanent process at work. Indeed, it has already been demonstrated that, even in positivist theories, facts cannot be easily discarded unless through a metaphysical loop. The idea is to go beyond the distinction between facts and law and demonstrate that sovereignty is inherent to the State. It appears with its construction. In international public law, for instance, the State is initially recognized as a fact. Moreover, such legal system is considered as the personification of sovereignty that manifests itself through marks or criteria, which are rendered visible by their exercise. The consequence is that sovereignty exists and is not created. This is why the methodology to find it needs to be explained in order to know when it appears.

Why does sovereignty appear and why does it have to be found? Law is not immediate.[97] It is not given instantaneously, in the sense that it is not initially present in the visible world.[98] Individuals come to the lawyer to know their rights. The legislator does much work in order to know what would be the adequate law. There is a methodology to find the law. Finding the law means that it is not immediately present in the same place as the people who need it. It is not present for the individual who did not study law but, before this, it is not present for the legislator who must determine what the law is. Originally,

93 D Baranger, 'Notes sur l'Apparition de la Souveraineté (et des Droits de l'Homme)' (2012) 4 Annuaire de l'Institut Michel Villey 260
94 ibid
95 ibid
96 ibid
97 ibid 264
98 ibid

the law is absent and finding law means to give up on immediacy.[99] Indeed, the world of facts is the world of 'is' (*sein*) while the world of law is the world of 'ought to be' (*sollen*). Its value gives its legitimacy to law.[100] If the law is a *sollen*, it means that it is not already realized but, as expected value, it must become knowable as a correction of the *sein*. If there is nothing to improve, there is no need for law.[101] Law appears through its interconnection with the visible world.

Hegel, in his *Principles of Legal Philosophy*, writes on the objective reality of law.[102] This reality has two aspects: law must exist for the conscience and be knowable; and law must have the power to be effectively real and valid for everybody.[103] The latter is its universal validity.[104] The law must be given in its empirical context in order to be not just universal but effectively universal and so valid. It means, for Baranger, that, when law must be interpreted to identify its right application, not only its content but also its context must be interpreted.[105] This is particularly true for sovereignty, which has no normative definition, and which is identified through its marks.

The State has been understood as the personification of sovereignty. As a legal person, the existence of the State has been made to parallel the existence of the human being.[106] However, sovereignty, as the main characteristic of this legal person, remains behind and only manifests itself through its marks, which are the power to make the law and, through this main power, to delegate its competences. Making the law means getting outside of the state of nature. The power to make the law can belong to a king or to the people but, in both cases, it belongs to the sovereign. This sovereign is the inevitable fact through which State and law become possible. In order to leave the state of nature for the normative sphere, a tangible sovereign is still necessary as the last impulsion in order to pass from one world to the other.[107] Even Kelsen, who made the sovereign a fiction, needs a point of imputation as a starting point.[108] He says that 'the will of the State is the anthropomorphic expression of the "ought to

99 ibid 266
100 ibid
101 ibid
102 GWF Hegel, *Elements of the Philosophy of Rights* (1820) para 210
103 ibid para 211
104 ibid
105 D Baranger, 'Notes sur l'Apparition de la Souveraineté (et des Droits de l'Homme)' (2012) 4 Annuaire de l'Institut Michel Villey 269
106 ibid 272
107 ibid
108 ibid 273

be" of the legal norms'.[109] In a way, the State, as legal system, can symbolize the transition from the visible world to the normative world. As a personification of its own sovereignty, it illustrates its necessity as impulsion from the visible world to the normative world. It must also be underlined that, in this perspective, the unity of sovereignty is the unity of the State.

Furthermore, if sovereignty is the unity of the State, why are there so many interpretations of the term? This legitimate question lies in the tangible necessity of sovereignty. When scholars want to avoid the concept of sovereignty, they use the term 'disappearance'.[110] Often, the existence of sovereignty in history is not put into question but the difficulty of finding it might make it easier to simply avoid such a concept. On the other side, as sovereignty manifests itself and is not only dependent on the will of the legislator, its apparition must be observed and analysed. Different scholars can identify different characteristics or be mistaken by some manifestations and end up creating different conceptions of sovereignty instead of finding its essence within its social and then legal construction. In his definition, Carré de Malberg is not wrong when he says there are different meanings of the term. However, not each of them corresponds to the essence of the term, but rather more to usages of it.[111] This is why Combacau writes about names of things in law. Names can mean something different than the things in themselves when the distance between facts and law is too strong and does not correspond to the reality of the social context. However, these names are still signs of the existence of the underlying things.

Nonetheless, it must be kept in mind that this argumentation is specific to the analysis of the concept of sovereignty and does not presuppose a general rule in law. Here, the methodology at work is to deepen consideration of its marks and characteristics to find its essential attributes. Bodin works this way in *The Six Books of the Republic*.[112] He analyses many different regimes at many different periods to find the essential characteristics of sovereignty. Thus, there are different kinds of political organisation he accepts (monarchy, democracy, aristocracy), but only one kind of sovereign with the same essential attributes. His leitmotif is that sovereignty is somewhere and must be found.

---

109 H Kelsen, *Pure Theory of Law* (1934)

110 D Baranger, 'Notes sur l'Apparition de la Souveraineté (et des Droits de l'Homme)' (2012) 4 Annuaire de l'Institut Michel Villey 278: mentioning Léon Duguit, who was an opponent of Carré de Malberg at the beginning of the 20th century. In his doctrine, he announces the disappearance of sovereignty.

111 D Baranger, 'Notes sur l'Apparition de la Souveraineté (et des Droits de l'Homme)' (2012) 4 Annuaire de l'Institut Michel Villey 274

112 J Bodin, *Les Six Livres de la République* (1576)

This is a recurrent theme among the authors on sovereignty.[113] Each author uses their own method to formulate their own methodology. It can be essence/marks or title/exercise, for example. In this sense, legal signs are witnesses of an underlying existence in the visible world. Even more, they are witnesses of an unavoidable interaction. Finally, this idea of interaction, coupled with that of apparition, belongs also to the vocabulary of recognition theory.

In the legal process of the apparition of sovereignty, as well as in international public law where facts must also be recognized, recognition theory is the driving element. The application of the theory is the same as that used to recognize the State. Indeed, the State, as a legal system, is the personification of sovereignty. Consequently, the declaratory position shall apply and the consequences of the definition of the recognition theory are:[114]

- Recognition means an apparition: it is the importance of the visible world in the process.
- Recognition implies the authority of what is recognized: recognition implies legal consequences (and in both theories: declaratory or constitutive).
- Recognition is an attestation: what is recognized becomes real in the legal sphere (proofs, for instance).
- Recognition is individuation: what is recognized is recognized as what it is and not as something else, it is a source of institutionalization.

Then, in the process of identifying the concept of sovereignty and its methodology, a parallel should be made with human rights as they are 'declared'.

3.3.1.2 The parallel with human rights

Human rights can be considered as 'perfect freedoms'.[115] They are individual actions vested of moral legitimacy[116] and, in a way, sovereign rights of the individuals. Within their fundamental rights, individuals received from the sovereign which they constituted their own personal and inviolable rights. In modern constitutional democracies, it can be said that the people, as original political sovereign, instituted their constitutional sovereign but with the guarantee to remain sovereign outside of the political sphere, meaning as individuals. The constitution, then, gives its legal legitimacy to these fundamentally human rights. There is an intimate connection between sovereignty and human

---

[113] D Baranger, 'Notes sur l'Apparition de la Souveraineté (et des Droits de l'Homme)' (2012) 4 Annuaire de l'Institut Michel Villey 280–81
[114] ibid 297
[115] ibid 299
[116] ibid

rights.[117] On one side, sovereignty is recognized by the subjects and is the State in action. On the other side, human rights are passively recognized by the State as personal actions. In a democracy both must coexist, otherwise there would not be any popular sovereignty. While sovereignty expresses itself through the power to edict positive law, human rights preserve individuals from abuse of this power. The State institutionalizes the society that leaves the state of nature. Similarly, when leaving this state of nature, as a parallel to the institution of sovereignty, individuals get civilized by human rights. This is a non-created law that must only be recognized as self-evident in the process of civilization. Hannah Arendt says herself about the American Declaration of Independence:

> Jefferson's famous words, 'We hold these truths to be self-evident', combine in a historically unique manner the basis of agreement between those who have embarked upon revolution, an agreement necessarily relative because related to those who enter it, with an absolute, namely with a truth that needs no agreement since, because of its self-evidence, it compels without argumentative demonstration or political persuasion. By virtue of being self-evident, these truths are pre-rational – they inform reason but are not its product – and since their self-evidence puts them beyond disclosure and argument, they are in a sense no less compelling than 'despotic power' and no less absolute than the revealed truths of religion or the axiomatic verities of mathematics.[118]

Nonetheless, the purpose is not to demonstrate an absolute connection between sovereignty and human rights in the field of law. When human rights need to be declared, it could be because of an abusive sovereign, but not only because of this (new fundamental rights can be declared in the relations between individuals). Similarly, there can be a sovereign without human rights. However, in modern democracies, it can be observed that they are bound in most constitutional regimes. Their mode of presentation is the same. Human rights are declared because they are self-evident. They must be found and then recognized. They follow the same path as the apparition of sovereignty. One can think that there is no absolute connection but that maybe there should be one. The concept of sovereignty must always have the same attributes but there are different possibilities to organize the State. Similarly, in their essence, human rights *are*, and they can only be declared, as in the sense of Hannah Arendt's words above. Similar to mathematical truths, there are intangible facts that have always been true. Law confirms their legitimacy but they should not need it. Here, the distinction between facts and law is so blurred that the distinction only appears through the specific mode of presentation that is the legal norm

---

117 ibid

118 H Arendt, *On Revolution* (Penguin Books 2006) 192

and it puts into question the fact that a norm is only valid or invalid.[119] With human rights, and in the sense of declarations such as the American Declaration of Independence or the French Declaration of Human and Civic Rights, a norm can be true or false.[120] Consequently, even if there is no absolute connection between human rights and sovereignty in the legal sphere, if both must only be revealed as already existing in the visible world, their connection should be reestablished in the same legal sphere as a balance between authority and individual freedom/dignity when it is needed. This balance is at work within the sphere of internal sovereignty through constitutional principles as it is within the sphere of external sovereignty through *jus cogens* (imperative norms).[121]

Finally, this process of apparition is meant to be specific to the concept of sovereignty.

3.3.2 A Specific Methodology

3.3.2.1 A concept of political law

The process of apparition of sovereignty has two aspects: the first is the blurred line between facts and law and the second is the importance of recognition theory as a legal tool for sovereignty to pass from the visible world to the legal sphere of norms. The specificity of this process to find sovereignty is similar to that used in order to declare human rights and that used in international public law for the recognition of the constitution of a new State. More accurately, there is a methodology, which corresponds to the field of political law.

Pimentel, on neighbouring bases to the ones used by Baranger for the apparition of sovereignty, gives elements for a theory of political law whose methodology would be the starting point in order to find sovereignty today.[122] 'What makes political law is its recognition by the subjects it governs.'[123] A

---

119 D Baranger, 'Notes sur l'Apparition de la Souveraineté (et des Droits de l'Homme)' (2012) 4 Annuaire de l'Institut Michel Villey 302

120 ibid

121 D Grimm, *Sovereignty: The Origin and Future of a Political and Legal Concept* (Columbia University Press 2015) 86; Vienna Convention on the Law of Treaties (1969) art 53: the *jus cogens* is imperative norms of general international law that must not be violated by conventions concluded between States. With time, an international legal order emerged with international human rights and the *jus cogens* (imperative norms) is no longer limited to international conventions: see eg AA Cançado Trindade, *The Construction of a Humanized International Law – A Collection of Individual Opinions (1991–2013)* (Brill Nijhoff 2014)

122 CM Pimentel, 'Reconnaissance et Désaveu: Contribution à une Théorie du Droit Politique' (2008) [1] Jus Politicum 1–6

123 ibid 1

rule is only words and what gives it its value is its recognition by the subjects of the State.[124] If there is no recognition, the rule is only a claim and it loses its imperative legal power. During the First English Revolution (1642–1651), both the King and the Parliament alleged their acts had a legal value on all of the subjects of the Kingdom.[125] Both were right and wrong because both were recognized by a part of the subjects and not by the other part. There is here a specificity of political law, which is due to the institutionalization of sovereignty. During a revolution, there is a new original constituent power, which is originally a fact, that creates the new legal system with a sovereign and a derived constituent power. What makes the success of the new political regime, which is an ideological choice to establish the new legal system, is the recognition of this regime by its subjects and so the recognition of the new sovereign within this political and legal system.

Even the imperative value of a norm is dependent on the relation between the command and the obedience to it.[126] It is the importance of law as a social link and a non-recognized sovereign cannot edict a norm with a legal value.[127] According to this idea, the importance of human rights in modern democracies can become crucial. It is article 16 of the French Declaration of Human and Civic Rights: 'any society in which no provision is made for guaranteeing rights or for the separation of powers, has no Constitution.'[128] The non-recognition of human rights by the legislator of a State having such a norm within its constitution, being the delegated body in order to make the law, inherently revokes the legal power of the acts it enacts and puts into question the entire legal system and its organization around the constitution as sovereign. It underlines the importance of the social link between sovereign and subjects in political law. Recognition, here, gives the legal value to the norm.[129] However, this recognition is based on collectivity.[130] If only one individual violates a norm, it is punished. Actually, it is punished by the collectivity, which chose and recognized the legal system that punishes it.

The recognition by the collectivity is not dependent on a specific kind of organization like democracy.[131] Even in a monarchy or any other kind of

---

124 ibid
125 ibid
126 ibi 2
127 ibid
128 French Declaration of Human and Civic Rights (1789) art 16 (Author's translation)
129 CM Pimentel, 'Reconnaissance et Désaveu: Contribution à une Théorie du Droit Politique' (2008) [1] Jus Politicum 2
130 ibid
131 ibid 3

regime, the collectivity of the subjects recognizes the king or any other sovereign. This can be observed through history because the recognition by the collectivity ceases when there is a revolution. Similarly, when only one individual refuses to recognize the legitimacy of the State, it does not put into question the latter. However, in a democracy, for instance, if the minority does not recognize the majority, it could put into question its legitimacy because the majority speaks in the name of the whole people and, in this situation, its legitimacy becomes a simple claim similar to those observed during the first English revolution.[132] At the level of the State, recognition and disallowance make the political law and the latter depends on collective actions.[133] What makes the State is its recognition, of itself and so of its authority. It is true in international public law, and so for external sovereignty, but also in political law, and so for internal sovereignty. In political law, recognition by an individual is an observation while recognition by the collectivity is a declaration of what exists in fact exists also in law.

Consequently, according to Pimentel, in this field of law interpretation cannot be limited to the content of norms and cases.[134] The context of the law must be considered. Thus, the interaction between facts and law must be observed. However, it is not only a factual observation of what could be a law but a permanent reconsideration of the relation between the sovereign and its subjects. Within this relation, collective recognition builds the State as a legal system, which is metaphorically alive and constantly evolving.

3.3.2.2 Finding sovereignty today

Sovereignty exists. The difficulty is to apprehend it and to understand it. It has not disappeared and it can still be found in any political system. It is an inherent element of any political and legal system. Scholars can define it as a supreme norm or as a fiction but its authority is necessary to the norm and to the political organization. Coming back to the notion of legal norm as expected value, as it is not immediate and so not obvious, it must first be imposed so it can become a part of the legal sphere. Then, this norm, which has been found or created depending on the kind of norm, is accepted and recognized by the collectivity. All imperative norms necessitate an original authority to impose them because their value is expected to become real but is not yet real (and so it originally needs to be imposed). This original authority is sovereignty.

Consequently, sovereignty is authority, but a specific kind of authority with a specific mode of presentation. First, concerning the kind of authority, there can

---

132 ibid

133 ibid

134 ibid 5

be many different conceptions of the political organization around the concept of sovereignty. However, concerning the concept in itself, it has attributes that never change and that are permanent. These attributes are the main elements of the concept in itself and they must be found, in a second phase, through the specific mode of presentation of the concept of sovereignty. The latter has two faces: external sovereignty and internal sovereignty. Concerning external sovereignty, independence or freedom in international law and as a negative quality of the concept is the main attribute of sovereignty. Concerning internal sovereignty, the main attribute is the absolute supreme authority. It is the highest authority in the State. The fact that it is the highest authority involves its unity (indivisibility) and its indeterminacy.[135] This highest supreme authority embodies the State.

Second, concerning the mode of presentation, sovereignty appears. In order to determine where sovereignty is and so who can be sovereign, it is not sufficient to look only at the content of the law; its context must also be considered. It is the specific methodology involved by the concept of sovereignty as a concept of political law and the line between facts and law should not be seen as a barrier. This does not mean that facts are the determinant element in order to find sovereignty but rather that sovereignty appears in a first step in a factual context that leads, in a second step, to legal decisions considered as sovereign decisions and recognized as such. In the end, it is the recognition that sovereignty can be found in a specific place and so held by a specific entity. The expression and so the apparition of the different attributes of sovereignty, in the visible world and in the sphere of norms together as context and content, should indicate where sovereignty is.

Today's international context could require a reassessment of the attributes of sovereignty and of its *locus* (location). Combacau explains that, for instance, too many self-limitations in international law could empty sovereignty of its substance: 'a deprivation of freedom and not a deprivation of power.'[136] International agreements and international organizations should not

---

[135] Bodin also presented permanence as a criterion. In international law, the State has a continuity, which is not put into question by a government change. The question on permanence and continuity would only be raised when there is a political change and so a revolution. Even in this case, as it is considered that sovereignty exists and must only be found, there is a continuity but through the concept in itself. So, permanence can be considered as an element of sovereignty but looking for it is looking for sovereignty in itself as it has no specific mode of presentation. It is the apparition of the other attributes in the visible world and the sphere of legal norms that would allow finding sovereignty in itself

[136] J Combacau, 'Pas une Puissance, une Liberté: la Souveraineté Internationale de l'Etat' (1993) [67] Pouvoirs 58

be considered as a risk in themselves for sovereignty but rather for the sovereignty of the State. The *locus* (location) of sovereignty can move, but always according to the inherent criteria of the concept. As such, what can change is not the concept of sovereignty but its manifestation through the State as personification.

3.4 CONCLUSION

While Kelsen and Carré de Malberg focused on the essential criteria of the concept of sovereignty to assess their consequent impact on the legal sphere, the purpose here is to come as close as possible to the origin of the concept. Indeed, the issue at stake is not only to assess what sovereignty is and how it manifests itself but whether it exists and, if yes, where it can be found. Such new interrogations become necessary because of the complexification of the global legal order and, when investigating, the process that led to this situation must not be ignored. Before the international legal order there were the States, which left the state of nature as social orders organized through what appears to be the concept of sovereignty. It means also that there cannot be a content of the law without a context of the law. Both can be interpreted. If a legal principle can be deduced from the content of a law or from the content of a case, the accumulation of legal decisions with specific legal orientations which create a context can also be interpreted, even if more complex. Then, theoretically, it might be easy to deduce that facts help in the creation of a legal context – with the example of the impact of political choices on the creation of the law – but this is difficult to analyse when the context becomes definitely legal. The creation of the norm is self-evident when it comes to the content of the law but not when it comes to its context. Yet, the attributes of sovereignty are so absolute – freedom and absolute supreme authority – that its location depends more on the legal context than on the legal content. An individual can proclaim itself king but, without recognition, this proclamation has no practical impact even if this individual edicts laws with a regular procedure. This individual would not have a supreme authority without a collective recognition within the legal sphere. Thus, nowadays, such attributes of the concept of sovereignty must be confronted with the impact of supranational integration such as the European Union (EU) to understand whether the concept of sovereignty can be found beyond the State.

PART II

The Sovereignty of the European Union and the Application of the Theory of Shared Sovereignty

4. Asserting the sovereignty of the European Union

4.1 INTRODUCTION

The European Union (EU) is a sovereign entity. When the definition and the methodology of the concept of sovereignty are applied, it can be found that sovereignty applies to a system that organizes the society and not only to the State as such. However, a reverse demonstration is necessary to demonstrate this. According to the concept of sovereignty, there is first internal sovereignty and second the recognition of external sovereignty on the international level. Indeed, external sovereignty is just a quality of internal sovereignty. However, the EU is the product of the powers of its Member States' through-making. Consequently, there was a supranational organization before the sovereign entity. The apparition of sovereignty at the EU level came progressively with the evolution of the Union. As there is a conventional origin, it is through the self-limitation of the external sovereignty of the Member States that the demonstration begins. This means that, for the EU, it begins at the level of external sovereignty. Thus, it is necessary to observe its situation on the international scene.

In this purpose, the technique of body of evidence is used. The confusion between the external sovereignty of the Member States and that of the EU can be demonstrated through the evolution of the Union itself. However, it is also necessary to spotlight the main elements that characterize its sovereignty. This is why the main manifestations of the sovereignty of the EU are highlighted. These manifestations must be important elements of its legal order and so general elements of its organization that are strongly implemented and so recognized by the Member States as belonging to the European legal order. It is the application of the methodology of the concept of sovereignty concerning the apparition of sovereignty. As such, recognition by the Member States has also a role to play.

Then, as the external sovereignty is only a quality of the internal sovereignty, it is asserted that the EU has an internal sovereignty. This is demonstrated through the analysis of the Court of Justice of the European Union

(CJEU), its function within the EU and the most important cases that it ruled upon in order to put in place the European order.

Finally, as is necessary to explain the sovereignty of the EU, the concept of shared sovereignty is introduced.

4.2 FROM THE EXTERNAL SOVEREIGNTY OF THE MEMBER STATES TO THE EXTERNAL SOVEREIGNTY OF THE EUROPEAN UNION: A CONFUSION

4.2.1 The Progressive Limitation of the Member States' External Sovereignty

4.2.1.1 From a conventional origin to the *acquis communautaire*

At the origin of the EU, there was a federal will.[1] However, knowing the reluctance specific to the old Europe, the Schuman Plan provided for a functionalist approach.[2] The full political integration had to smoothly follow integration by sector, and especially by economic sector, through a gear system.[3] Therefore, in the declaration of 9 May 1950, it is specified that 'by pooling basic production and by instituting a new High Authority, whose decisions will bind France, Germany and other member countries, this proposal will lead to the realization of the first concrete foundation of a European federation indispensable to the preservation of peace'.[4]

Thus began the complex evolution of the EU, with the conclusion of three different treaties between the six Founding States. First, on 18 April 1951, the treaty establishing the European Coal and Steel Community (ECSC) was signed in Paris.[5] It established, for 50 years, a common market for free trade in this specific sector, where the management would be entrusted to a political and supranational institution.[6] Extinguished since 2002, this treaty laid

1 M Blanquet, *Droit Général de l'Union Européenne* (Sirey 2018) 2; see also A Cuyvers, *The Scope, Nature and Effect of EU Law in East African Community Law: Institutional, Substantive and Comparative EU Aspects* (E Ugirashebuja and others eds, Brill/Nijhoff 2017) 25–28

2 ibid

3 ibid

4 R Schuman, 'Declaration of 9 May 1950' <www.robert-schuman.eu/en/declaration-of-9-may-195> accessed 19 November 2025

5 Treaty establishing the European Coal and Steal Community [1951] 261 UNTS 140

6 See M Blanquet, *Droit Général de l'Union Européenne* (Sirey 2018) 3; see also A Cuyvers, *The Scope, Nature and Effect of EU Law in East African*

the first stones of the EU. It provided for a High Authority independent from the Member States and with effective powers to manage the internal market.[7] Also, this High Authority had its own Court of Justice and its own resources.[8] It was thanks to this sectored success that the European Economic Community (EEC) and Euratom could come to life years later.

The six Founding Member States agreed at the Messine conference in June 1955 that it was necessary to move beyond the ECSC.[9] The Spaak report opened the door to two new communities: a general one and one on atomic energy.[10] Two treaties were concluded on 25 March 1957, one on the European Atomic Energy Community (Euratom)[11] and one on the EEC.[12] The latter instituted 'ultimate objectives and immediate commitments'.[13] According to its preamble, the Member States are 'determined to establish the bases of an always closer Union between the European people'.[14] This sentence underlines the fact that the EU is based on objectives and is a dynamic order. This aspect is crucial for the construction of its own sovereignty. On the institutional side, this treaty created the internal market and the customs union in combination with common sectored policies in areas such as agriculture.[15] The institutions in themselves generally followed the model of the ECSC, but with less importance given to the supranational authority (Commission), even if the objective was already integration and not just intergovernmental cooperation.[16]

In the process of the construction of the EU, an initial period began in the 1960s and ended with the treaty of Maastricht in 1992. First, in 1957, the Treaty of Rome still respected unanimity voting and so the veto right of the

---

Community Law: Institutional, Substantive and Comparative EU Aspects (E Ugirashebuja and others eds, Brill/Nijhofff 2017) 28

[7] ibid

[8] ibid

[9] M Blanquet, *Droit Général de l'Union Européenne* (Sirey 2018) 4; see also A Cuyvers, *The Scope, Nature and Effect of EU Law in East African Community Law: Institutional, Substantive and Comparative EU Aspects* (E Ugirashebuja and others eds, Brill/Nijhoff 2017) 28

[10] ibid

[11] Treaty establishing the European Atomic Energy Community [1957] 298 UNTS 167

[12] Treaty establishing the European Economic Community [1957] 294 UNTS 3

[13] M Blanquet, *Droit Général de l'Union Européenne* (Sirey 2018) 4

[14] Treaty establishing the European Economic Community [1957] 294 UNTS 3 preamble

[15] Intergovernmental Committee on the Common Market and Euratom, 'Report of the Heads of Delegation to the Foreign Ministers' (1956)

[16] See eg M Blanquet, *Droit Général de l'Union Européenne* (Sirey 2018) 4

Member States.[17] Respectful of the usual rule in international organizations, it was not in line with the final objective of political integration. This is why this rule was condemned to be progressively replaced by qualified majority voting (QMV) until 1 January 1966.[18] This provoked the empty chair crisis[19] that led to the Compromise of Luxembourg.[20] France, and especially De Gaulle, refused to abandon unanimity voting for QMV as a general rule. It was too damaging for the sovereignty of the Member States and so was denounced as a supranational deviation.[21] As a sign of protestation, France's chair at the Council stood empty from 30 June 1965 until 30 January 1966. With the Compromise, the search for a consensus was prioritized over QMV and the latter was abandoned in crucial sectors such as taxation. Consequently, QMV is still not a general rule in the EU. This incident demonstrates that the European integration process is slow and built on compromises.

In a second step during this period, the EEC improved its integration process in such a way that, as announced by Combacau,[22] it becomes difficult to assert that the limitations accorded by the Member States to their independence at the international level and understood as their external sovereignty did not affect their sovereignty in their relations with the EU. This step is characterized by the Single European Act (SEA)[23] and the treaty of Maastricht.[24] The SEA can be considered as the prelude to the treaty of Maastricht. This treaty provided for the achievement of the common market at the end of 1992, achieving promises of the treaty of Rome that could not be held to before.[25] It strengthened the institutional organization of the EEC but also the intergov-

---

[17] M Blanquet, *Droit Général de l'Union Européenne* (Sirey 2018) 6; see also, on political resistance from the governments of the Member States, A Cuyvers, *The Scope, Nature and Effect of EU Law in East African Community Law: Institutional, Substantive and Comparative EU Aspects* (E Ugirashebuja and others eds, Brill/Nijhoff 2017) 29

[18] See M Blanquet, *Droit Général de l'Union Européenne* (Sirey 2018) 6

[19] M Blanquet, *Droit Général de l'Union Européenne* (Sirey 2018) 6; A Cuyvers, *The Scope, Nature and Effect of EU Law in East African Community Law: Institutional, Substantive and Comparative EU Aspects* (E Ugirashebuja and others eds, Brill/Nijhoff 2017) 29

[20] European Council, 'Compromise of Luxembourg' (1966)

[21] M Blanquet, *Droit Général de l'Union Européenne* (Sirey 2018) 6

[22] See pt 1, ch 3, especially the conclusion

[23] Single European Act [1987] OJ L169 30/1

[24] Treaty on European Union [1992] OJ C 191 35/1

[25] M Blanquet, *Droit Général de l'Union Européenne* (Sirey 2018) 7; A Cuyvers, *The Scope, Nature and Effect of EU Law in East African Community Law: Institutional, Substantive and Comparative EU Aspects* (E Ugirashebuja and others eds, Brill/Nijhoff 2017) 29

ernmental cooperation between the Member States.[26] Still, it is the treaty of Maastricht that was the turning point for the institutionalization of the EU. Since the 1970s, with the Tindemans report, the objective had been to reinforce the external and internal cooperation of the European communities.[27] In 1984, the European Parliament adopted a project of a European Union, which was a real project of constitution for the European communities.[28] Consequently, the treaty of Maastricht (which is the treaty on the European Union (TEU)) was signed on 7 February 1992, around three pillars:

- The first pillar is the European Community in itself.[29] The EEC became the EC because it is no longer limited to economic sectors. This was symbolized by the apparition of the European citizenship. Also, monetary union was created, and it entered into force in 1999. Even if the latter still does not involve all the Member States, it is a big step towards the political integration of the Union. It came with institutional improvements such as the association of the European Parliament to the legislative power of the EU with the Council (codecision). It illustrates the success of the functionalist approach towards European political integration.
- The second pillar is the Common Foreign and Security Policy (CFSP).[30]
- The third pillar is Cooperation in Justice and Home Affairs.[31]

Even if the three pillars all belong to the European project, only the first pillar concerns European integration, while the two others are based on coordination. The two other European treaties, on the ECSC and Euratom, are included

---

[26] M Blanquet, *Droit Général de l'Union Européenne* (Sirey 2018) 6; A Cuyvers, *The Scope, Nature and Effect of EU Law in East African Community Law: Institutional, Substantive and Comparative EU Aspects* (E Ugirashebuja and others eds, Brill/Nijhoff 2017) 30

[27] See L Tindemans, 'Report to the European Council' (1976) [Supplement 1/76] Bulletin of the European Communities

[28] M Blanquet, *Droit Général de l'Union Européenne* (Sirey 2018) 11; see also KD Borchardt, *The ABC of EU law* (European Union 2017) 15-18

[29] M Blanquet, *Droit Général de l'Union Européenne* (Sirey 2018) 14; A Cuyvers, *The Scope, Nature and Effect of EU Law in East African Community Law: Institutional, Substantive and Comparative EU Aspects* (E Ugirashebuja and others eds, Brill/Nijhoff 2017) 30; see also KD Borchardt, *The ABC of EU Law* (European Union 2017) 15-18

[30] M Blanquet, *Droit Général de l'Union Européenne* (Sirey 2018) 16; A Cuyvers, *The Scope, Nature and Effect of EU Law in East African Community Law: Institutional, Substantive and Comparative EU Aspects* (E Ugirashebuja and others eds, Brill/Nijhoff 2017) 30

[31] ibid

within the first pillar and, despite the important progress that has been reached through the treaty of Maastricht, the Union was still considered as a political organization at that time as it did not yet have the legal personality and a real capacity for international commitments. This came in a second period for the EU.

Thus, the treaty of Amsterdam,[32] concluded on 2 October 1997, and the treaty of Nice,[33] concluded on 26 February 2001, brought some evolutions in European integration, but nothing as important as the treaty of Maastricht.[34] It was only with the treaty of Lisbon,[35] signed on 13 December 2007, that the European Community (EC) became the EU and accomplished a further step towards political integration. The first initiative before the signature of this treaty was a project of constitution for Europe.[36] Even if the CJEU already qualified the European treaties as a constitution, and some scholars already considered them as a European constitution, a European constitution in itself would have been a formalization of this process[37] and would have been a new treaty repealing the older ones.[38] Too politically radical, this reform has been refused and the treaty of Lisbon, on a revisionist basis, has been adopted. The treaty of Rome, under the name 'Treaty on the Functioning of the European Union' (TFEU), and the treaty of Maastricht, as the TEU, were retained. However, this revision still brought many modifications towards the constitutionalization of the EU. For example, there is no European law, but legislative acts.[39] Similarly, the Charter of Fundamental Rights (CFR) is not within the treaties but article 6 TEU gives it its legal value. Also, the idea of the three pillars disappeared and became a distinction between exclusive competences,

---

[32] Treaty of Amsterdam amending the Treaty on European Union, the Treaties establishing the European Communities and certain related acts [1997] OJ C 340 40/1

[33] Treaty of Nice amending the Treaty on European Union, the Treaties establishing the European Communities and certain related acts [2001] OJ C 80 44/1

[34] M Blanquet, *Droit Général de l'Union Européenne* (Sirey 2018) 27; see also KD Borchardt, *The ABC of EU Law* (European Union 2017) 15–18

[35] Treaty of Lisbon amending the Treaty on European Union and the Treaty establishing the European Community [2007] OJ C 306 50/1

[36] Draft Treaty establishing a Constitution for Europe [2003] OJ C 169 46/1

[37] See eg M Blanquet, *Droit Général de l'Union Européenne* (Sirey 2018) 34; A Cuyvers, *The Scope, Nature and Effect of EU Law in East African Community Law: Institutional, Substantive and Comparative EU Aspects* (E Ugirashebuja and others eds, Brill/Nijhoff 2017) 31

[38] M Blanquet, *Droit Général de l'Union Européenne* (Sirey 2018) 34; see also KD Borchardt, *The ABC of EU Law* (European Union 2017) 15–18

[39] M Blanquet, *Droit Général de l'Union Européenne* (Sirey 2018) 37

shared competences and competences of coordination.[40] Furthermore, the EU now has the legal personality and a defined capacity for international commitments.[41] More than a political integration, this treaty demonstrates a real constitutional integration. Thus, the process of European integration led to the constitution of the *acquis communautaire* (EU acquis), which grew over time and imposes itself upon all Member States and acceding States. The *acquis communautaire* limits the external sovereignty of the Member States by limiting their international independence.

Still, the process of European integration remains based on compromises. From these compromises resulted a Europe with different speeds. Some examples deserve to be mentioned and confronted with the European integration process to assess the effective limitation of the external sovereignty of the Member States by this process.

First, the expansion of the EU can be contradictory in its development, in the sense that having 27 Member States is not the same as having 6 States. This is especially obvious in the fields where unanimity voting is still required. Consequently, to avoid European agreements or associations outside the EU, it has been decided to accept some distinctions between the different Member States, to the detriment of the *acquis communautaire.* It is a Europe with different speeds, where not all the Member States are in the Schengen area or participate in the monetary union (there is an opt-out option in the Maastricht treaty). Also, with article 114 paragraph 4 TFEU, a Member State can justify national dispositions in contradiction with a new European legislative act that is adopted by the majority. In the Lisbon treaty this is translated by many protocols, such as protocol no 16 on specific dispositions concerning Denmark[42] or protocol no 30 on the application of the CFR to Poland and the UK.[43]

Second, there is the procedure of enhanced cooperation that has been introduced by the treaty of Amsterdam and that is now defined by the Lisbon treaty at article 20 TEU and articles 326 to 334 TFEU. It is a distinction in the pace of participation. Because of unanimity voting, which results in a veto right for the Member States in some areas, a minimum of nine Member States can choose to implement a measure only for them. Other Member States may participate even if the measure will not bind them. The idea is to create a knock-on effect to encourage the non-participating Member States to finally implement such

---

40 TFEU, art 3, 4 and 6

41 TEU, art 47

42 Protocol on Certain Provisions relating to Denmark [2007] OJ C 306 50/182

43 Protocol on the Application of the Charter of Fundamental Rights of the European Union to Poland and to the United Kingdom [2007] OJ C 306 50/156

measures.[44] However, at the time of writing, enhanced cooperation has been used only five times.[45] It can be considered that it has a limited impact.

Third, the right to voluntarily leave the EU must be mentioned. Indeed, when it comes to the independence of the Member States and so to their external sovereignty, it is the independence of their own will that is considered and not measures of exclusion or suspension included in the treaties such as article 7 TEU. Hence, the Lisbon treaty introduced a new article 50 in the TEU. It is a principle: 'every Member State may decide to withdraw from the Union in accordance with its own constitutional requirements.'[46] The purpose of this provision was to reassure the Member States and help them to ratify the treaties but also to organize the withdrawal of a Member State, if it really happens, over a two-year period in order to forecast the outcome.[47] This came to pass with 'Brexit' and the departure of the United Kingdom (UK) from the EU on 31 January 2020. However, what is important to underline is that the Member States have a sovereign right to leave the EU that does not depend on article 50 TEU. It is a characteristic of their own sovereignty, as underlined by the CJEU:

> That being so, the Court notes that Article 50 TEU pursues two objectives, namely, first, that of enshrining the sovereign right of a Member State to withdraw from the European Union and, secondly, that of establishing a procedure to enable such a withdrawal to take place in an orderly fashion.[48]

The Member States have a fully independent right to leave the EU that is based on their own will.

As such, there are some exceptions to the *acquis communautaire*. The process of European integration does not always take the same pace for each Member State.[49] These limitations to full European integration are nonethe-

---

[44] M Blanquet, *Droit Général de l'Union Européenne* (Sirey 2018) 58–59; see also KD Borchardt, *The ABC of EU Law* (European Union 2017) 38–40

[45] M Blanquet, *Droit Général de l'Union Européenne* (Sirey 2018) 63–66

[46] TEU, art 50

[47] M Blanquet, *Droit Général de l'Union Européenne* (Sirey 2018) 54; see, on the whole procedure: A Cuyvers, *The Scope, Nature and Effect of EU Law in East African Community Law: Institutional, Substantive and Comparative EU Aspects* (E Ugirashebuja and others eds, Brill/Nijhoff 2017) 36–40

[48] Case C-621/18 *Wightman and Others v Secretary of State for Exiting the European Union* [2018] EU:C:2018:999

[49] Thus, the legitimacy of the *acquis* for the new adhering Member States can also be questioned. Indeed, to adhere, the Copenhagen criteria already require from the candidates that they are a democracy respecting the rule of law and human rights and have a functioning market economy able to cope with

less allowed by the European treaties concerning enhanced cooperation, or, on the other side, are negotiated by specific treaties. This means that there is still a process of European integration and an adhesion to the *acquis communautaire*, even if lighter. It is only with the fully sovereign right to voluntarily leave the EU that the Member States can preserve their external sovereignty. Yet, the right to voluntarily leave the EU should be understood as a change of legal sphere and of political organization. An example of this is the Brexit referendum held in the UK on 23 June 2016.

Concerning this precise referendum, there was, on the facts, confusion as to whether it was a legislative referendum or a consultative referendum, even if, legally, in the UK it was considered as a consultative referendum.[50] However, on the facts, it brought a constitutional change in the UK's legal organization: the UK, as a constitutionally organized legal system, is no longer bound to the EU as a constitutional system.[51] The English people, through the referendum, acted as the constituent power.[52] This gave impulse to the new legal organiza-

---

competitive pressure. Furthermore, the candidate State must be able to take over all the European implications such as the euro. As such, the candidate is prepared to implement the *acquis* and it is its will to adhere. However, there are interests to the adhesion, and opening the EU to eastern Europe asks such questions of legitimacy. New adherents did not participate in the negotiations on the fundamental treaties of the EU and their internal political, legal and economic functioning might not correspond to that of a western European Member State. Such disparities have already been observed with the reunification of Germany, and the EU might need to be flexible concerning the implementation of the *acquis communautaire* in such new Member States: see FW Scharpf, 'La Diversité Légitime: Nouveau Défi de l'Intégration Européenne' (2002) 52 [5–6] Revue Française de Science Politique 618–20

[50] C Invernizzi Accetti, G Oskian, 'What is a Consultative Referendum? The Democratic Legitimacy of Popular Consultations' (2020) 18 [3] Perspectives on Politics 10

[51] Understanding that the EU is a constitutional order: see Case 294/83 *Les Verts* [1986] ECR 1339

[52] Constitutional issues related to the EU will be further developed in ch 5. Yet, the result in this chapter is the same: the UK left the legal order constituted by the EU and the Member States. However, the referendum can be considered as a constituent referendum or as a revolution (as a fact) depending on whether the constitutional participation of the UK in the Union is considered as a material constitutional disposition. Such aspect is seen in ch 5 for the EU and its constituent sovereignty. Here, concerning the UK, what is important to demonstrate is that adhering to and leaving the EU does not impact its sovereignty as a legal system (as long as it does not empty it of its substance). As such, it also demonstrates how facts can influence the legal sphere.

tion of the UK. The effect is, here, more important than its cause. Legally, if it was clear that it was just a consultative referendum, Parliament would not have been bound by the decision and not following the people's vote would not have impacted democracy in the UK. Actually, as already underlined, it was legally a consultative referendum. However, on the other side, politically, whether the referendum is legislative or consultative did not affect its legitimacy and it can be considered that the political importance of the referendum had a legal impact on the decision to follow the people's vote:

> Many countries believe they can get away cheaply by allowing only consultative referendums. In our view, the distinction between advisory and binding referendums must be considered but also relativized. In practice, what makes the result of a referendum to be implemented or not is less its legal scope than its legitimacy, which itself depends upon various factors [...] Thus, one can argue that it is politically difficult to ignore an advisory referendum in conditions of high legitimacy of its result. Such a referendum may therefore be equivalent to a binding referendum.[53]

On the facts, this resulted in a Brexit at any cost under the impulse of the people, which factually acted as constituent power[54] as a result of the confusion between the two kinds of referendum or of Parliament's will to not act to the detriment of the people's decision in a democratic State. It is an example of the kind of fundamental and political fact with legal effects that is inherent to the apparition of sovereignty in a specific sphere. Consequently, the Member States have external sovereignty but not towards the EU as long as they are Member States. There is a confusion between the two legal spheres, which become one as long as the State is a Member State. Sovereignty is always present but can appear differently according to the kind of civil society to which it applies. When a Member State leaves the EU, unity is no longer accomplished with the EU but rather with the State alone. The adherence to the EU and so to its legal sphere appears to be a moment in time similar to the different kinds of political organizations that knew the different States throughout history. Democratic and constitutional improvements might have led to these kinds of

---

53 L Morel, 'Types of Referendums, Provisions and Practice at the National Level Worldwide' in L Morel and M Qvortrup (eds), *The Routledge Handbook to Referendums and Direct Democracy* (Routledge 2017) 32

54 Even in terms of constitutional theory (see ch 5, section 5.2), legally, the adhesion to the EU with the treaty of Maastricht can be considered as a revolution by modifying material constitutional dispositions in the Member States' constitutions. As such, leaving the EU when it leads to such a constitutional change is in parallel a revolution. On this aspect and to fully understand, please see what is said about the material theory of constitutional law and its implications for the EU: ch 5, section 5.2.

softer revolutions (understood as a change of system). Therefore, there must be a demonstration of how, through the process of European integration, the EU developed its internal sovereignty under the impulsion of the Member States themselves. This process began by increasingly self-limiting their own external sovereignty.

4.2.1.2 The burden of the limitation of their external sovereignty for the Member States: about the competences of the European Union

The organization between the EU and the Member States relies on the attribution of competences between the two levels. It must be demonstrated that what has been conventionally defined by treaty-making is overridden by the reality of the EU as a legal system. The principles of the attribution and of the exercise of the EU competences can be found in article 5 TEU.[55] The attribution of competences is ruled by the principle of conferral.[56] This principle defines the limits of the competences conferred to the EU and the notion of 'conferral' should express itself the sovereign limits of the EU. The Union receives competences from the Member States through the European treaties and can use them in the limits established by the Member States. Every competence not conferred to the EU must remain with the Member States.[57] Thus, such a provision should endorse the sovereignty of the Member States over the EU, and this was the case at the beginning of the Union. However, the competences are conferred to the EU to attain objectives. They are the powers through which the EU can effectively act in a specific area to attain its general objectives.[58] Consequently, the lines defined by the principle of conferral are blurred and it must be demonstrated that the logic of the system has overridden the logic of the treaties.[59]

Thus, generally speaking, the EU has supervisory competences and action competences (power to act).[60] The latter are divided between exclusive competences (article 3 TFEU), shared competences (article 4 TFEU) and assistance competences (article 6 TFEU). The Member States' attribution of these powers to the EU is irreversible and invulnerable.[61] The CJEU, in line with the European integration process and so the institutionalization of the EU,

---

[55] TEU, art 5

[56] TEU, art 5 para 2

[57] TEU, art 5 para 2

[58] M Blanquet, *Droit Général de l'Union Européenne* (Sirey 2018) 79; see also KD Borchardt, *The ABC of EU Law* (European Union 2017) 54–57

[59] M Blanquet, *Droit Général de l'Union Européenne* (Sirey 2018) 85

[60] M Blanquet, *Droit Général de l'Union Européenne* (Sirey 2018) 74; see also KD Borchardt, *The ABC of EU Law* (European Union 2017) 54–57

[61] M Blanquet, *Droit Général de l'Union Européenne* (Sirey 2018) 86

confirmed the definitive character of the attribution of competences.[62] The non-exercise of one competence[63] or the failure to use another[64] does not mean their extinction. These aspects of the institutional construction of the EU led the Member States and the EU itself to wonder whether the attribution of competences through the principle of conferral should be considered as a real attribution (the EU having its own competences) or as a transfer of competences (by delegation).[65] With a transfer of competences, preexisting competences are conferred to the EU and limit the sovereignty of the Member States,[66] while with an attribution of competences, newly created competences are attributed to the EU.[67] The latter has sometimes been considered in the literature as a division of sovereignty.[68] However, it is through the question of sovereignty that the attribution of competences should be questioned. Competences follow sovereignty, not the other way around. Specific competences should not be followed to find an amount of sovereignty at the EU level or at the Member State level. Indeed, through the European integration process, preexisting competences will persist while newly created competences will appear. It is the institutional construction of the EU that must be observed, such as the affirmation by the CJEU and the respect by the Member States of the irreversibility and invulnerability of the EU competences. On the same line, the EU strengthened its autonomy by adjusting its competences through subsidiary competences and implied competences. These adjusting powers correspond to the criterion of absoluteness in the concept of sovereignty as they express its indeterminacy.

First, concerning the subsidiarity competences, article 352 TFEU[69] is known as the flexibility clause.[70] These competences exist to complement the explicit competences.[71] They are the direct consequence of the process of European integration. Indeed, the treaties cannot be revised too often because of a burdensome procedure, but the European integration process must remain

---

[62] Case 6/64 *Costa v ENEL* [1964] ECR 585; Case 106/77, *Simmenthal* [1978] ECR 629, para 18

[63] Case 7/71 *Commission v France* [1971] ECR 1003

[64] Case 32/79 *Commission v United Kingdom* [1980] ECR 2403

[65] See eg M Blanquet, *Droit Général de l'Union Européenne* (Sirey 2018) 88

[66] ibid

[67] ibid

[68] ibid

[69] TFEU, art 352. It must be completed withDeclaration 42 on article 352 TFEU.

[70] M Blanquet, *Droit Général de l'Union Européenne* (Sirey 2018) 96; see also KD Borchardt, *The ABC of EU Law* (European Union 2017) 54–57

[71] M Blanquet, *Droit Général de l'Union Européenne* (Sirey 2018) 95; see also KD Borchardt, *The ABC of EU Law* (European Union 2017) 54–57

dynamic over time.[72] This reserve of competences is supposed to keep the dynamic process of integration adapted to the European treaties. This clause remains strictly delimited and uses unanimity voting.[73] However, it is an overture towards EU competences not defined in the treaties and delimited only by the general fields of competence of the EU.

Yet, it is really with the implied competences that the EU proves the indeterminacy of its authority. Such theory of implied powers exists in international law[74] but was paradoxical with the principle of conferral.[75] Nonetheless, as early as 1956, the CJEU recognized implied competences to the EU.[76] Then, in 1960, it generally admitted that implied competences can be the consequence of the interpretation of the European treaties or of their general implications.[77] It can be an adjustment of the general field of competence or of a power itself. This can even involve an interpretation of the objective for which the EU received a competence.[78] Essentially, the implied competences concern the EU competences as powers but, among others, due to the dynamic approach and the evolution of its fields of competences, it happens that it can lead to an interpretation or an adaptation of the general field of competence of the EU and of its objectives.[79] The CJEU recognized both external[80] and internal competences[81] but it has a restrictive approach. The implied competences should be considered as a specific interpretation of the principle of conferral and so be deemed necessary for the application of the European treaties.[82] Nonetheless, concerning the criterion of indeterminacy, the implied competences of the EU confirm that its limit in terms of competences, or powers to act, is not the prin-

---

72 M Blanquet, *Droit Général de l'Union Européenne* (Sirey 2018) 85

73 TFEU, art 352 para 1

74 *Reparation for Injuries Suffered in the Service of the United Nations* [1949] Advisory Opinion ICJ 174

75 M Blanquet, *Droit Général de l'Union Européenne* (Sirey 2018) 97

76 Case 8/55 *Fédération Charbonnière de Belgique* [1956] ECR 245

77 Case 20/59 *Italy v High Authority* [1960] ECR 325

78 Opinion 1/78, *International Agreement on National Rubber* [1979] ECR 2871: the objective of liberalization of global trade could more largely include the organization (even restrictively understood) of global trade

79 See Case 45/86 *Commission v Council* [1987] ECR 1493

80 See Case 22/70 *Commission v Council* [1971] ECR 263

81 See Cases 281/85, 283/85, 284/85, 285/85 and 287/85 *Germany, France, Netherlands, Denmark and United Kingdom v Commission* [1987] ECR 3203

82 See Cases 281/85, 283/85, 284/85, 285/85 and 287/85 *Germany, France, Netherlands, Denmark and United Kingdom v Commission* [1987] ECR 3203: the reasoning of the judge to find implied competences has been made according to the principles of effectiveness (effet utile) and necessity; M Blanquet, *Droit Général de l'Union Européenne* (Sirey 2018) 99

ciple of conferral in itself and so the attribution of competences, but rather its interpretation by the CJEU and so the general objectives of the Union. Indeed, the general objectives of the Union define its sphere of general competence as legal order.

The exercise of competences is regulated by the principles of subsidiarity (article 5 paragraph 3 TEU), proportionality (article 5 paragraph 4 TEU) and loyal cooperation (article 4 paragraph 3 TEU). The principles of proportionality and loyal cooperation are not pertinent for the strict assessment of the sovereignty of the EU. The principle of subsidiarity impacts the criterion of indeterminacy for the determination of the sovereignty of the EU. It is a principle governing the EU exercise of competences but with a concrete impact on its own attribution of competences. Consequently, as written in paragraph 3 of article 5 TEU, this principle does not apply to the explicit competences of the Union or of the Member States, but to shared competences (and supposedly to implied competences when pertinent). According to this principle, the EU should exercise its competence when such exercise at the State level would be insufficient and better efficiency could be reached at the EU level.[83] However, it must be kept in mind that it is the lowest efficient level that must have the competence first.[84] The EU must act only if efficiency cannot be reached at a more local level. This particularity improved the dialogue between the Member States and the EU but it can be an important administrative burden for both the Member States and the Union.[85] There are important control procedures such as political control and the Committee of the Regions.[86] However, the emphasis must be put on the national Parliaments and on the role of the CJEU. In a first step, the national Parliaments always wanted to avoid an 'evasion of legal competences'.[87] Therefore, there is a second subparagraph to paragraph 3 of article 5 TEU: 'the institutions of the Union shall apply the principle of subsidiarity as laid down in the Protocol on the application of the principles of subsidiarity and proportionality. National Parliaments ensure compliance with the principle of subsidiarity in accordance with the procedure set out in that Protocol.'

---

[83] M Blanquet, *Droit Général de l'Union Européenne* (Sirey 2018) 114; see also KD Borchardt, *The ABC of EU Law* (European Union 2017) 56–57

[84] ibid

[85] See M Blanquet, *Droit Général de l'Union Européenne* (Sirey 2018) 115: the dialogue put in place between the Member States and the EU in order to execute the principle of subsidiary increased the exchange of reports and documents. It is the obligation to open for the Commission

[86] M Blanquet, *Droit Général de l'Union Européenne* (Sirey 2018) 117; see also KD Borchardt, *The ABC of EU Law* (European Union 2017) 56–57

[87] M Blanquet, *Droit Général de l'Union Européenne* (Sirey 2018) 118; see also KD Borchardt, *The ABC of EU Law* (European Union 2017) 56–57

In this Protocol there is a role given to parliamentary cooperation through the Conference of Parliamentary Committees for Union Affairs,[88] but it is the control by each individual national Parliament that is relevant here. It is an a priori control: each national Parliament can address a reasoned opinion to the presidents of the European Parliament, the Council and the Commission explaining how the proposal does not respect the subsidiarity principle.[89] Each unicameral Parliament has two voices and each chamber of bicameral Parliaments has one voice.[90] If the reasoned opinions represent one third of the voices, the author of the proposal must reexamine it (yellow card procedure).[91] The author of the proposal can then withdraw, modify or even keep it, but always with a reasoned opinion too.[92] The same procedure applies to the legislative ordinary procedure and the Commission. However, this time, there must be a simple majority among the national Parliaments.[93] If the Commission maintains its position, it writes a reasoned opinion and sends it with the reasoned opinions of the national Parliaments to the European Parliament and the Council.[94] The proposal can hence be rejected with 55 per cent of the voices in the Council or a simple majority in the European Parliament.[95] It is then the orange card procedure.[96] What is interesting to note is that it is the EU that has the final word in such procedure. Furthermore, the yellow card procedure has been used three times. Twice the EU maintained its position and justified it through

[88] There are actually two protocols and the role of the Conference is in the Title II of the first one: Protocol n 1 on the Role of National Parliaments in the European Union to the Treaty on the Functioning of the European Union [2016] OJ 202/203; Protocol n 2 on the Application of the Principles of Subsidiarity and Proportionality annexed to the Treaty on European Union and to the Treaty on the Functioning of the European Union [2008] C-115/01

[89] Protocol n 2 on the Application of the Principles of Subsidiarity and Proportionality annexed to the Treaty on European Union and to the Treaty on the Functioning of the European Union [2008] C-115/01, art 6

[90] Protocol n 2 on the Application of the Principles of Subsidiarity and Proportionality annexed to the Treaty on European Union and to the Treaty on the Functioning of the European Union [2008] C-115/01, art 7

[91] M Blanquet, *Droit Général de l'Union Européenne* (Sirey 2018) 119

[92] Protocol n 2 on the Application of the Principles of Subsidiarity and Proportionality annexed to the Treaty on European Union and to the Treaty on the Functioning of the European Union [2008] C-115/01, art 7

[93] ibid

[94] ibid

[95] ibid

[96] M Blanquet, *Droit Général de l'Union Européenne* (Sirey 2018) 119

a communication[97] and once it withdrew it – not because of an infringement of the principle of subsidiarity, but because it estimated that the proposal would not pass because of a lack of political support.[98] Besides an important political dialogue, the EU holds the reins in terms of subsidiarity control. This can also be proved by the role of the CJEU in such matter. Indeed, there is a jurisdictional control of the principle of subsidiarity, but by the CJEU, which acts as a 'Federal constitutional court'.[99] Contrary to the control of the principle of proportionality, which is a minimum control (control of the absence of manifest error of interpretation), for the subsidiarity principle full control is operated.[100] This full control led to the appreciation by the Court of the motivations of a European act and even to its justification when it found no breach of the subsidiarity principle:

> In the context of Article 81(1) EC, the principle of subsidiarity is given concrete form by the limitation of the prohibition contained therein to agreements between undertakings, decisions by associations of undertakings and concerted practices which may affect trade between Member States. [...] Where that action takes the form of a Commission decision, the Commission is therefore acting in accordance with the principle of subsidiarity where it establishes to the requisite legal standard that trade between Member States is capable of being affected by the agreement between undertakings, the decision by an association of undertakings or the concerted practice the legality of which it is examining.[101]

The CJEU, therefore, also assimilated this principle to the main principles of the European market.[102] It is exemplified in the *Alliance for Natural Health* case:

> To leave Member States the task of regulating trade in food supplements which do not comply with Directive 2002/46 would perpetuate the uncoordinated development of national rules and, consequently, obstacles to trade between Member States and distortions of competition so far as those products are concerned. It follows that the objective pursued by Articles 3, 4(1) and 15(b) of Directive 2002/46 cannot be

97 European Commission, 'Subsidiarity Control Mechanism' < https://commission.europa.eu/law/law-making-process/adopting-eu-law/relations-national-parliaments/subsidiarity-control-mechanism_en> accessed 23 November 2025

98 ibid

99 M Blanquet, *Droit Général de l'Union Européenne* (Sirey 2018) 120

100 M Blanquet, *Droit Général de l'Union Européenne* (Sirey 2018) 121; see also KD Borchardt, *The ABC of EU Law* (European Union 2017) 56–57

101 Case T-168/01 *GlaxoSmithKline Services v Commission* [2006] ECR II-2969, paras 201–202

102 M Blanquet, *Droit Général de l'Union Européenne* (Sirey 2018) 122; see also JL Clergerie and others, *Droit Institutionnel et Matériel de l'Union Européenne* (14th edn, Dalloz 2022) 288–90

> satisfactorily achieved by action taken by the Member States alone and requires action to be taken by the Community. Consequently, that objective could be best achieved at Community level.[103]

Consequently, it can be very subjective to appreciate what would be the most adequate level of efficiency to authorize the exercise of a shared competence. What is interesting here is that the EU has the last word when it comes to control of the principle of subsidiarity. Furthermore, the CJEU could have kept the minimum control as a principle in such a sensitive role, but it preferred to promote a deeper control in order to respect the main principles and so the main objectives of the EU. It is in the end a promotion of the European integration process and, above all, another aspect of the indeterminacy of the power of the EU (understood as its public power and so its internal sovereignty), limiting the Member States' independence. Indeed, when the CJEU uses the subsidiarity principle like a general principle and confirms the competence of the EU, in a way it reverses the principle in favour of the EU. The role of the CJEU is extremely important when it comes to the apparition of the EU's sovereignty.

Therefore, the limits of the EU as written in the treaties are blurred. Through both the European treaty evolution and the action of the CJEU, it is demonstrated that the limits set in the treaties are not that clearly defined. Concerning its powers (or competences), the EU has a margin of interpretation which is only limited by its general objectives. A first criterion is revealed in relation to the sovereignty of the EU: the indeterminacy of its powers. As such, it must be understood that the limits of the EU, as written in the European treaties, are also limits of the external sovereignty of the Member States, which concluded these European treaties, in their relationship with the Union. Thus, through the European integration process and so through the institutionalization of the EU, the independence between the EU and the Member States disappears. Through the process of the apparition of EU sovereignty the Member States lose their independence in relation to the Union, which gives rise to their shared sovereignty.

---

103 Case C-154/04 *Alliance for Natural Health and others* [2005] ECR I-6451, paras 106–107

4.2.2 The Superposition of the European Union's External Sovereignty on the Member States' External Sovereignty

4.2.2.1 The European Union's power to limit the external sovereignty of the Member States: about the legislative power of the European Union

The European treaties are the primary law of the EU. However, when it comes to using their competences for the EU, the question is how. It is through the secondary law of the EU, which is partly constituted by its legislative power. There is a paradox specific to the Union. The acts it adopts are derived from and in application of the treaties.[104] Nonetheless, the EU has a real legislative power similar to the Member States' legislative powers. Initially, there was a reluctance to name such acts as laws, but, incrementally and eventually, doubts have been dispelled.[105] The original treaties did not use the term 'law',[106] erasing the classic distinction between law and regulation[107] through the use of regulations, directives and decisions, but the CJEU qualified the Union as a legislative order in 1970[108] and confirmed this assertion in 1978.[109] With the amending treaties, the Member States jumped ahead and now articles 288 TFEU and following refer to legislative acts and legislative procedures. However, as explained in article 289 paragraph 3 TFEU, it is the procedure that defines the legislative act: the same kind of act can be legislative or not.[110] There is also an organic identification of the legislative power of the EU through its institutions in the TEU: it is exercised jointly by the Council and the European Parliament.[111] The Council can be understood as representing the Member States and the European Parliament the European citizens.[112] However, on the facts, the legislative power of the EU depends on the attribution of competences.[113] For each kind of competence, the EU has to

---

[104] M Blanquet, *Droit Général de l'Union Européenne* (Sirey 2018) 370; see also KD Borchardt, *The ABC of EU law* (European Union 2017) 98–107

[105] M Blanquet, *Droit Général de l'Union Européenne* (Sirey 2018) 371–72

[106] ibid 371

[107] ibid

[108] Case 25/70 *Köster* [1970] ECR 1161, para 6: 'the legislative scheme of the Treaty'

[109] 'Case 106/77, *Simmenthal* [1978] ECR 629, para 18: 'within which the Community exercises its legislative power.'

[110] M Blanquet, *Droit Général de l'Union Européenne* (Sirey 2018) 372

[111] TEU, art 14 para 1 and 16 para 1

[112] M Blanquet, *Droit Général de l'Union Européenne* (Sirey 2018) 372

[113] See M Blanquet, *Droit Général de l'Union Européenne* (Sirey 2018) 385; see also KD Borchardt, *The ABC of EU Law* (European Union 2017) 98

use the adequate act in accordance with the adequate legal base.[114] This means that, when the precise category of acts that can be used is not defined, there is again room for interpretation. Thus, it is the material characteristics of the legislative acts that help to assimilate them to 'laws' in their definition. Indeed, the law is one mark of sovereignty and if the EU concretely enacts laws it means there is a rupture with its conventional origin and a paradox to solve with the notions of conferral and derived powers. More than organ theory, it depends on the concrete characteristics of the European legislative acts.

Three kinds of acts must be mentioned: regulations, directives and decisions. Their definition is in article 288 TFEU and only these acts can have binding force. They are the only acts to be mentioned as possible legislative acts tantamount to laws. First, regulation is the European act that can be considered as a pure European law. It has a general scope, it is mandatory in all of its provisions and it has direct effect.[115] Concerning its general scope, its provisions must be abstract (general and impersonal)[116] and the CJEU qualified this act as the legislative function of the EU.[117] However, some distinctions must be made: there are the basic regulations adopted according to a legislative procedure but also implementing regulations based on a different procedure (like comitology and generally adopted by the Commission).[118] The latter can be assimilated to what is known as a regulation in domestic law by opposition to the law while the first one is similar to the law in itself.[119] Then, the regulation is mandatory in all of its provisions. There is no margin of application of its provisions.[120] The Member States must fully apply all the provisions of a regulation. Finally, it has direct effect. It is the only legislative act that creates a direct relation between the European citizens and the Union.[121] By its direct effect, the regulation is directly applicable on the territory of all the Member States, like the treaties,[122] and does not need an intervention from

114 See eg TFEU, art 43 or 48; M Blanquet, *Droit Général de l'Union Européenne* (Sirey 2018) 385

115 TFEU, art 288

116 M Blanquet, *Droit Général de l'Union Européenne* (Sirey 2018) 376; see also KD Borchardt, *The ABC of EU Law* (European Union 2017) 99–100

117 Case C-73/97 P *France v Comafrica* [1999] ECR I-185

118 M Blanquet, *Droit Général de l'Union Européenne* (Sirey 2018) 377; see also KD Borchardt, *The ABC of EU Law* (European Union 2017) 98–107

119 M Blanquet, *Droit Général de l'Union Européenne* (Sirey 2018) 377

120 M Blanquet, *Droit Général de l'Union Européenne* (Sirey 2018) 377; see also KD Borchardt, *The ABC of EU Law* (European Union 2017) 99–100

121 See Case C-43/71 *Politi* [1971] ECR 1039; CJEU, Case 34/73 *Variola* [1973] ECR 981

122 Case 61/77 *Commission v Ireland* [1978] ECR 417

the national authorities.[123] Any intervention by the national authorities would actually be forbidden because contrary to the doctrine of direct effect.[124] Thus, the European definition of a regulation has the same material characteristics as general domestic law. Consequently, there are European laws, which are accepted and applied by the Member States.

Second, there is the directive. Its main distinction from the regulation is that it does not have direct effect.[125] The Member States are the recipients and must implement it.[126] Consequently, in principle, the directive does not have a general scope.[127] However, the CJEU still qualified it as having this normative general scope because it is still a legislative instrument, even if indirect.[128] The directive can be compared to a framework law, which needs additional instruments in order to be executed.[129] Similarly, the absence of direct effect must be tempered because the directive is still a mandatory instrument and the Member States have a result-based obligation and a delay period for implementation.[130] If a Member State fails to implement and exceeds the delay, individuals can still invoke a non-implemented directive.[131] The result-based obligation and the delay prove also that the directive can be assimilated to a law because, even if the Member States can choose the instrument they want to use in order to implement it,[132] they can be condemned if they fail to do it.[133] Furthermore, they always must interpret domestically their national law in the light of the directive,[134] if applicable.

---

123 M Blanquet, *Droit Général de l'Union Européenne* (Sirey 2018) 378; see also KD Borchardt, *The ABC of EU Law* (European Union 2017) 99–100

124 Case 39/72 *Commission v Italy* [1973] ECR 101

125 TFEU, art 288

126 ibid

127 M Blanquet, *Droit Général de l'Union Européenne* (Sirey 2018) 379; see also KD Borchardt, *The ABC of EU Law* (European Union 2017) 99, 101–05

128 Case T-99/94 *Asocarne* [1994] ECR II-871, summary of the order: 'normative measure of general application'

129 M Blanquet, *Droit Général de l'Union Européenne* (Sirey 2018) 378; see also KD Borchardt, *The ABC of EU Law* (European Union 2017) 99, 101–05

130 M Blanquet, *Droit Général de l'Union Européenne* (Sirey 2018) 379-380; see also KD Borchardt, *The ABC of EU Law* (European Union 2017) 99, 101–05

131 Cases C-6/90 and C-9/90 *Francovich* [1991] ECR I-5357

132 TFEU, art 288

133 M Blanquet, *Droit Général de l'Union Européenne* (Sirey 2018) 380; see also KD Borchardt, *The ABC of EU Law* (European Union 2017) 101–05

134 ibid

Third, the decision is mentioned because some kinds of European decisions can have a general scope.[135] Through practice appeared atypical kinds of decisions named *Beschluss* decisions (*Beschluss* means decision in German) by reference to their German origin.[136] They do not have specific recipients and the Lisbon treaty incorporated them in article 288 TFEU.[137] Consequently, they have similar characteristics to the law. The decision, when it has a general scope, can be compared to the regulation even if it remains mainly an executive instrument. The CJEU itself qualified a decision as an act with a general scope.[138]

Finally, the material similarities and the jurisprudence of the CJEU confirm that the EU has real legislative power. Through the possibility to make laws, the Union demonstrates that the main mark of sovereignty does not belong only to the Member States and that its conventional origin is not a limit in the construction of its own legal system. Still, what is important to highlight here is that the legislative power of the EU, besides working on the construction of its own legal system, is another limit to the independence of the Member States and so to their sovereignty. Legislative acts enacted by the Union are constant and unpredictable limits to the independence of the Member States. Yet, sovereignty cannot disappear. As such, it does not imply the end of the external sovereignty of the Member States and so of their full sovereignty but rather a shift that includes the EU level, forming a unity with the EU and the Member States altogether.

4.2.2.2 The absence of independence between the European Union and the Member States at the international level

The EU has had legal personality only since the Lisbon treaty. Article 47 TEU means that it is a subject of international law alongside the Member States without depriving them of their own personality. Nevertheless, the legal personality of the EU is not in itself the origin of its external competences on the international scene.[139] The external competences of the Union are determined by the treaties. Still, the legal personality of the EU involves a capacity of rep-

[135] M Blanquet, *Droit Général de l'Union Européenne* (Sirey 2018) 383; see also KD Borchardt, *The ABC of EU Law* (European Union 2017) 99, 105–07

[136] M Blanquet, *Droit Général de l'Union Européenne* (Sirey 2018) 383

[137] M Blanquet, *Droit Général de l'Union Européenne* (Sirey 2018) 383; see also KD Borchardt, *The ABC of EU Law* (European Union 2017) 105–07

[138] Case T-396/09 *Vereniging Milieudefensie et Stichting Stop Luchtverontreiniging Utrecht v Commission* [2012] ECLI:EU:T:2012:301

[139] M Blanquet, *Droit Général de l'Union Européenne* (Sirey 2018) 309; JL Clergerie and others, *Droit Institutionnel et Matériel de l'Union Européenne* (14th edn, Dalloz 2022) 1009

resentation on the international scene and a real existence at the international level.[140] It strengthens its existence as a legal order codependent with the legal orders of the Member States.

Concerning the capacity of representation on the international scene, it evolved and changed with almost every new amending treaty.[141] Initially, the Commission was representing the EU in matters of CFSP, so in matters of cooperation.[142] Then, with the treaty of Maastricht, the presidency of the EU had to take on this role, assisted by the general secretary.[143] However, even this representation is dependent on the attribution of competences to the EU, meaning there are several fields of representation with different procedures. Still, institutionally, the Commission must ensure the representation of the EU on the international scene except for the CFSP according to article 17 TEU. In these fields, as explained in article 18 TEU, the European Council appoints the High Representative of the Union for Foreign Affairs and Security Policy, but still with the agreement of the President of the Commission. Furthermore, this High Representative must be one of the Vice-Presidents of the Commission.[144] This means that, even if the EU has different strands in its external relations, the High Representative is the Union's institutional junction point concerning its presence on the international scene.[145] Then, what is important is what this international capacity of representation of the EU involves. What impact the sovereignty of the Member States and the emerging sovereignty of the EU are the EU's real powers to act and live at the international level and, through these powers, the capacity to bind the Member States.

First, the EU right to conclude treaties is a reminder of the attribution and exercise of competences by the EU. Before the Lisbon treaty, there was a European community without legal personality, which was able to conclude agreements in relation with the CFSP when it was necessary.[146] Nowadays, the EU capacity to conclude treaties entirely depends on the attribution of compe-

140 M Blanquet, *Droit Général de l'Union Européenne* (Sirey 2018) 308; see also KD Borchardt, *The ABC of EU Law* (European Union 2017) 92–96

141 M Blanquet, *Droit Général de l'Union Européenne* (Sirey 2018) 309; JL Clergerie and others, *Droit Institutionnel et Matériel de l'Union Européenne* (14th edn, Dalloz 2022) 1009ff

142 ibid

143 ibid

144 TEU, art 18 para 4

145 M Blanquet, *Droit Général de l'Union Européenne* (Sirey 2018) 311; see also JL Clergerie and others, *Droit Institutionnel et Matériel de l'Union Européenne* (14th edn, Dalloz 2022) 1009ff

146 M Blanquet, *Droit Général de l'Union Européenne* (Sirey 2018) 312; JL Clergerie and others, *Droit Institutionnel et Matériel de l'Union Européenne* (14th

tences. There is again the distinction between exclusive competences, shared competences and implied competences. Thus, there can be mixed agreements when both the EU and the Member States on their own can be parties to the same agreement.[147] Also, before the Lisbon treaty, the CJEU ruled that the Union has a general power to conclude international agreements as a consequence of the logic of the European treaties.[148] It has been codified into the TFEU as article 216. It is a logical consequence of the EU's objectives, and the Member States are bound by such agreements. Thus, concerning the external sovereignty of the Member States, such provision impacts the relation between the Member States and the EU but also between the Member States and third States. In a first step, if the EU can conclude an international agreement that binds the Member States, it means that there is no independence between them. Furthermore, it is doubtful to consider that the EU is just a representative of the Member States because such agreements are concluded to achieve the own objectives of the EU. A Member State would not have these objectives if it were not a Member of the EU. The EU uses its own competences, which are specific competences, exclusive or not, in relation to the internal market (like customs). The Member States are bound by the exercise of such competences by the EU. Consequently, it is not possible to establish an international independence of the Member States in their relationship with the EU. In addition, in a second step, when a third State concludes an agreement with a Member State, it knows that some EU rules might apply. Similarly, if the third State concludes an agreement with the EU, it means that the agreement applies in the relations with each Member State, as the territories and the people of both the EU and the Member States are the same. There is a confusion between the external sovereignty of the Member States and the European order on the international scene. Consequently, what can be wondered is whether it means that the EU also has an external sovereignty because of this confusion between both kinds of orders. Thus, remaining at the international level, signs can be found through the process of recognition of the EU on the international scene.

Hence, accordingly and second, the EU has a right of legation both passive and active. It is the right to send or receive permanently diplomatic representatives.[149] Passively, the Member State where an EU institution is established

---

edn, Dalloz 2022) 1009ff; see also KD Borchardt, *The ABC of EU Law* (European Union 2017) 92–96

147 M Blanquet, *Droit Général de l'Union Européenne* (Sirey 2018) 331

148 See eg Case 12/86 *Meryem Demirel v Stadt Schwäbisch Gmünd* [1987] ECR 3719

149 M Blanquet, *Droit Général de l'Union Européenne* (Sirey 2018) 335; JL Clergerie and others, *Droit Institutionnel et Matériel de l'Union Européenne* (14th edn, Dalloz 2022) 1022–25

must grant to the diplomatic delegations of third States accredited by the EU the same privileges and rights given to a classic diplomatic delegation.[150] Actively, the EU is also accredited in order to have diplomatic delegations in third States or international organizations.[151] However, in practice, and also because the Member States feared that their own delegation would be supplanted by those of the EU, the Council is represented by the delegation of the Member State having the presidency of the EU. Furthermore, the Commission representatives are the 'Union delegations' and placed under the authority of the High Representative of the Union for Foreign Affairs and Security Policy (article 221 TFEU).[152] These delegations always receive diplomatic statute in the third States and they must collaborate with the Member States' diplomatic representatives for the execution of European policies and for the protection of EU citizens in third States.[153] The Union also has the right to impose international penalties.[154] On the facts, this right has existed since the beginning of the European Community and depends on the competences attributed to the EU.[155] Sanctions were mainly decided in the name of the Member States through unanimity voting and within the framework of coordination.[156] However, and especially with the fight against terrorism since 2001, autonomous sanctions coming from the Union exploded under the CJEU's supervision.[157] Then, it must be highlighted that what applies between the EU and the third States applies also between the EU and the international organizations, putting the emphasis on the fact that, as a consequence of its international capacity, the EU can be a member of an international organization.[158]

These material elements demonstrate that the EU is recognized as a legal person with an international capacity on the international scene. Yet, this

---

150 Protocol no 7 on the Privileges and Immunities of the European Union, C-326/1, 26 October 2012, article 6

151 M Blanquet, *Droit Général de l'Union Européenne* (Sirey 2018) 336; see also JL Clergerie and others, *Droit Institutionnel et Matériel de l'Union Européenne* (14th edn, Dalloz 2022) 1022–25

152 ibid

153 ibid

154 M Blanquet, *Droit Général de l'Union Européenne* (Sirey 2018) 336

155 ibid 337–40

156 ibid 337

157 See eg Case C-229/05 P *PKK and KNK v Council* [2007] ECR I-00439; Case T-47/03 *Sison v Council* [2007] ECR II-73; Case T-327/03 *Stichting Al-Aqsa v Council* [2007] ECR II-79

158 See eg Joined cases 3/76, 4/76 and 6/76 *Kramer* [1976] ECR 01279; Opinion 1/76 *Draft Agreement establishing a European Laying-up Fund for Inland Waterways* [1977] ECR 741; M Blanquet, *Droit Général de l'Union Européenne* (Sirey 2018) 343

recognition is not a recognition of the EU as a fully separate entity from the Member States. The Union can act on its own but always in the interest of the internal market, which is a common interest of the Member States. Similarly, the Member States should not act to the detriment of the EU as it is the result of their common interests and so, ultimately, of their own general interest. What must be pointed out here is the confusion between the external sovereignty of the Member States and the external sovereignty of the EU.[159] There is no full independence between the two levels on the international scene. Internationally, the EU cannot be recognized as being fully independent from the Member States and the Member States themselves are recognized as Member States of the EU. This fact must be legally considered for the context of the law. The confusion between the EU and the Member States on the international scene demonstrates the legal evolution of the EU to create a new legal sphere with the Member States, leading to the concept of shared sovereignty.[160]

4.3 ASSERTING THE INTERNAL SOVEREIGNTY OF THE EUROPEAN UNION

4.3.1 The Supreme Authority of the European Union

4.3.1.1 The primacy of European law: the supreme authority

The EU did not constitute its supreme authority upon its creation with the European treaties. It came later with the assertion of the primacy of EU law in the *Costa* case by the CJEU.[161] It should be understood that EU law has had primacy over the domestic laws of the Member States since its creation but the *Costa* case had to clarify the specificities of the European order by opposition to the international order. In this case, the CJEU argued through a logic of system that is specific to the EU, while the Italian Constitutional Court had ruled some months before in the same case[162] according to an internationalist point of view and so according to the dualist position that is taken in Italy. The

---

159 Keeping in mind that it is a reverse demonstration and that the external sovereignty of the EU can be asserted only through its internal sovereignty

160 This concept is the conclusion of this chapter on the EU but it is conceptually explained as a concept of absolute (and so indivisible) sovereignty in ch 5, section 5.3.2. What must be explained for now is the attraction of sovereignty at the EU level.

161 Case 6/64 *Costa v ENEL* [1964] ECR 585

162 Corte Costituzionale, Sentenza n 14/1964 *Costa v ENEL* [1964] ECLI:IT:COST:1964:14

Italian view was in opposition with the logic of the European treaties.[163] The CJEU had to clarify at this specific moment the primacy of EU law and, being done explicitly, it was possible for the Member States to recognize and accept this principle from this precise moment.

Concretely, as there was no basis in the treaties in order to assert the primacy of EU law, the CJEU could have used three different methods.[164] However, the Court refused to base its reasoning on international law, and so on the Vienna Convention, or on domestic law, and so on the provisions on international law in the constitutions of the Member States. Had it done this, the primacy would not have been complete because the Member States could have organized the transposition of EU law as they want and there would not have been primacy over the Member States' constitutions.[165] This is why the Court had to clarify the principle through a different reasoning in order to assert the supreme authority of EU law.

This reasoning was, first, based on the logic of the European system. The first argument for this logic is the immediate integration of EU law:[166] 'by contrast with ordinary international treaties, the EEC Treaty has created its own legal system which, on the entry into force of the Treaty, became an integral part of the legal systems of the Member States and which their courts are bound to apply.'[167] This means that a Member State cannot avoid the application of EU law by enacting a different domestic law. Then, the second argument is based on the attribution of competences to the EU. The Court listed all the competences of the EU repeating what it said in the *Van Gend & Loos*

---

163 M Blanquet, *Droit Général de l'Union Européenne* (Sirey 2018) 472; see also KD Borchardt, *The ABC of EU Law* (European Union 2017) 44–47 and A Cuyvers, *The Scope, Nature and Effect of EU Law in East African Community Law: Institutional, Substantive and Comparative EU Aspects* (E Ugirashebuja and others eds, Brill/Nijhofff 2017) 161–81

164 M Blanquet, *Droit Général de l'Union Européenne* (Sirey 2018) 472; see also A Cuyvers, *The Scope, Nature and Effect of EU Law in East African Community Law: Institutional, Substantive and Comparative EU Aspects* (E Ugirashebuja and others eds, Brill/Nijhoff 2017) 176

165 M Blanquet, *Droit Général de l'Union Européenne* (Sirey 2018) 472-473; see also, reversely, A Cuyvers, *The Scope, Nature and Effect of EU law in East African Community Law: Institutional, Substantive and Comparative EU Aspects* (E Ugirashebuja and others eds, Brill/Nijhofff 2017) 161-181

166 M Blanquet, *Droit Général de l'Union Européenne* (Sirey 2018) 473; A Cuyvers, *The Scope, Nature and Effect of EU Law in East African Community Law: Institutional, Substantive and Comparative EU Aspects* (E Ugirashebuja and others eds, Brill/Nijhoff 2017) 177; see also KD Borchardt, *The ABC of EU Law* (European Union 2017) 44-47

167 Case 6/64 *Costa v ENEL* [1964] ECR 585

case[168] but adding one important specificity: the Member States, through the attribution of competences to the EU, have in specific sectors limited their sovereign rights *and this limitation is definitive and no posterior domestic law incompatible with EU law can be enacted.*[169] Without this definitive character, the attribution of competences to the EU would not have had any significance. The collective exercise of some competences must be efficient. Finally, the third argument was the consistency in the application of EU law:[170] 'the executive force of Community law cannot vary from one State to another in deference to subsequent domestic laws, without jeopardizing the attainment of the objectives of the Treaty set out in Article 5(2) and giving rise to the discrimination prohibited by Article 7.'[171] The argument is simple: common rules must be similarly applied in all the Member States and only the primacy of EU law can guarantee this consistent application.[172]

Then, in a second step, the Court based its reasoning on the coherence of the treaty.[173] Specific provisions in the EU treaties allow for derogations to the application of EU law and, if it were possible to avoid the application of EU law just by enacting a posterior domestic law, these provisions would be purposeless.[174] Also, the mandatory and direct effect of the European regulations would not have any significance. However, this last argument of the Court is

---

168 Case 26/62 *Van Gend & Loos* [1963] ECR 1

169 M Blanquet, *Droit Général de l'Union Européenne* (Sirey 2018) 474; A Cuyvers, *The Scope, Nature and Effect of EU Law in East African Community Law: Institutional, Substantive and Comparative EU Aspects* (E Ugirashebuja and others eds, Brill/Nijhoff 2017) 176; see also KD Borchardt, *The ABC of EU Law* (European Union 2017) 44–47

170 M. Blanquet, *Droit Général de l'Union Européenne*, p. 474 (2018), Sirey; see also A Cuyvers, *The Scope, Nature and Effect of EU law in East African Community Law: Institutional, Substantive and Comparative EU Aspects* (E Ugirashebuja and others eds, Brill/Nijhofff 2017) 177

171 Case 6/64 *Costa v ENEL* [1964] ECR 585

172 M Blanquet, *Droit Général de l'Union Européenne* (Sirey 2018) 475; see also KD Borchardt, *The ABC of EU Law* (European Union 2017) 44–47 and A Cuyvers, *The Scope, Nature and Effect of EU law in East African Community Law: Institutional, Substantive and Comparative EU Aspects* (E Ugirashebuja and others eds, Brill/Nijhoff 2017) 177

173 M Blanquet, *Droit Général de l'Union Européenne* (Sirey 2018) 475; see also KD Borchardt, *The ABC of EU Law* (European Union 2017) 44-47

174 M Blanquet, *Droit Général de l'Union Européenne* (Sirey 2018) 475; see also KD Borchardt, *The ABC of EU Law* (European Union 2017) 44–47 and A Cuyvers, *The Scope, Nature and Effect of EU law in East African Community Law: Institutional, Substantive and Comparative EU Aspects* (E Ugirashebuja and others eds, Brill/Nijhofff 2017) 176–77

ambiguous because it could also justify the primacy of only instruments such as regulations.[175]

Lastly, it can be observed that the main arguments to clarify the primacy of EU law are the arguments based on the system as a whole and not on specific provisions:

> It follows from all these observations that the law stemming from the Treaty, an independent source of law, could not, because of its special and original nature, be overridden by domestic legal provisions, however framed, without being deprived of its character as Community law and without the legal basis of the Community itself being called into question.[176]

These concluding words of the Court in its arguments in the *Costa* case underline the fact that it is the specific nature of the EU that is the basis of the principle of the primacy of EU law. As said by Pescatore, it is an existential principle.[177] It is inherent to the nature of the EU and the consequence of this existential nature is that it is the general European order that has primacy over the domestic laws of the Member States.[178] Thus, it means that all EU laws have primacy over all domestic laws without any question of time and that national judges must also apply this primacy in internal relations. This principle must not be applied only by the CJEU.[179] It also means that the relation between EU law and domestic laws is not a simple relation of hierarchy of norms.[180] Indeed, the nature itself of the EU is the pooling of competences that can be better achieved on a common basis or that improve the personal situations of the Member States thanks to this pooling of competences. Consequently, it is a relation of general law (EU law) to particular law (domestic laws of the Member States).[181] EU law is autonomous but still part of the domestic laws of the Member States. The reasons for its existence themselves necessitate its primacy to preserve the consistent application of the

175 M Blanquet, *Droit Général de l'Union Européenne* (Sirey 2018) 475

176 Case 6/64 *Costa v ENEL* [1964] ECR 585

177 P Pescatore, *Le Droit de l'Intégration* (Bruylant 1972) 85

178 M Blanquet, *Droit Général de l'Union Européenne* (Sirey 2018) 477; see also KD Borchardt, *The ABC of EU Law* (European Union 2017) 44–47

179 M Blanquet, *Droit Général de l'Union Européenne* (Sirey 2018) 477–82; see also KD Borchardt, *The ABC of EU Law* (European Union 2017) 44–47

180 M Blanquet, *Droit Général de l'Union Européenne* (Sirey 2018) 479; see also A Cuyvers, *The Scope, Nature and Effect of EU Law in East African Community Law: Institutional, Substantive and Comparative EU Aspects* (E Ugirashebuja and others eds, Brill/Nijhoff 2017) 177–78

181 ibid

common competences.[182] The reasons for the existence of the EU give to it its total supremacy. Furthermore, this assertion and so the nature itself of the EU have consequences according to the concept of sovereignty. They have been revealed by the *Costa* case: it is the supreme authority of the EU. The supreme authority of the EU was not asserted before this case and so without any possibility of recognition by the Member States. As such, there was a before and an after the *Costa* case. With this case, within its field of competence, the CJEU affirmed that the European order has a full authority. There is no higher power and no possibility to avoid the authority of the EU. By its nature and so the reasons for its existence, the EU is sovereign. This sovereignty is shared with the Member States but, in the same way that the European order has no existence outside its scope of competence, within its scope of competence it has an authority that is supreme due to the principle of primacy of EU law. This supremacy is absolute due to the indeterminacy of the EU competences. Consequently, in its sphere, the EU is sovereign.

Then, this sovereignty of EU law through the principle of primacy must be endorsed through two confirmations. The first concerns the principle of subsidiarity and the second is the principle of autonomy. Thus, first, concerning the principle of subsidiarity, it has been introduced by the treaty of Maastricht to reassure the Member States of their own sovereignty.[183] However, it has also been seen that, in its application, it is the EU that decides whether there is a breach of the principle or not. The principle is written in European terms. Cahill argues that the principle of subsidiarity, instead of affirming the ultimate authority of the Member States, is a kind of parody of the principle of subsidiarity due to its mode of operation.[184] Indeed, in order to apply it, there is a dialogue between the EU and regional government levels (Committee of the Regions), not with the Member States in their ultimate authority (despite the introduction of the Early Warning System by the treaty of Lisbon, the EU remaining the final decision-maker); it applies only to the shared competences of the EU; and its appreciation is made according to the European objectives.[185] Marquardt also says that 'in the longer run', the subsidiarity principle would 'contribute to the erosion of effective sovereignty and autonomy' of the Member States, as disputing the idea 'that the authority of existing States is somehow

[182] M Blanquet, *Droit Général de l'Union Européenne* (Sirey 2018) 477; see also KD Borchardt, *The ABC of EU Law* (European Union 2017) 44–47

[183] M Cahill, 'Subverting Sovereignty's Voluntarism Pluralism and Subsidiarity' in G Davies and M Avbelj (eds), *Cahoots in Research Handbook on Legal Pluralism and EU Law* (Edward Elgar Publishing 2018) 32–36

[184] ibid

[185] ibid

a good in itself'.[186] Grainne de Búrca also emphasizes the fact that this principle displaces sovereignty's assumption that ultimate authority only belongs to the nation state.[187] This is confirmed by Nicholas Barber, who thinks that national self-determination as having the nation as the only *locus* (location) of sovereignty is questioned by this procedure of article 5(3) TEU.[188] As such, the principle of subsidiarity can be understood as a tool of centralization at the EU level and not as a tool of decentralization.[189] Thus, as the supreme authority in its application belongs to the EU, the principle of subsidiarity, as it is shaped in the TEU, cannot be an obstacle to the EU's sovereignty. On the contrary, it is another argument for the empowerment of the EU in the sense of the concept of sovereignty. Accordingly, second, the principle of autonomy of EU law is constantly asserted since the *Van Gend & Loos* case.[190] This case must explain how the doctrine of direct effect contributes to the autonomy of the European order and so to its sovereignty. Nonetheless, before that, an explanation must be given of the principle of autonomy of EU law, which is provided by the CJEU in its opinion 2/13 about the relation between the EU and the European Court of Human Rights (ECtHR).[191] Thus, according to Koen Lenaerts, the principle of autonomy of EU law has two sides: a negative side and a positive side.[192] Negatively, EU law is not ordinary international law.[193] The idea is to define what EU law is not.[194] There is a European legal order in relation to which the individual can rely on the legal norms and rights it promotes, even in front of national courts.[195] The Member States cannot infringe EU law and

---

186 P Marquardt, 'Subsidiarity and Sovereignty in the European Union' (1994) 18 Fordham International Law Journal 653

187 G de Búrca, 'Reappraising Subsidiarity's Significance after Amsterdam' (1999) 7/99 Harvard Jean Monnet Working Paper < https://jeanmonnetprogram.org/archive/papers/99/990701.html> accessed 21 November 2025

188 N Barber, 'The Limited Modesty of Subsidiarity' (2005) 11 European Law Journal 308

189 M Cahill, 'Subverting Sovereignty's Voluntarism Pluralism and Subsidiarity' in G Davies and M Avbelj (eds), *Cahoots in Research Handbook on Legal Pluralism and EU Law* (Edward Elgar Publishing 2018) 32–36

190 Case 26/62 *Van Gend & Loos* [1963] ECR 1

191 Opinion 2/13 *Accession of the European Union to the ECHR* [2014] ECLI:EU:C:2014:2454

192 K Lenaerts, 'The Autonomy of European Union Law' (2019) I Post di AISDUE, I, 2 <https://www.aisdue.eu/wp-content/uploads/2019/04/001C_Lenaerts.pdf> accessed 21 November 2025

193 ibid

194 ibid

195 ibid

must give it its full effect.[196] In this sense, the CJEU applies the principle of res judicata.[197] Its decisions are immediately effective and they do not need to be taken back by the national courts.[198] Then, positively, in opinion 2/13, the European Court explains that:

> The concept of autonomy relates to the constitutional structure of the EU,[199] the nature of EU law, the principle of mutual trust between the Member States, the system of fundamental rights protection provided for by the CFR, the substantive law of the EU that directly contributes to the implementation of the process of European integration, the principle of sincere cooperation, and the EU system of judicial protection of which the preliminary reference procedure laid down in article 267 TFEU is conceived as a keystone.[200]

Thus, positively, autonomy seeks to define the EU as 'an autonomous legal order that has the capacity to operate as a self-sufficient system of norms'.[201] As such, the EU order is defined negatively as an independent legal order; and its counterpart is the totality of all the positive actions that are inherently involved by the empowerment of the European legal order through the EU treaties and the CFR as 'living instruments'.[202] Such process through the negative and positive aspects of the concept of autonomy in EU law corresponds to the external and internal sides of the concept of sovereignty. Indeed, there are scholars who

---

[196] ibid 3–4: the EU is not an external component to the Member States like other international orders but an internal component to the Member States.

[197] K Lenaerts, 'The Autonomy of European Union Law' (2019) I Post di AISDUE, I, 5 <https://www.aisdue.eu/wp-content/uploads/2019/04/001C_Lenaerts.pdf> accessed 21 November 2025

[198] For the application of EU law, in case of a defaulting Member State, individuals can seek damages against it: Case C-234/17 *XC and Others* [2018] ECLI:EU:C:2018:853

[199] Here, it must be said that the constitutional evolution of the EU structure and so of the EU treaties is not put into question. However, the question of the constitutionality of the EU based on constituent sovereignty, so institutionally similar to a constitutional State, must be answered. Besides that, the evolution of the EU legal order to strengthen the constitutional value of the EU treaties seems to correspond to a different evolution and context: see ch 5, section 5.2.

[200] K Lenaerts, 'The Autonomy of European Union Law' (2019) I Post di AISDUE, I, 6 <https://www.aisdue.eu/wp-content/uploads/2019/04/001C_Lenaerts.pdf> accessed 21 November 2025, mentioning: CJEU, Opinion 2/13, *Accession of the European Union to the ECHR*, 18 December 2014, paras 165–176

[201] K Lenae rts, 'The Autonomy of European Union Law' (2019) I Post di AISDUE, I, 2 <https://www.aisdue.eu/wp-content/uploads/2019/04/001C_Lenaerts.pdf> accessed 21 November 2025

[202] Case C-673/16 *Coman and Others* [2018] ECLI:EU:C:2018:385, paras 49–50

compare the principle of autonomy of EU law to a claim for sovereignty.[203] Yet, conceptually speaking, autonomy does not correspond to sovereignty[204] but, concerning the EU, it can be a way to characterize the factual evolution of the European order without having to put a word on a new reality that can put into question the stand-alone sovereignty of the Member States.

4.3.1.2 Direct effect in European law and the recognition of the supreme authority

The doctrine of direct effect participates in the autonomy of the European order to affirm its sovereignty and especially its internal sovereignty through its public power. As such, an explanation must be provided of how the CJEU applies the doctrine of direct effect since the *Van Gend & Loos* case,[205] before explaining the general implication of the application of this doctrine in terms of recognition of the EU's sovereignty.

Thus, the direct effect of EU law is the immediate integration of EU law within the Member States' orders.[206] Therefore, it is a source of law and it creates a direct relation between the EU and the European citizens in a legal order.[207] As such, it has a political dimension because it gives a legal status to the European citizen.[208] The individuals can invoke EU law that directly creates for them rights and obligations. EU law does not need the Member States' orders to have a binding force.[209] On the contrary, the Member States must preserve this application of EU law.[210] The latter creates rights and obligations for the individuals. They can invoke EU law in front of the domestic judge, and

---

[203] See eg C Eckes, 'The Autonomy of the EU Legal Order' (2020) 4 [1] Europe and the World: A Law Review

[204] Ch 6, section 6.1

[205] Case 26/62 *Van Gend & Loos* [1963] ECR 1

[206] M Blanquet, *Droit Général de l'Union Européenne* (Sirey 2018) 552; A Cuyvers, *The Scope, Nature and Effect of EU Law in East African Community Law: Institutional, Substantive and Comparative EU Aspects* (E Ugirashebuja and others eds, Brill/Nijhoff 2017) 165

[207] M Blanquet, *Droit Général de l'Union Européenne* (Sirey 2018) 552; A Cuyvers, *The Scope, Nature and Effect of EU Law in East African Community Law: Institutional, Substantive and Comparative EU Aspects* (E Ugirashebuja and others eds, Brill/Nijhoff 2017) 166

[208] ibid

[209] M Blanquet, *Droit Général de l'Union Européenne* (Sirey 2018) 552; A Cuyvers, *The Scope, Nature and Effect of EU Law in East African Community Law: Institutional, Substantive and Comparative EU Aspects* (E Ugirashebuja and others eds, Brill/Nijhoff 2017) 167

[210] M Blanquet, *Droit Général de l'Union Européenne* (Sirey 2018) 552

the domestic judge must guarantee the application of EU law.[211] Accordingly, there is a general presumption of direct effect of EU law.[212] There is an objective of integration that assumes the application of the doctrine of direct effect.[213] It is due to the specificity of the European order and to the initial will of its founders.[214] In this sense, even when a European norm is not directly involved in front of the domestic judge, it must be taken into consideration.[215] It is the indirect scope of direct effect and a logical consequence of the EU as legal order, justifying its absolute supreme authority. Thus, there is a true distinction with direct effect in international law. Concerning international treaties, they have a direct effect depending on the contracting will of the parties.[216] It depends on the recipient of the treaty, especially because the relations between States are the initial object of international law.[217] Furthermore, in order to apply an international norm, the State must give it its effect in domestic law and the norm must be sufficiently complete and precise.[218] The European order, here, marks its difference with international law. EU law is not based on

---

211 M Blanquet, *Droit Général de l'Union Européenne* (Sirey 2018) 553; A Cuyvers, *The Scope, Nature and Effect of EU Law in East African Community Law: Institutional, Substantive and Comparative EU Aspects* (E Ugirashebuja and others eds, Brill/Nijhoff 2017) 167

212 M Blanquet, *Droit Général de l'Union Européenne* (Sirey 2018) 556; A Cuyvers, *The Scope, Nature and Effect of EU Law in East African Community Law: Institutional, Substantive and Comparative EU Aspects* (E Ugirashebuja and others eds, Brill/Nijhoff 2017) 166–67

213 M Blanquet, *Droit Général de l'Union Européenne* (Sirey 2018) 556; A Cuyvers, *The Scope, Nature and Effect of EU Law in East African Community Law: Institutional, Substantive and Comparative EU Aspects* (E Ugirashebuja and others eds, Brill/Nijhoff 2017) 168

214 M Blanquet, *Droit Général de l'Union Européenne* (Sirey 2018) 557; A Cuyvers, *The Scope, Nature and Effect of EU Law in East African Community Law: Institutional, Substantive and Comparative EU Aspects* (E Ugirashebuja and others eds, Brill/Nijhoff 2017) 167–68

215 M Blanquet, *Droit Général de l'Union Européenne* (Sirey 2018) 554

216 M Blanquet, *Droit Général de l'Union Européenne* (Sirey 2018) 555; A Cuyvers, *The Scope, Nature and Effect of EU Law in East African Community Law: Institutional, Substantive and Comparative EU Aspects* (E Ugirashebuja and others eds, Brill/Nijhoff 2017) 174

217 ibid

218 M Blanquet, *Droit Général de l'Union Européenne* (Sirey 2018) 556; A Cuyvers, *The Scope, Nature and Effect of EU Law in East African Community Law: Institutional, Substantive and Comparative EU Aspects* (E Ugirashebuja and others eds, Brill/Nijhoff 2017) 174

the recipient but it is an obligation of system, which reveals a self-identity like other legal systems such as the Member States.[219]

Then, in practice, not all EU legal provisions have direct effect (similar to the States) and the CJEU decides which norm has it.[220] The legal provision must be sufficiently clear and precise, unconditional and not in need of additional measures.[221] Then, it can have a complete direct effect or only a vertical direct effect. A complete direct effect entails a horizontal and a vertical direct effect. A horizontal direct effect creates a justiciability between citizens and a vertical direct effect creates justiciability between the citizens and the Member States. Thus, concerning primary law, depending on the criteria, it has a complete direct effect except when the Member States have a margin of discretion concerning its implementation.[222] Accordingly, regulations, as written in article 288 TFEU, have a complete direct effect and directives have a vertical direct effect when the Member States fail to properly implement them.[223] Moreover, concerning the international agreements, there is no presumption of direct effect but they may have it depending on the criteria already mentioned and on their relation with the European legal order.[224] In this manner, the doctrine of direct effect in EU law participates in the autonomy of the European order as providing for its own existence as a sovereign order through the assertion of its absolute supreme authority on the European citizens. As such, it is the latter that recognize the EU order as sovereign through their political function (it is an application of the theory of recognition in political law, by applying and invoking EU law).

Hence, concerning the recognition of the EU's absolute supreme authority, the *Van Gend & Loos* case came in 1963 and the *Costa* case in 1964. The direct effect in the relations between the EU and the European citizens was

---

219 M Blanquet, *Droit Général de l'Union Européenne* (Sirey 2018) 557; A Cuyvers, *The Scope, Nature and Effect of EU Law in East African Community Law: Institutional, Substantive and Comparative EU Aspects* (E Ugirashebuja and others eds, Brill/Nijhoff 2017) 167–68

220 M Blanquet, *Droit Général de l'Union Européenne* (Sirey 2018) 557; A Cuyvers, *The Scope, Nature and Effect of EU Law in East African Community Law: Institutional, Substantive and Comparative EU Aspects* (E Ugirashebuja and others eds, Brill/Nijhoff 2017) 166

221 M Blanquet, *Droit Général de l'Union Européenne* (Sirey 2018) 558ff; A Cuyvers, *The Scope, Nature and Effect of EU Law in East African Community Law: Institutional, Substantive and Comparative EU Aspects* (E Ugirashebuja and others eds, Brill/Nijhoff 2017) 166

222 Case 8/81 *Becker* [1982] ECR 53

223 Case 41/74 *Van Duyn v Home Office* [1974] ECR 1337

224 Case 12/86 *Meryem Demirel v Stadt Schwäbisch Gmünd* [1987] ECR 3719

recognized only just before the primacy of EU law. The principle of primacy of EU law is the necessary consequence of the doctrine of direct effect in EU law. As such, it must be highlighted how the reception and so the recognition of direct effect in EU law instituted the sovereignty of the European legal order. Indeed, primary law written in the treaties is the legal content of the source of the sovereignty of the EU but it is through the evolution of the legal context that the EU became a sovereign legal order; mainly through the role of the CJEU but also through the recognition of this sovereign legal order by the Member States and by the European citizens who are the people who must recognize the sovereignty of the EU. Therefore, the recognition by the Member States of the primacy of EU law was recognized in the *Costa* case but it was mainly focusing on the relations between the EU and the Member States to underline the supreme authority of the EU in its field of competence which constitutes its legal order. Consequently, it is especially through the doctrine of direct effect that recognition of the EU's sovereignty (the absolute supreme authority, according to the *Costa* case) can be achieved by the European citizens. This legal context that is embodied by the direct relation between the EU and the people, and so, for instance, by the justiciability of EU law, became certain, and so has been written in the European legal content to remove any doubts, through the *Van Gend & Loos* case. It is said:

> The conclusion to be drawn from this is that the Community constitutes a new legal order of international law for the benefit of which the States have limited their sovereign rights, albeit within limited fields, and the subjects of which comprise not only Member States but also their nationals. Independently of the legislation of Member States, Community law therefore not only imposes obligations on individuals but is also intended to confer upon them rights which become part of their legal heritage. These rights arise not only where they are expressly granted by the Treaty, but also by reason of obligations which the Treaty imposes in a clearly defined way upon individuals as well as upon the Member States and upon the institutions of the Community.[225]

Therefore, what is important is the direct effect of the European legal order as a whole. Indeed, this case can be considered as an important step in the evolution of the legal context of the EU. Consequently, it is also an important step for the legal content of the EU. The recognition of the principle of direct effect gives rights and obligations to the European citizens as inherent to the European legal order and not just as the consequence of clearly written provisions contained in the European treaties:

[225] Case 26/62 *Van Gend & Loos* [1963] ECR 1

> These rights arise not only where they are expressly granted by the Treaty, but also by reason of obligations which the Treaty imposes in a clearly defined way upon individuals as well as upon the Member States and upon the institutions of the Community.[226]

The rights and obligations of the citizens 'arise not only where they are expressly granted by the Treaty'.[227] This means that there are European rights and obligations of the citizens, and not of the Member States, that are the consequence of the EU as a legal context, and so as a legal order and not as the sole consequence of written provisions. Furthermore, when the Court says 'but also by reason of obligations which the Treaty imposes in a clearly defined way',[228] it means that the EU is still limited by its field of competence, which constitutes its legal order. However, this attribution of competences is not limited by a list of sovereign rights but only by the objectives that constitute its rationale and that are written in the European treaties. This direct relation between the European legal order and the European citizens is permanently alive as EU law can still be invoked by the individuals and so can still create rights and obligations. In this respect, the EU has the recognition of its authority as legal order, and which has been recognized as supreme in this precise legal order through the *Costa* case.

Therefore, the EU has an absolute supreme authority in its own legal order. It is sovereign in this order in its relations with the Member States and the European citizens. However, even if it has this absolute supreme authority and so an internal sovereignty, the EU is not independent from the Member States and so there is a confusion between the European order and the Member States' orders as observed through the definition of external sovereignty.[229] The EU

---

226 ibid

227 ibid

228 ibid

229 Here, this aspect must be explained. As independence (external sovereignty) is a quality of internal sovereignty, there cannot be one external sovereignty and two internal sovereignties. Thus, it is explained in ch 5, section 5.2 that the constitution of a legal order (EU treaties for the EU) is the sovereign of the legal order as manifesting the constituent sovereign. The real original sovereign is the constituent sovereign during the constitutional moment. Then, the constitution remains its constituent act (act of sovereignty), which actually is the expression of the will of the constituent sovereign and which manifests it. Saying that the constitution is sovereign is a shortcut. Thus, the supreme authority remains in the hands of the constituent sovereign but there is a habilitation within the constitution. Similarly, the public power is expressed through this habilitation within the constitution. As such, each constitution in each legal order (the EU and the Member States) manifests sovereignty but sovereignty in itself remains a higher concept that reunites

is sovereign, but with the Member States. Hence, it must be highlighted how the EU became sovereign despite its conventional origin to enshrine the evolution of the EU to become a sovereign legal order. Yet, this legal order is sovereign, autonomous through its internal sovereignty, but not independent. The autonomy of the EU justifies its sovereignty as absolute supreme authority but also its shared sovereignty with the Member States. The concept of shared sovereignty explains this paradox.

4.3.2 The Sovereignty of the EU in Action

4.3.2.1 Recognizing the role of the Court of Justice of the European Union

Against the sovereignty of the EU can be considered the regular argument of its conventional origin which implies that its powers are derived powers and that it cannot be sovereign because it is only the result of the will of the Member States benefiting only from an attribution of competences. Nonetheless, even if this was the original structure of the European treaties, it is not the case any longer. One institution mostly symbolizes the autonomy and the supremacy of the EU in its legal sphere. It is the CJEU, through its work of interpretation.

Thus, the European treaties are based on objectives and the EU is conceived as a dynamic order. This dynamism is based on the different roles of the EU institutions and especially on the role of the CJEU, which must interpret the treaties and be the judge of all European acts.[230] Through this work, the Court defines the general principles of EU law and, in contrast with the international judge, it does not respect a principle of limited interpretation in accordance with the sovereignty of the States.[231] A European judge has already ruled that the objectives of European integration contained in the EU treaties allow interpretations that go against the sovereignty of the Member States.[232] The

both orders together. What can be observed in each legal order are its manifestations. Such explanation is provided in ch 5, section 5.3.2. Hence, here, there are two manifestations of the internal sovereignty within the legal orders of the EU and of the Member States but, concerning the external sovereignty, as it is a negative quality, the only manifestation that can be observed is that there is no independence between the two different orders. Therefore, due to this manifestation, to apply the concept of sovereignty, both orders cannot be separated. The manifestations of the internal sovereignty and of the external sovereignty must just be assessed according to their characteristics

230 TFEU, art 263

231 M Blanquet, *Droit Général de l'Union Européenne* (Sirey 2018) 432

232 See eg Case 232/78 *Commission v France* [1979] ECR 2729

CJEU has the monopoly of interpretation of EU law[233] and, in this sense, it is not in the same situation as an international judge. The specificity of the EU and its rationale justify the interpretation methods of the CJEU.[234] For instance, beyond the use of the systematic method[235] and of the teleological method[236] as specific methods of interpretation, the Court always favours an evolving interpretation in order to have a modern interpretation of the treaties even in domains that could not have been anticipated when they were written.[237] Similarly, and more similar to a domestic judge than an international judge,[238] the CJEU can apply a deductive reasoning and not an inductive reasoning in order to establish all the consequences of the notion of Community, and so the *acquis communautaire* (EU acquis) of the European order.[239]

Through this role, the CJEU put in place a full panel of general principles of EU law that became part of the *acquis communautaire* (EU acquis) and that must be mandatorily applied by the Member States. For instance, the French Conseil d'Etat refuses the primacy of the general principles of international law[240] but recognizes the same value of the European treaties and of the general principles of EU law.[241] Based on the treaties, the discovery of these principles can be inspired by international law or by common laws of the different Member States but they can also have a pure community-based inspiration.[242] Concerning the latter, it is based on the logic of the treaties[243] (or the logic of the system as the treaties are the basis of a full system) or it can also be the generalization of a written provision of the treaties.[244] This generalization, in

233 TFEU, art 267

234 M Blanquet, *Droit Général de l'Union Européenne* (Sirey 2018) 428ff

235 See eg Case 59/75 *Manghera* [1976] ECR 91: example of an interpretation of a norm in its relations with other norms and the full legal and hierarchical system.

236 See eg Case 61/72 *Mij PPV* [1973] ECR 301: example of an interpretation of a norm in the light of its goals.

237 See eg Opinion 1/75 [1975] ECR 1355

238 M Blanquet, *Droit Général de l'Union Européenne* (Sirey 2018) 433

239 See eg Case 9/65 *San Michele* [1965] ECLI:EC:C:1965:63

240 Conseil d'Etat *Aquarone* [1997] Recueil Lebon n 148683, 206; Conseil d'Etat *Paulin* [2000] Recueil Lebon n 217017, 685

241 Conseil d'Etat *SNIP* [2001] Recueil Lebon n 226514, 624

242 M Blanquet, *Droit Général de l'Union Européenne* (Sirey 2018) 435–37

243 M Blanquet, *Droit Général de l'Union Européenne* (Sirey 2018) 437; see eg Case 294/83 *Les Verts* [1986] ECR 1339; see also A Cuyvers, *The Scope, Nature and Effect of EU lLaw in East African Community Law: Institutional, Substantive and Comparative EU Aspects* (E Ugirashebuja and others eds, Brill/Nijhoff 2017) 161–81

244 M Blanquet, *Droit Général de l'Union Européenne* (Sirey 2018) 438; see eg Case 44/84 *Hurd* [1986] ECR 29

the process of discovery, is usually the consequence of the logic of the system itself or of modernization in accordance with the dynamic objectives of the treaties (which is, again, ultimately a consequence of the logic of the European system). Furthermore, whether or not the CJEU recognizes a specific general principle is discretionary and it does not seem possible to predict the legal value it will give to each principle that is taken into account in each specific case.[245] However, what is interesting to notice is that the Court does not limit itself to the declaration of general principles in order to judge on a case but it declares also fundamental rights and democratic principles.[246] The evolution of the EU towards political and constitutional integration has already been seen through the lens of the modification of the European treaties but the CFR and article 6 TEU can only be dated back to the Lisbon treaty. Still, the CJEU began its work on fundamental rights in 1970.[247] Many revision treaties were codifications of jurisprudential principles. This proves the fundamental role of the CJEU in the accomplishment of the EU objectives and also towards a deeper political integration according to the initial federal will. Thus, the EU mostly intervenes on an a posteriori basis and its evolution is limited by the cases on which it must judge. Still, while the European treaties can be considered as international law treaties at their origin, they were still founding treaties and the work of interpretation of the CJEU strengthened their constitution-like value. Similarly, the *Costa* case and the *Van Gend & Loos* case are the result of European judges' interpretations. The sovereignty of the EU and its evolution as a complete legal order are the consequences of the work of interpretation of the CJEU which has the monopoly of interpretation of EU law. Through this monopoly and through this work of full interpretation, the EU has been able to develop itself, rending possible the concrete application of its objectives. These objectives constitute the sovereignty of EU law in the treaties as being its constitutional objectives, but their recognition has been brought by the work of interpretation of the CJEU. Recognition is necessary for the existence of a legal order.

245 See eg M Blanquet, *Droit Général de l'Union Européenne* (Sirey 2018) 440; Case 32/67 *Van Leuwen* [1968] ECR 43; see also A Cuyvers, *The Scope, Nature and Effect of EU Law in East African Community Law: Institutional, Substantive and Comparative EU Aspects* (E Ugirashebuja and others eds, Brill/Nijhofff 2017) 161–81

246 See eg M Blanquet, *Droit Général de l'Union Européenne* (Sirey 2018) 447; see also A Cuyvers, *The Scope, Nature and Effect of EU law in East African Community Law: Institutional, Substantive and Comparative EU Aspects* (E Ugirashebuja and others eds, Brill/Nijhofff 2017) 163

247 Case 11/70 *Internationale Handelsgessellschaft* [1970] ECR 1125

4.3.2.2 Two systems but one system: about shared sovereignty

The bases established by the *Costa* case and the *Van Gend & Loos* case mean two things: first, EU law is not a foreign law but the personal law of each Member State, which must be applied on their territories as well as their own domestic law;[248] and second, the EU is still a specific legal order with its own characteristics.[249] There is a principle of autonomy of the European legal order but also a principle of immediate integration of EU law.[250]

First, about the autonomy of EU law, the EU has been recognized as a real legal order with its own characteristics.[251] In this sense, it must not be diluted within the different laws of the different Member States,[252] and this is why it is said that it is autonomous. The CJEU is the sole interpreter of EU law and the primacy of EU law has been asserted. It was necessary to preserve the specific characteristics of the EU. EU law is one of the sources of the domestic law of the Member States but as EU law and it must remain EU law.[253] This has been translated as the particular internal sovereignty of the EU in its own legal sphere. The EU has the public power in its sphere of competence and it cannot be put into question by the Member States, which are also sovereign and have also the public power in their own legal sphere. Thus, the legal sphere of the Member States did not change when they attributed derived competences to the EU but rather when the EU asserted its supremacy in its own legal order. Consequently, the legal sphere in which the Member States are sovereign changed and there are now two equivalent public powers, but each one in its own specific sphere of competence: the EU and each Member State.

Second, even if there are two different public powers, there are not two different sovereignties. Indeed, there is the principle of immediate integration of EU law that only accepts a monist view and that is concretely translated by the direct effect of EU law. The citizens and the territory of the EU are the same as the citizens and the territories of the Member States. There is unity between the EU and the Member States and that can be explained through the

---

[248] See Case 6/64 *Costa v ENEL* [1964] ECR 585

[249] See Case 6/64 *Costa v ENEL* [1964] ECR 585

[250] M Blanquet, *Droit Général de l'Union Européenne* (Sirey 2018) 462; see also A Cuyvers, *The Scope, Nature and Effect of EU Law in East African Community Law: Institutional, Substantive and Comparative EU Aspects* (E Ugirashebuja and others eds, Brill/Nijhoff 2017) 161–81

[251] See Case 6/64 *Costa v ENEL* [1964] ECR 585

[252] M Blanquet, *Droit Général de l'Union Européenne* (Sirey 2018) 463; see also A Cuyvers, *The Scope, Nature and Effect of EU Law in East African Community Law: Institutional, Substantive and Comparative EU Aspects* (E Ugirashebuja and others eds, Brill/Nijhoff 2017) 161–81

[253] See eg Case 106/77, *Simmenthal* [1978] ECR 629, para 18

lack of independence of one order towards the other. Thus, there is no relation of external sovereignty between the national legal spheres and the European legal sphere, but just a relative autonomy: there is a confusion at the level of the external sovereignty.

However, there is here a contradiction. The external sovereignty is only a quality of the internal sovereignty and if there are two public powers and so two different internal sovereignties, it means that there must be two different external sovereignties. This is where the concept of shared sovereignty comes into play. The concept of sovereignty is indivisible but it is a concept for which concrete manifestations are marks revealing this concept. Sovereignty is an abstract concept for which each concrete manifestation in the legal sphere, and so in the organization of the civil society, is not the concept in itself but one of its marks. This is the case for EU law and the CJEU's work of interpretation as a delegated power of the European legal order. Thus, the subtlety is that there have been found two manifestations of one internal sovereignty embracing the EU and the Member States. These two manifestations are the EU legal order and the still persistent legal orders of the Member States through their own constitutions for each legal order.

There are two paradoxes. First, as said in the *Costa* case, the European order is and is not part of the Member States' orders. It is consequently said in this case that there is no independence between the two orders. There is unity and they form, as a logical consequence, one bigger order that encompasses the European legal order and the national orders of the Member States. However, there is no higher level that encompasses them. The bigger order is the Member States' order and the EU order forming one unity. Both orders are on the same level. The concept of sovereignty must be found in the perfect unity between both orders because the EU could not ask for independence from the Member States and, as long as the Member States are part of the EU, they accept its supreme authority regarding the European order. As such, the concept of sovereignty must be found for this unity as a bigger order that encompasses the two different kinds of orders. The specific public powers of the EU and of the Member States are the manifestations of the concept of sovereignty, which is the real public power, in each specific legal sphere. Each of the legal spheres are complete on their own but they still are part of a united and bigger legal sphere. Unity can be fully accomplished only through this larger sphere.

Second, the mark of sovereignty as the manifestation of the concept of sovereignty cannot be itself the sovereign. Moreover, there cannot be two internal sovereignties at the level of the Member States and of the EU, but also at their level and at the level of the legal system that encompasses them both. This aspect must be explained through the constitutional theory but some inputs must already be given here.[254] The constitutions of the EU and of the Member States act as sovereign in their respective legal orders, but it is a shortcut. The constitution is the constituent act and so the act of sovereignty of the constituent power. As such, it is a mark of sovereignty and so a manifestation of the concept of sovereignty. In the constitutional theory, the constituent sovereign acts during the constitutional moment and then, as it is the people, remains as subject of the constitution. Then, the people can act as constituent sovereign, during the life of the legal order, only at specific moments. Thus, the constitution remains the sovereign during the life of the legal order and organizes its public power. However, it still has an author in the world of facts: the constituent sovereign. The concept of sovereignty expresses itself through the constituent sovereign, which is in the world of facts as it must create the legal order. As such, the constitution is a manifestation of the concept of sovereignty but it embodies the sovereign during the life of the constitutional order. Therefore, with the EU and the Member States, the constituent sovereign is their common people, which unites them in a common constitutional system. However, the EU did not acquire its political sovereignty at the same time as its constitutional sovereignty in terms of full democratic legitimacy (the constitutional system is one of the possible forms of the State while the latter always has a political sovereignty).[255] Thus, there is here a specific situation created by the EU where it could affirm its public power through the EU treaties in relation to its people, thanks to the doctrine of direct effect, but where there was initially a democratic deficit from an institutional point of view. Thus, a distinction must be made here. International founding treaties can be considered as constitutional treaties.[256] Also, institutionally, in terms of democratic legitimacy, a constituent referendum can be required as well as democratic principles such as representation. Therefore, here, it is considered that the EU treaties are founding treaties that can be considered as constitutional treaties as institutionalizing the EU through its institutions.[257] However, the institutional

---

[254] See ch 5

[255] In this paragraph, it is not said that the EU lacks a full democratic legitimacy as a whole. It can acquire it through multiple means, depending on what is involved, like the agreement of the national Parliaments. However, with the latter for instance, it is an indirect democratic legitimacy. It is similar with output democratic legitimacy. Here, it is question of an institutional democratic legitimacy of the EU as sovereign legal order, which requires some aspects of direct legitimacy and so direct democratic requirements like a regular constitutional State: see ch 5, section 5.2.

[256] See eg in the context of the EU: Case 294/83 *Les Verts* [1986] ECR 1339

[257] Thus, who is the sovereign? Abstractly, the EU treaties as still being the manifestation of the concept of sovereignty for the EU order and organizing it as

democratic legitimacy of the EU still needs deeper investigation.[258] Then, as such, the EU treaties remain a manifestation of the concept of sovereignty as public power. As a matter of fact, the constitutional State and so the constitutional sovereignty is one form of the State, but the State exists through its political sovereignty. Thus, here, the question is about the political sovereignty of the EU. The EU is sovereign in relation to the European citizens, with the EU treaties manifesting the concept of sovereignty. The EU and the Member States share sovereignty in a common system with two orders and two manifestations of the concept of sovereignty.

Finally, the EU treaties and the constitutions of the Member States are the materialization that is necessary within the legal sphere in order to manifest the concept of sovereignty, which is abstract but inevitable. This is what is meant by shared sovereignty. There cannot be a legal order without sovereignty and so without unity. So, there is still an indivisible concept of sovereignty, but one that materializes dually into two really sovereign orders.

4.4 CONCLUSION

The particularity of the EU is that it did not begin with an authority which constituted itself at one time as internal sovereignty and that had to be recognized on the international level in a second time. Rather, it had a pure conventional origin, but with the objective to be more than just an international organization. At its origin, it was a supranational organization with the objective of becoming a supranational integration. This is why a reverse demonstration had to be done. Through the technique of the body of evidence, it has been demonstrated that through its evolution the EU grew in importance until it came to take up inherent elements of the concept of sovereignty. This has been done through the content of the law (provisions written in the treaties with the general construction based on EU objectives) but also through the context of the law (recognition).

Thus, the thoughts of Combacau must be recalled when he wondered whether too much self-limitation of the own external sovereignty of a State would lead to the disappearance and the alienation of its sovereignty. Concerning the external sovereignty of the Member States, this situation happened with the evolution of the EU treaties and the work of interpretation of the CJEU. Still, the sovereignty of the Member States did not disappear; it has been reorganized in a bigger order encompassing the States and the EU. Indeed, the EU

constitutional treaties in their founding value. Similarly, for Bodin, abstractly, the people in a democracy or several people in an aristocracy can be sovereign.

258 See ch 5, section 5.2

asserted its sovereignty within its own legal order on the same people and in the same territories as the Member States. This has been done through the work of interpretation of the CJEU, which confirmed the supreme authority of the EU through the principle of primacy of EU law and its recognition through the doctrine of direct effect within the European legal order.

As such, there are two different legal orders but with one indivisible concept of sovereignty which internally manifests itself through the constitutions (or constitution-like treaties) in each legal order. Indeed, sovereignty, more than internal sovereignty as public power and external sovereignty as independence, is the concept that organizes a legal sphere around a supreme authority, which is necessary to impose the norm on the civil society which constitutes this legal sphere. This organization of the legal order through the concept of sovereignty is symbolized by its unity.

5. The theory of shared sovereignty and its application to the EU

5.1 INTRODUCTION

Political sovereignty is inherent to each kind of political system. However, each kind of political system must take a specific political form (monarchy, aristocracy, democracy). The Member States are democracies, which take juridically the form of the constitutional State. As such, to explain how the theory of shared sovereignty applies to the EU and the Member States as coexistent constitutional systems, the constitutional implications of the political sovereignty of the EU in its relations with the Member States must be set out beforehand. Thus, the theoretical bases must be provided to understand the sovereignty of the EU from a constitutional perspective as the shape of modern European States. With these bases, the theory of shared sovereignty can be concretely applied to the EU in a constitutionalist system.

5.2 THE IMPORTANCE OF THE CONSTITUENT SOVEREIGNTY FOR THE SOVEREIGNTY OF THE EUROPEAN UNION

5.2.1 The Importance of the Distinction between the Constituent Sovereignty and the State's Sovereignty

5.2.1.1 About the constituent power and the constituent act

This section concerns the European Union (EU) as having its own sovereignty in the context of the European modern democracies and so of the constitutional State. The latter is especially important to assess the legitimacy of the sovereignty of the EU not only in terms of supreme power but also in terms of democratic legitimacy, as it is the current context of the Member States and so of the EU in terms of political and legal design of the States' systems. Thus, modern European countries are democratic regimes, and the EU is based on the same democratic ideal. Consequently, what must be explained is how the people can be both the sovereign and the subjects of the State to give it its democratic dimension (representative democracy). This is about the distinction between the original constituent power and the derived constituent power.

First, Dieter Grimm proposes a modern definition of the constitution: 'it is characterized by the pretention to govern globally and unitarily, by a higher law to all other norms, the political power in its formation and its conditions of exercise.'[1] Legally, since the American and French revolutions, the constitution can be considered as a legal act that also fixes the political organization of a State.[2] It defines both the political order and the legal order of the State.[3] Thus, the constitution is the constituent act and the constituent power is its author.[4] Indeed, in modern democracies based on popular sovereignty, the constituent power is the people that decides the political organization of the State by fixing legal rules.[5] The consequence of this decision is the constitution as constituent act.[6] Furthermore, the association of the constituent power and the constituent act is defined as the constituent sovereignty, which is different from the sovereignty of the State.[7]

Consequently, in modern States, constituent sovereignty means that the sovereign is the one who makes the constitution. The people is sovereign because it gives itself a constitution.[8] However, the notion of constitution remains different from the notion of the State.[9] They coexist in the constitutional State.[10] The distinction between both is defined by Beaud as the distinction between the power and its limitation.[11] The constituent sovereignty is related to the control of the constitution and the sovereignty of the State is related to the content of the powers of the State, in other words sovereignty as the public power.[12] This means that a rule-of-law State is different from the State.[13] Any kind of State has a sovereignty but only constitutional States have a constituent sovereignty, and the State preexists the constitutional State.[14] Indeed, the State

1 D Grimm, *Entstehungs- und Wirkungsbedingungen des Modernen Konstitutionalismus in Die Zukunft der Verfassung* (1991) 37
2 O Beaud, *La Puissance de l'Etat* (PUF 1994) 206
3 ibid
4 ibid
5 ibid 207
6 ibid 206
7 ibid 207
8 ibid
9 ibid
10 ibid
11 ibid
12 ibid
13 ibid
14 ibid

is permanent even if its organization changes through a new constituent power. In modern history, changes of constitutions within the States did not mean that the States did not exist during these periods of transformation.

Hence, when there is a change due to a new constituent sovereignty, there is a two-step process. The first step is the deconstituent phase by the deconstituent power, which includes the fact of a revolutionary phase.[15] Thus, at the origin of the formation of the State through its sovereignty, there is a fact as there is no legal order at this moment. Then, there is a similar process with the constituent sovereignty. A constitution cannot be legally abolished.[16] The only possibility is through a fact, qualified as revolution, to put in place another constitutional order. Then, the act of putting in place another constitutional order is the reconstituent phase by the reconstituent power, which has a legal aspect.[17] It is the act of putting in place a new procedure in order to create a new constitution (through a constituent assembly, for instance).[18] The consequence of this second phase is that the constitution is a law that has been elaborated through a procedure. As the supreme law, it defines what is legal or illegal and it can be difficult to legally determine its creation as it is both political and legal. Indeed, the constituent power is the creative power of the legal order.[19] Thus, for Bodin the constitution can be compared to the law (la loy) as act of sovereignty.[20] Similarly, according to Beaud, as the constitution is a constituent act, the distinction between original constituent power and derived constituent power is superficial. Indeed, the original constituent power is the constituent power in relation to the creation of the constituent act.[21] On the other side, all other powers are constituted by the constitution, which creates the legal order, and a derived constituent power is simply a constituted power.[22]

This last distinction highlights another particularity of the constituent sovereignty. As already mentioned, a procedure must be put in place to create the constitution. Generally, it is a constituent assembly. However, even if the constitutional State is based on representation, the question of the acceptance of the constitution by the people has been raised throughout history.[23] Indeed, once within the sphere of the constitution, the representation regime is established but before it, the people remains the constituent power. Thus, nowadays,

---

15 ibid 223
16 It is explained in the next paragraphs
17 ibid 226
18 ibid
19 See eg ibid 237
20 ibid 234
21 ibid 314–15
22 ibid
23 ibid 265

the dominant theory is the theory of the popular sanction.[24] Even if it is the constituent assembly that creates the constitution, the latter must be accepted by the people as constituent sovereign through a constituent referendum.[25]

5.2.1.2 About the distinction between revision and revolution

Then, the limits of the act of constitutional revision must be defined. Nowadays, especially with the constitutional judge or the political power, there is a permanent risk that the constitution can be changed on non-democratic bases and so a permanent risk for the constituent sovereignty. Indeed, the modern State lies on a democratic foundation by the popular sovereignty but, then, the same people is governed by the political power and the political institutions even if they are constituted powers within the sphere of the sovereignty of the State. Concerning the constitution as constituent act, this risk lies in the possibility of revision of the constitution without having any regard for the constituent sovereignty and it must be demonstrated that the constitution cannot be abrogated but only abolished, in the sense that it is not possible to legally change the constitution and that only a revolution can do that. Here, it must be defined under which conditions a constitution can be revised.

First, it is important to recall the distinction between the constituent power and the constituted power. The first is unrestricted and puts in place the constitution while the second is instituted by the constitution and consequently restricted by it. The authority that has the power to revise and modify the constitution is a constitutional power but as a constituted power (limited by the constitution). According to this distinction, the constituent authority is a factual authority while the power to revise the constitution, as a constituted power, is a legal authority. The consequence is that there is a fundamental distinction between the constitution as constituent act and the act of revision as constituted act.[26]

This distinction means that the power of revision cannot be sovereign and cannot change the constitution if it is exercised by a constituted power. Only the constituent power can change the constitution. However, there are different theses in opposition on this aspect. A first thesis in favour of the sovereignty of the power of revision says that, normatively, the superiority of the constitutional laws over the ordinary laws allows to deduct the supremacy of the power of revision.[27] This would be the consequence of the identification between the revision and the abrogation of the constitution but also of the

---

24 ibid
25 ibid 287
26 ibid 321
27 ibid 318

hierarchy of norms.[28] The revision would be 'the sovereign revolution as legal activity'[29] and the organ of revision would dominate all other public authorities.[30] Another thesis with the same objective is based on the German notion of *Kompetenz-Kompetenz*.[31] It is the possibility for the federal State to modify its own competence to the detriment of the federative States.[32] The federal organ of revision would be the sovereign organ of the State.[33]

However, this idea of the sovereignty of the power of revision is criticized from two different points of view. The first is the positivist attitude from a formal point of view and the second is the non-positivist attitude from a material point of view. The distinction between these two points of view is of extreme relevance for the theory applied here. Hence, concerning the formal critics of the theory of sovereignty of the power of revision, scholars such as Carré de Malberg and Kelsen have significantly the same position.[34] The organ of revision is instituted by the constitution and cannot be sovereign because of this subordination.[35] It is similar to the impossibility of a parliamentary sovereignty regime, as the Parliament must be subordinated to the national sovereignty, for Carré de Malberg.[36] The power of revision is a competence provided by the constitution in positive law.[37] However, the ambiguity here is that positive law does not consider and rejects the constituent fact.[38] Consequently, such authors still give the organ of revision a constituent function even if it is paradoxical. Thus, it must be considered the material theory on the power of revision. This thesis finds its origin in Sièyes and Hauriou and it is supported by authors such as Schmitt and Burdeau.[39] Similar to the positivist attitude, they consider that

---

28 ibid

29 F Saint-Girons, *Manuel de Droit Constitutionnel* (2nd edn, 1885) 641

30 ibid

31 O Beaud, *La Puissance de l'Etat* (PUF 1994) 318

32 See R Carré de Malberg, *Contribution à la Théorie Générale de l'Etat,* vol 1 (Sirey 1920) 174

33 O Beaud, *La Puissance de l'Etat* (PUF 1994) 318

34 R Carré de Malberg, *Contribution à la Théorie Générale de l'Etat,* vol 1 (Sirey 1920) 227; H Kelsen, *Allgemeine Staatslehre* (1925) 253

35 H Kelsen, *Allgemeine Staatslehre* (1925) 253

36 R Carré de Malberg, *Contribution à la Théorie Générale de l'Etat,* vol 1 (Sirey 1920) 227

37 O Beaud, *La Puissance de l'Etat* (PUF 1994) 319

38 ibid 320

39 See ibid: he quotes the constitutional theory of Carl Schmitt who himself quotes Sièyes and Hauriou. Sièyes has been defined as one of the main theorists of the constituent sovereignty and Hauriou is quoted in the next paragraph for his theory of the institution and its importance for the constituent sovereignty; see also G Burdeau, *Traité de Science Politique Tome III* (LGDJ 1950) 209

the power of revision is just a competence subordinated to the constitution, even if it is an extraordinary competence.[40] However, this time, the constituent power is considered. The constituent sovereignty defines the political and legal order and there is a radical distinction between this sovereignty and the power of revision, which is a constituted power that cannot be sovereign in any case despite its extraordinary function.[41] Finally, sovereignty is inalienable.[42] This means that the power of revision cannot exercise a constituent function. The public powers can only act, even through the power of revision, in the limits of their habilitation from the constituent sovereignty.[43] Therefore, what would be the concrete limits of this power of revision as constituted power?

Thus, second, it must be concretely seen when there is a revision and when there is a constituent action. For the positivists, it is possible to abrogate the constitution by revision while the doctrine of the material limitation refuses a legal possibility of suppressing the constitution (only abolition through a revolution is possible). This opposition must help to determine when the act of revision is an act of sovereignty. Thus, on one side, from a positivist point of view, the revision of the constitution can be made according to the form (a competence and a procedure) and, on the other side, it can only be made according to substantive provisions. The first doctrine is the formal limitation of the constitutional revision and the second is the material limitation of the constitutional limitation of the revision. Consequently, an example of a substantive limitation (a material limitation) can be found in article 89 of the French constitution, where it is said that the republican form of the government cannot be the object of a revision.[44] Nonetheless, the positivist doctrine still follows this idea of the constituent function of the organ of revision: as long as there is a competence and a respected procedure that provides for it, the power of revision is unlimited.[45] There is no material restriction and, in

40 C Schmitt, *Verfassungslehre* (1928) 102

41 See G Burdeau, *Traité de Science Politique Tome IV* (LGDJ 1950) 194

42 O Beaud, *La Puissance de l'Etat* (PUF 1994) 323

43 ibid: the idea of inalienability and of habilitation from the constituent power gives its legal dimension to the theory.

44 ibid 330

45 Indeed, Carré de Malberg, according to the organ theory, must admit that the power of revision is perfectly independent as, as an organ, it gives birth to and expresses the will and the personality of the Nation as a moral person. He follows his positivist doctrine based on competence and procedure and, to balance this power of the organ of revision, he opposes the electoral body, but it does not change the unlimited power of the organ of revision: see R Carré de Malberg, *Contribution à la Théorie Générale de l'Etat,* vol 2 (Sirey 1922) 605

this sense, the constitution could be legally abolished.[46] For such theory, text such as article 89 paragraph 5 of the French constitution has no legal importance.[47] Then, concerning the theory of the material limitation, a distinction must be made between the different limitations that can be found within the constitution.[48] There are explicit limits written in the constitution and implicit limits deduced by the interpreter.[49] Also, there are material limitations as such (*ratione materiae*) and circumstantial limitations (*ratione temporis*).[50] The latter is relative while the former is absolute.[51] For instance, article 89 paragraph 4 of the French constitution is a circumstantial limit: no revision can be made when the integrity of the territory is under attack.[52] Next, the idea of the theory of the material limitation is that the authors of the constitution could not foresee and justify the annihilation of this constitution by a revision.[53] If you plan for the best form of government, you do not plan also for its destruction.[54] It would be inconsistent to organize its own 'legal murder'.[55] Thus, this theory is in opposition to the neutrality of the theory of the formal limitation.[56] The possibility of revision is not supposed to provide for a legal method for the abolition of its own legality or, even more, of its own legitimacy.[57] Beaud argues that a constitutional revision is never neutral.[58] Indeed, the constitution conveys the constitutional values.[59] Still, the positivist doctrine opens the door for a modification of the republican form of the government, for instance, and this should be considered as a non-sense.[60] The idea of constitutionalization exists to avoid such disagreements and, with the formal doctrine, the revision becomes a weapon instead of a shield.[61] Consequently, the material doctrine proposes a more coherent vision of the revision: it is supposed to safeguard

46 O Beaud, *La Puissance de l'Etat* (PUF 1994) 331
47 ibid 332
48 ibid 335
49 ibid
50 ibid
51 ibid
52 ibid
53 ibid 338
54 See eg A Esmein, *Eléments de Droit Constitutionnel Français et Comparé* (6th edn from Joseph Barthélémy, Sirey 1914) 1073
55 O Beaud, *La Puissance de l'Etat* (PUF 1994) 335
56 ibid
57 See eg C Schmitt, *Legalität und Legitimität* (3rd edn, Duncker and Humblot 1980, 1932) 61
58 O Beaud, *La Puissance de l'Etat* (PUF 1994) 335
59 ibid 335–36
60 ibid 335
61 ibid 336

the constitution in addition to giving the possibility to legally modify it.[62] It is supposed to ensure its perennity, its supremacy on other rules and its existence towards the powers that could threaten it.[63] Thus, through this idea of ensuring the perennity of the constitution, a hierarchy is determined.[64] For the material theory, what is important is the significance of the revision.[65] A higher power than the constitution must not be created through the possibility of revision.[66] The extraordinary character of the revision procedure demonstrates the solemnity of the act but the formal respect of this procedure (and of the competence) is not sufficient in order to guarantee the integrity of the constitution.[67] In this sense, Constant identifies legal violations that can be repaired and legal violations that cannot be repaired.[68] The latter concerns fundamental guarantees for the survival of the constitution. Accordingly, the power of revision can modify the constitution but not in its foundations, meaning its fundamental guarantees or fundamental rights. It could be said that the power of revision, as a constituted power, cannot derogate to the constitution. The consequence is that there are constitutional dispositions that can be revised and constitutional dispositions that cannot be revised.[69] The constitutional dispositions that cannot be revised can only be abolished by a new constituent power. Similarly, there is no possibility of abrogation of the constitution as a whole, as it can only be abolished by a constituent fact (deconstituent power and then reconstituent power).

Furthermore, this hierarchy of constitutional norms can be found in current constitutional law[70] but also in EU law when the Court of Justice of the European Union (CJEU) declares it impossible to revise some dispositions of the EU treaties.[71] While the formal theory of the revision envisages only the external legality, the material theory also takes into account the internal

---

62 ibid 336–37

63 ibid

64 ibid 344

65 ibid 340

66 B Constant, *Fragments d'un Ouvrage Abandonné sur la Possibilité d'une Constitution Républicaine dans un Grand Pays* (Aubier 1991, between 1795 and 1810) 423

67 O Beaud, *La Puissance de l'Etat* (PUF 1994) 340

68 B Constant, *Fragments d'un Ouvrage Abandonné sur la Possibilité d'une Constitution Républicaine dans un Grand Pays* (Aubier 1991, between 1795 and 1810) 423

69 O Beaud, *La Puissance de l'Etat* (PUF 1994) 340

70 ibid 363

71 See Opinion 1/91 [1991] ECR I-6079

legality.[72] The constituent act puts in placc thc fundamental principles of the political regime and it is not possible to change the substance of the constitution.[73] In this sense, it cannot be derogated to fundamental democratic principles in modern constitutional States. Consequently, an attempt to revise such fundamental constitutional principles such as the representative form, the separation of powers or the fundamental rights of individuals[74] is a revolution according to the material conception of the power of revision. A revision of such intangible principles is a constituent act that cannot take a legal form but that can only be a fact, and so a revolution. On the other side, non-essential dispositions of the constitution can be revised under the adequate legal procedure. Still, there are limits to consider between the power of revision and the constituent power of the people, which is the constituent sovereign, through the notion of referendum.

5.2.2 The Constituent Sovereignty of the European Union

5.2.2.1 The people as constituent power: the limits

Here, the question lies in the fact that the people is the constituent sovereign: why would it obey the constitution it gave itself and why would any referendum not be a constituent referendum? There are again two theses in opposition. According to the first, the people is a permanent sovereign and the power of revision of the people (through the referendum) can be identified to the constituent power: the constitution can always be modified according to the concept of sovereignty.[75] According to the second, there is an original constituent sovereign and the constituent power cannot be used at any moment once the constitution has been enacted.[76] The people would be self-limited in the name of the democracy and by the original constituent power. The constituent sovereignty would be relative, and it is in this sense that the constitution can be understood as sovereign.[77]

Philosophically, the theory of the absoluteness of the constituent sovereignty has been justified by the impossibility to bind the will of the people.[78] As sovereign, it is always free to modify its will.[79] Constitutionally, it questions

---

72 O Beaud, *La Puissance de l'Etat* (PUF 1994) 385

73 See eg ibid 366

74 See eg for material constitutional dispositions the French Declaration of the Rights of Man and of the Citizen [1789] art 16

75 O Beaud, *La Puissance de l'Etat* (PUF 1994) 403

76 ibid 404

77 ibid

78 ibid 405

79 J Locke, *Second Treatise of Government* (1689) s 116

whether the people can always retake its constituent power once the constitution is already defined.[80] The answer is yes when the constituent power is identified to the power of revision and exercised by the people through a referendum.[81] The idea behind it would be that one generation of people cannot bind another generation of people and that the sovereignty of the people must be real.[82] There is a primacy of the immediate will of the people as sovereignty must be permanent.[83] In this sense, according to Beaud, the material democracy could be suppressed in the name of the formal democracy.[84] In other words, as the people would always express its will as constituent sovereign, it could always change any provision of the constitution and so its substance. This is paradoxical as the idea of constitution is to prevent such authoritarian actions from a Prince, an aristocracy or even the people.[85] Thus, even when it is in the hands of the people, the power of revision should not be identified with the constituent power. There is a distinction, and this is why the second theory is a more adequate approach of the power of revision and of the constituent power of the people.

Thus, here we follow the material theory already evoked. Madison, at the beginning of the American democracy, saw the political dangers of a permanent sovereignty of the people.[86] He recognized the necessity for the people to be able to express its will on some extraordinary occasions, but thought this should not be a permanent possibility in a constitutional democracy.[87] There must be a stability of the constitution: 'an institutionalized Constitution can favorize democracy as well as stabilize it.'[88] The self-limitation of the people with a preestablished constitution is a tie but also offers deliverance from important burdens.[89] Thus, some German scholars follow the same idea; while the Prince in a monarchy is a permanent sovereign, the democratic sovereign can only act when the constitution is put between parentheses.[90] The idea is that 'the democratic sovereign sleeps as long as the Constitutional State

---

80 O Beaud, *La Puissance de l'Etat* (PUF 1994) 408
81 ibid
82 ibid
83 ibid
84 ibid 410
85 ibid 412
86 ibid 427
87 See J Madison, *The Federalist Papers n 49* (1787–88)
88 S Holmes, *Passions and Constraints: On the Theory of Liberal Democracy* (Chicago University Press 1995) 216
89 ibid 223
90 O Beaud, *La Puissance de l'Etat* (PUF 1994) 428

exists'.[91] The material thesis makes a coherent opposition between the constituent sovereign in a constitutional democracy and the Prince in a monarchy.[92] According to Beaud, in the constitutional State, there is a sovereign over the constitution but not within the constitution.[93] The sovereign people is *constitutione solutus* (it makes the constitution) while the Prince is *legibus solutus* (it makes all the laws).[94] Consequently, the people can abolish the constitution, but it is not legal and not anticipated in the constitution. On the other side, the Prince can modify all the laws and even a constitution as an absolute sovereign. There is a distinction between both. In the constitutional State, there is no permanent sovereign during its life, and this is why the constitution embodies this function for the State. There is no sovereign within the constitution but only constituted powers. As such, this second theory is considered as a more adequate theory by considering the idea of the constitution for the preservation of the democracy.

Nevertheless, there is a final contradiction that must be highlighted. It is the application of the idea of the limitation of the constituent sovereignty from a legal point of view (knowing that the concept of sovereignty is absolute).[95] Beaud, in order to not give up on the thesis of the immutability of the constituent act, proposes a different approach to explain it: from the point of view of the institution of the State.[96] Indeed, the theory of the absoluteness of the constituent sovereignty lies in the idea of the social contract and so in absolute voluntarism and individualism.[97] Each individual must be in relation with the State under the idea of contract and so each generation of people is supposed to renew this intuitu personae social contract, and so the constitution.[98] However, this theory is problematic for the continuity of the State. Each new generation of people could get rid of the rights and obligations of the State contracted by the previous generation that the State represents.[99] There is a need for institutionalization that has even been admitted by voluntarist

[91] M Kriele, *Einführung in der Staatslehre: Die Geschichtlichen Legitimitätsgrundlagen des Demokratischen Verfassungsstaates* (2nd edn, 1994) 226

[92] See O Beaud, *La Puissance de l'Etat* (PUF 1994) 426

[93] ibid 429

[94] ibid

[95] ibid 441

[96] ibid 442

[97] ibid 443

[98] MF Rigaux, *La Théorie des Limites Matérielles à l'Exercice de la Fonction Constituante* (Larcier 1985) 249

[99] ibid

philosophers.[100] Such corrections find their bases in civil law: the transmission of heritage and the legal personality.[101] There is a permanence of the State through its legal personality and, consequently, there is a transmission of its heritage as the sum of its rights and obligations as a legal unity.[102] Thus, once such limitations have been admitted as necessary, the door is open for a theory of the State as institution. The people as constituent sovereign needs to be institutionalized for the preservation and the continuity of the State in its components (its rights and obligations as the elements of its sovereignty in action).

This theory comes from Hauriou and is named the constituent foundation.[103] Its advantage is that it considers the original constituent power and the constituent moment as the moment of foundation. Still, the notion of foundation also accepts an evolutive conception of the constitution.[104] In this sense, there is no total subjectivism under the theory of the social contract, but the constituent act can still evolve in its social and political context and in its own limits. This theory found its basis in the more general theory of the institution that Hauriou developed at the beginning of the 20th century, while Carré de Malberg was putting in place his own theory of the organ.[105] While the latter was a positivist, the former had jusnaturalist influences.[106] For Hauriou, institutions represent, in law as in history, the category of duration, continuity and reality.[107] Thus, there are three moments for institutionalization: the idea of the work, its incorporation by power and its personification by adhesion.[108] In this process, the foundation is primordial and acts through four elements: 'the manifestation of the common will with the intention of foundation, the redaction of the statutes, the factual organization of the corporative institution and the recognition of the legal personality.'[109] In this sense, the constituent power can be analysed

---

100 See eg H Grotius, *De Iure Belli ac Pacis* (1625) Book II, ch 14, s 10; J Locke, *Second Treatise of Government* (1689) ch 6, s 73

101 O Beaud, *La Puissance de l'Etat* (PUF 1994) 444

102 O Beaud, *La Puissance de l'Etat* (PUF 1994) 444 quoting J Carbonnier, *Droit Civil, tome 1: Les Personnes* (6th edn, 2000) 143 for a definition of heritage.

103 M Hauriou, 'Aux sources du Droit. Le Pouvoir, l'Ordre et la Liberté' (1933) [23] Cahiers de la Nouvelle Journée

104 O Beaud, *La Puissance de l'Etat* (PUF 1994) 446

105 On Carré de Malberg and the theory of the organ, see pt 1, ch 3, para 3.2.2.1

106 O Beaud, *La Puissance de l'Etat* (PUF 1994) 446

107 M Hauriou, 'Aux sources du Droit. Le Pouvoir, l'Ordre et la Liberté' (1933) [23] Cahiers de la Nouvelle Journée 89

108 M Hauriou, 'Aux sources du Droit. Le Pouvoir, l'Ordre et la Liberté' (1933) [23] Cahiers de la Nouvelle Journée

109 ibid 120

as a power of foundation.[110] The constituent act is a legal act of foundation of the State and the common will is the constitutional ideal that can be found, for instance, in different declarations of human rights.[111] Such human rights orders can be considered as giving constitutional legitimacy to the modern republican regimes.[112] Then, the constituent power needs the adhesion of the citizens as popular majority.[113] It is a moment of 'communion'[114] between the founders and the consent of the nation (see the Tennis Court Oath, for instance).[115] Finally, the moment of foundation, revolutionary in its essence, becomes a process of 'continued foundation'[116] through the organs of the State and so, legally, through the constituted powers.[117] The original constitutional discontinuity becomes a constitutional continuity through the work of interpretation of the constitution.[118] The hierarchy between the different powers and the continuity of the constitutional State is preserved.[119] Then, with time, the constitution is supposed to loosen its bond with the original generation of people in order to embody the State and get the adhesion of subsequent generations.[120] Thus, as Hauriou's theory is a theory of the moral personality of the State, the constitution is supposed to adopt its qualities, which are impersonality and timelessness.[121] There is an institutionalization. Such theory finds an echo nowadays, especially among American constitutionalists.[122]

---

110 M Hauriou, *Précis Elémentaire de Droit Constitutionnel* (2nd edn, Sirey 1930) 252

111 O Beaud, *La Puissance de l'Etat* (PUF 1994) 447: example of the French Declaration of the Rights of Man and of the Citizen in 1789 but the same is true for each constitutional State with fundamental rights.

112 O Beaud, *La Puissance de l'Etat* (PUF 1994) 447

113 ibid

114 M Hauriou, 'Aux sources du Droit. Le Pouvoir, l'Ordre et la Liberté' (1933) [23] Cahiers de la Nouvelle Journée 105

115 O Beaud, *La Puissance de l'Etat* (PUF 1994) 448

116 ibid

117 ibid

118 O Beaud, *La Puissance de l'Etat* (PUF 1994) 448; M Hauriou, 'Aux sources du Droit. Le Pouvoir, l'Ordre et la Liberté' (1933) [23] Cahiers de la Nouvelle Journée 118

119 O Beaud, *La Puissance de l'Etat* (PUF 1994) 448

120 ibid

121 ibid

122 See eg S. Holmes, *Precommitment and the Paradox of Democracy in Passions and Constraints: On the Theory of Liberal Democracy* (Chicago University Press 1995) 134–77; O Beaud, *La Puissance de l'Etat* (PUF 1994) 448 quoting J Elster, *Ulysses and the Sirens: Studies in Rationality and Irrationality* (Cambridge University Press 1984)

Furthermore, this theory takes a proper account of the facts, which is the argument of validity for a theory.[123] Yet, what does this constitutional framework involve for the EU as political sovereign?

5.2.2.2 The case of the European Union

It is agreed that the sovereignty of the State is different from the constituent sovereignty and that the State must preexist through its sovereignty to get its modern form of constitutional democracy through its constituent sovereignty. Similarly, the constituent power that can give this constitutional form through a constituent act is the people as constituent sovereign. The act must be previously defined as a constituent act, and it can then be constituently sanctioned by the people through a constituent referendum. Furthermore, the EU acquired its sovereignty through the interpretation of the CJEU by defining principles such as the supremacy of EU law and the doctrine of direct effect. Yet, it must be admitted that, because of the distinction between the sovereignty of the State and the constituent sovereignty, it did not constitute the EU as a constitutional legal order from an institutional perspective. Nevertheless, it is not said that the EU is not a democratic system because it remains integrated in a democratic process through democratic Member States. Furthermore, material democratic dispositions can be found within the EU treaties, similarly to the constitutions of the Member States. Yet, it must not be determined here what should or should not be a democratic disposition, other than dispositions already accepted and determined as such. That is a debate for elsewhere.

Hence, for some commentators on the ratification of the treaty of Maastricht, this treaty was a violation of the sovereignty of the Member States.[124] According to Beaud, for instance, some material dispositions of the treaty were material constitutional dispositions and the constitutional revision that followed in France was a constituent action.[125] In this sense, the popular referendum was a constituent referendum. A similar thesis is followed here. The sovereignty of the EU is self-constituted but the sovereignty of the Member States is preserved through the theory of shared sovereignty. Furthermore, it must be explained how the Member States constitutionally deal in practice with the revolution of the EU and how shared sovereignty applies. Thus, the idea is that the popular referendums in the Member States concerning the EU at the moment of the treaty of Maastricht, considering the democratic or substantive dispositions in terms of competence it contained, must be considered as constituent referendums. Yet, these referendums were also constituent

123 O Beaud, *La Puissance de l'Etat* (PUF 1994) 449

124 O Beaud, *La Puissance de l'Etat* (PUF 1994) 457–86

125 ibid 478

referendums for the EU as sovereign legal order due to the doctrine of direct effect.[126] Also, the constitution gives its form to the State. It is a democratic form based on democratic principles such as representation and separation of powers. In this sense, as the EU treaties contain such democratic material dispositions (articles 2 and 6 of the treaty on the European Union (TEU)) and because the EU is institutionalized on democratic principles, these treaties can be considered as the constitution of the EU. As such, the EU has the political sovereignty but is also a constitutional system. Thus, it must be explained how different constitutional orders can coexist within the unity of sovereignty in one single legal system thanks to the theory of shared sovereignty.

5.3 THE OBSERVATION OF THE CURRENT CONSTITUTIONAL RELATIONS BETWEEN THE EUROPEAN UNION AND THE MEMBER STATES

5.3.1 The Relations between the Member States' Constitutional Orders and the European Union

5.3.1.1 Monist state and dualist state: the examples of France and Germany

Monism and dualism are two different approaches of the legal system. They represent two different perceptions of the relations between the internal legal system of the State and the international legal order. With monism, an international treaty is considered as a law of the State once it is ratified.[127] There is a unique system, and the treaty is usually placed between the law and the constitution in the hierarchy of norms. On the other side, with dualism, it is considered that there are two distinct systems and the ratified international treaty must be transposed as an internal law.[128] The EU, with the *Costa* case, chose monism in its relations with the Member States.[129] However, among the Member States themselves, some are of a monist tradition while others are of a dualist tradition.[130] Furthermore, even in monist States, the constitution is superior to the international treaties, which seems paradoxical with the prin-

---

[126] The treaty of Maastricht changed the paradigm of the EU giving it a decisive political importance. It seems that the democratic importance of the treaty can be summarized in the creation of the European citizenship.

[127] See M Blanquet, *Droit Général de l'Union Européenne* (Sirey 2018) 448: the French Constitution of 1946 contained this principle in its article 26.

[128] See eg the case of Italy: M Blanquet, *Droit Général de l'Union Européenne* (Sirey 2018) 519–23

[129] See M Blanquet, *Droit Général de l'Union Européenne* (Sirey 2018) 488ff

[130] ibid

ciple of primacy of EU law. This is why the way in which the supremacy of EU law is accepted within the internal constitutional systems of the Member States must be envisaged from both perspectives: monism and dualism.

The example of France as a monist State:

France has been chosen as an example of a monist State. Initially, in the French Constitution, the relations between the international order and the French order are dependent on article 55 of the Constitution. However, this article deals with the ordinary relations between international treaties and the French order but does not take into account the specificities of the EU.[131] It says that the treaties are immediately applicable from their publication and superior to the law, under the condition of reciprocity. Thus, in order to take into account the specificities of the Union, a new article 88-1 was introduced in the French Constitution in order to ratify the treaty of Maastricht, which was found unconstitutional. This article says that France participates in the EU with other States, which have chosen to exercise in common some of their competences.[132] The *Conseil Constitutionnel* (French Constitutional Court) recognized that the internal order and the EU are two different orders, with the latter integrated within the first one.[133] The EU is different from the international order.[134] It is this aspect that was criticized by Beaud at the moment of the treaty of Maastricht. The constitutional revision to take into account the specificities of the EU was not a simple revision but a constituent action. Indeed, from a sovereignty point of view the question was between a limitation of competences and a transfer of competences.[135] A limitation is a limitation of the external sovereignty and is not a threat to the unity of the concept and so to the concept in itself.[136] The external relations between different legal orders are based on this approach. However, a transfer of competences would divide the sovereignty and would be a transfer of sovereignty. The concept of sovereignty should not be approached under this point of view,[137] but this was one of the positions during the debates on the treaty of Maastricht. Thus, France modified its constitution in order to

---

131 M Blanquet, *Droit Général de l'Union Européenne* (Sirey 2018) 490

132 See M Blanquet, *Droit Général de l'Union Européenne* (Sirey 2018) 496. With a specific article, France accepts the specificities of the EU as legal order and especially the constitutional consequences of the *Simmenthal* case (primacy of EU law even over a posterior national law: Case 106/77, *Simmenthal* [1978] ECR 629).

133 DC n 2004-505 *Traité établissant une Constitution pour l'Europe* [2004] Recueil 175

134 ibid

135 M Blanquet, *Droit Général de l'Union Européenne* (Sirey 2018) 499

136 See ch 3, section 3.2.1.2

137 See ch 4, section 4.2.1.2

take into account the specificities of the EU order.[138] This means that France took into account the principle of primacy of EU law but the French courts called it the principle of effectiveness.[139] As highlighted by Blanquet, there is a logic of 'relationships between the systems'.[140] From each point of view – EU or Member State – each order sees itself as the supreme order: as the State that originally took an engagement in order to participate to the Union on the side of the Member State and with the principle of primacy of EU law as basis on the side of the EU. Constitutional pluralism is based on this ambiguity, but it must first be envisaged how this ambivalence is dealt with by the constitutional courts of the Member States.

In France, the a priori control of constitutionality during the existence of the EU was put in place only with the constitution of 1958.[141] As it was not possible to create retroactive control, the founding treaties of the EU could not be controlled.[142] From 1958, the Constitutional Court found itself competent to create a control on constitutionality.[143] However, even when the Court found some unconstitutionalities, conciliation was found through a constitutional revision.[144] Nonetheless, even if a conciliation has always been found, some limitations have been raised against the European integration process. Initially, in 1976, the Court used the distinction between the limitation of sovereignty and the transfer of sovereignty.[145] It accepted the limitation but any transfer would need a constitutional revision.[146] The idea was to protect

---

138 Loi Constitutionnelle relative à l'Autorisation de Ratifier le Traité sur l'Union Européenne [1992] n 92-554 JO 8483: to ratify the treaty of Maastricht and with the introduction of the new article 88-1 within the Constitution.

139 M Blanquet, *Droit Général de l'Union Européenne* (Sirey 2018) 496: French judges prefer to refer to a principle of effectiveness rather than to the principle of primacy.

140 M Blanquet, *Droit Général de l'Union Européenne* (Sirey 2018) 497

141 ibid 497–98

142 DC n 70-39 *Loi relative à Certaines Dispositions concernant la Banque de France* [1970] Recueil 19

143 M Blanquet, *Droit Général de l'Union Européenne* (Sirey 2018) 498; see eg DC n 70-39 *Loi relative à Certaines Dispositions concernant la Banque de France* [1970] Recueil 19

144 M Blanquet, *Droit Général de l'Union Européenne* (Sirey 2018) 498; Loi Constitutionnelle relative à la Charte de l'Environnement [2005] n 2005-205 JO 3697; Loi Constitutionnelle relative à la Ratification du Traité de Lisbonne [2008] n 2008-103 JO 2097

145 DC n 76-71*Election de l'Assemblée des Communautés Européennes au Suffrage Universel Direct* [1976] Recueil 33

146 M Blanquet, *Droit Général de l'Union Européenne* (Sirey 2018) 499

national sovereignty, but this conception was abandoned in 1992.[147] Thus, at the moment of the treaty of Maastricht, the Constitutional Court said that the national sovereignty could accept, under the condition of reciprocity, some transfers of competences for the creation or the development of a permanent international organization.[148] It abandoned the distinction between limitation and transfer, and it validated the European integration process.[149] Still, a distinction has been preserved between the European dispositions that could be authorized through the law and the dispositions that would need a constitutional revision.[150] For the latter, these dispositions would be those that jeopardize the essential conditions of exercise of the national sovereignty.[151] The latter should be understood as the criterion of the constitutional identity of France. Such criterion, by avoiding the confrontation between limitation and transfer, is a way to avoid sovereignty debates and conciliate with the European integration process through a dialogue of judges.[152]

Concerning the a posteriori control, it was only in 2004 that the French constitutional judge accepted indirect control of European directives[153] (as only the European judge can invalidate a European act of secondary law)[154] and it systemized its jurisprudence in 2006 through this criterion of the constitutional identity of France: 'the transposition of a directive could not go against a rule or a principle inherent to the constitutional identity of France except if the constituent [sovereign] accepts.'[155] The idea behind such distinctive criterion is that the French Constitutional Court cannot judge a law of transposition of a directive as long as it means controlling the directive when its leading legal principle is also a European principle.[156] Only the CJEU could control such a secondary law act. However, in order to create the control according

147 DC n 92-308 *Maastricht 1* [1992] Recueil 55

148 ibid

149 M Blanquet, *Droit Général de l'Union Européenne* (Sirey 2018) 500

150 DC n 92-308 *Maastricht 1* [1992] Recueil 55

151 ibid

152 On the dialogue between the CJEU and the French Courts and on the relations between both in general, see B Bonnet, *Les Rapports entre Droit Constitutionnel et Droit de l'Union Européenne, de l'Art de l'Accommodement Raisonnable* (2019) [n 2] De l'Intégration des Ordres Juridiques : Droit Constitutionnel et Droit de l'Union Européenne Titre VII <www.conseil-constitutionnel.fr/publications/titre-vii/les-rapports-entre-droit-constitutionnel-et-droit-de-l-union-europeenne-de-l-art-de-l-accommodement> accessed 23 November 2025

153 DC n 2004-496 *LCEN* [2004] Recueil 80

154 Case 314/85 *Foto-Frost* [1987] ECR 4199

155 DC n 2006-540 *DADVSI* [2006] Recueil 88; DC n 2006-543 *Loi relative au Secteur de l'Energie* [2006] Recueil 120

156 M Blanquet, *Droit Général de l'Union Européenne* (Sirey 2018) 504

to the French constitutional principles, if the principle at stake is specific to the French constitutional order, the French constitutional judge could control it.[157] Concretely, such approach relies on three elements: the notion of constitutional identity of France; a threat to an inherent aspect of this identity; and the possible validation of such threat by the constituent power.[158] However, to date, the Constitutional Court has identified only one principle that would be inherent to the French constitutional identity.[159] Thus, as there is only one identified principle, each scholar is able to dress its own list of possible inherent principles to the French constitutional identity.[160] Nonetheless, one approach could be linked to the material theory of the constituent sovereignty. The inherent principles of the French constitutional identity would be the inherent democratic principles written in the constitution or deduced from it. Then, some French democratic specificities could also be part of this constitutional identity, substantively or formally. In any case, a parallel can be made between this approach of the constitutional judge and the idea behind the material theory of the constitutional power as it would place within the constituent sovereign's exclusive competences similar democratic and constitutional dispositions, even if a constitutional revision following the formal theory remains possible for the Constitutional Court. What has been recognized is the constitutional value of some material dispositions according to the material theory. In this sense, Blanquet also underlines that such constituent consent has been given in 1992 with, for instance, the right to vote in the municipal elections for the European citizens, and also with the monetary competence given to the Union.[161] Furthermore, if a French democratic and constitutional principle can be controlled at the EU level by being also a European principle, it is for the CJEU to control it.[162] Thus, the French constitutional judge, through this solution, respects the European order and the principle of primacy of EU law. As such, such principle should be controlled by the French constitutional judge only if there is no equivalent principle at the EU level.[163] Also, the French Constitutional Court said in 2017 that, for a mixed agreement, the dispositions dependent on shared competences can be normally and constitutionally con-

---

157 See DC n 2025-144 QPC *Association Cimade et Autre* [2025] JO 0149 n 94; M Blanquet, *Droit Général de l'Union Européenne* (Sirey 2018) 504

158 M Blanquet, *Droit Général de l'Union Européenne* (Sirey 2018) 504

159 See DC n 2021-940 QPC *Société Air France* [2021] JO 0242 n 52

160 D Rousseau, 'L'Identité Constitutionnelle, Bouclier de l'Identité Nationale ou Branche de l'Etoile Européenne in L'Identité Constitutionnelle saisie par les Juges en Europe' in L Burgorgue-Larsen (ed), *1 Cahiers Européens* (2011) 96

161 M Blanquet, *Droit Général de l'Union Européenne* (Sirey 2018) 505

162 ibid 506

163 ibid

trolled but for dispositions dependent on the exclusive competences of the EU the control should be limited to the inherent principles relative to the French constitutional identity, the latter being a kind of minimum standard.[164]

Furthermore, the Priority Preliminary Ruling of Constitutionality (PPRC) (*Question Prioritaire de Constitutionnalité* in French) was created in France in 2008.[165] The disposition insists on priority and gives priority to the control of constitutionality over the control of conventionality (control according to international treaties) without saying anything about EU law.[166] Thus, the French *Cour de Cassation* (French Judicial Supreme Court) asked for a preliminary ruling from the CJEU.[167] The idea was to establish whether it is possible to ask for a preliminary ruling during the PPRC and whether a constitutionally approved disposition can be found inapplicable because it is contrary to EU law. Yet, the constitutional judge and the French *Conseil d'Etat* (French Administrative Supreme Court) gave their opinions before the answer of the CJEU.[168] The Constitutional Court underlined the distinction between the two kinds of control. The control of constitutionality is created exclusively by the constitutional judge and the common courts can, in parallel, still act as the judges of conventionality.[169] The two procedures can be applied in parallel. Moreover, the *Conseil d'Etat* followed the same position and this solution has been confirmed by the CJEU.[170] During a PPRC, the ordinary judge can seize the CJEU for a preliminary ruling and a national law can be found inapplicable due to EU law, even if constitutional. Such findings follow the peacemaker views between the national judges and the European judge.[171] In the end, the *Cour de Cassation* decided that, as long as it cannot put in place the conservative and provisory measures in order to protect EU law, it cannot apply the PPRC.[172] The judiciary judge gave the priority to the control of conventionality in order to respect EU law as in the present case it did not have the powers to put in place the conservative and provisory measures. The paradox is that,

---

164 ibid 505

165 Loi Constitutionnelle de Modernisation des Institutions de la Ve République [2008] n 2008-724 JO 171

166 M Blanquet, *Droit Général de l'Union Européenne* (Sirey 2018) 511

167 Cour de Cassation, Assemblée Plénière *Melki et Abdeli* [2010] n 10-40002

168 DC n 2010-605 *Loi relative à l'Ouverture à la Concurrence et à la Régulation du Secteur des Jeux d'Argent et de Hasard en Ligne* [2010] JO 0110 n 1; Conseil d'Etat *Rujovic* [2010] n 312305

169 See M Blanquet, *Droit Général de l'Union Européenne* (Sirey 2018) 512

170 Joined Cases C-188/10 and C-189/10 *Melki and Abdeli* [2010] ECR I-5667

171 See M Blanquet, *Droit Général de l'Union Européenne* (Sirey 2018) 512

172 Cour de Cassation, Assemblée Plénière *Melki* [2010] n 10-40.001

internally, the PPRC still has a character of priority. There is always a balance, which can be hard to find in the dialogue between the judges.

Finally, the only inherent principle of the French constitutional identity must be mentioned. It was defined in 2021 after a PPCR.[173] In the judgment, the Constitutional Court confirmed that the private sector cannot get delegated competences of general administrative police inherent to the public force and necessary to the guarantee of rights.[174] This is the public monopole of the legal force.[175] Before this decision, in accordance with European law, the migrant code was obliging air carriers to reconduct migrants that could not be admitted to the territory.[176] Thus, as an answer to this judgment, the CJEU said at the end of 2021 that national judges must keep unapplied the constitutional courts' decisions that go against the primacy of EU law.[177] This last case illustrates the increasing tension between the recent opposing constitutional claims of the EU and of the Member States.[178] Such debate is omnipresent in Germany as a Member State.

The example of Germany as a dualist State:

Germany is a dualist State. However, similar to France as a monist State, it had to take into account the specificities of the EU. With the treaty of Maastricht, it also introduced through a constitutional revision a disposition on the EU, which is article 23 of the German Fundamental Law. However, it is article 24(1) of the German Fundamental Law that is the basis for the transfer of competences to international organizations, including the EU.[179] Through decisions from 1967 and 1971, Germany recognized the autonomy of the EU and the primacy of EU law.[180] However, the German Federal Constitutional Court also put in place important counter-limits to the principle of primacy of EU law.[181] The dialogue between the Court of Karlsruhe (German Federal Constitutional Court) and the European judge has sometimes been intense and

---

173 See DC n 2021-940 QPC *Société Air France* [2021] JO 0242 n 52

174 ibid

175 ibid

176 See ibid

177 Joined Cases C-357/19, C-379/19, C-547/19, C-811/19 and C-840/19 [2021] ECLI:EU:C:2021:1034

178 See eg Case C-561/19 *Consorzio Italian Management* [2021] ECLI:EU:C:2021:799; Case C-564/19 *Pesti Központi Kerületi Birosag* [2021] ECLI:EU:C:2021:949

179 See M Blanquet, *Droit Général de l'Union Européenne* (Sirey 2018) 524

180 BVerfGE 22, 293 I [1967]; BVerfGE, 2 BvR 225/69 [1971]

181 M Blanquet, *Droit Général de l'Union Européenne* (Sirey 2018) 524

it perfectly embodies the relation between the national constitutional systems and the EU as legal order.[182]

First, the German Federal Constitutional Court insisted on the protection of fundamental rights.[183] Accepting the primacy of EU law, it underlined at the beginning of the EU that it could control EU regulations as long as the EU had not codified fundamental rights enacted by an assembly elected by direct universal suffrage (Solange I).[184] Then, in 1986, the constitutional judge considered that the EU had reached a sufficient level of protection of the fundamental rights, especially through the reference to the ECHR, and it decided to cease control of secondary law (Solange II).[185] However, with the treaty of Maastricht, the Court of Karlsruhe self-declared as available in order to control the treaty in its respect of the EU competences and concerning fundamental rights.[186] Only in 2000 did it assert that it will work in cooperation with the CJEU, admitting a European standard for the protection of fundamental rights, but still with the conditional reserve for its own control that the EU would maintain a level of protection of such fundamental rights (Solange III).[187]

Second, as early as 1974, the German Federal Constitutional Court put in place the criterion of the national constitutional identity.[188] Article 24 of the German Fundamental Law, which allows a transfer of competences, does not allow, however, that the fundamental structure of the constitution could be modified without a constitutional revision.[189] The fundamental rights are considered as being part of this fundamental structure and so of the German constitutional identity.[190] In this sense, at the moment of the ratification of the treaty of Lisbon, the Court insisted on the 'eternity clause' of article 79(3) of the German Fundamental Law.[191] There are dispositions of the German con-

---

182 On this dialogue, see C Langenfeld, 'La Jurisprudence Récente de la Cour Constitutionnelle Allemande relative au Droit de l'Union Européenne' (2019) [n 2] De l'Intégration des Ordres Juridiques : Droit Constitutionnel et Droit de l'Union Européenne Titre VII <www.conseil-constitutionnel.fr/publications/titre-vii/la-jurisprudence-recente-de-la-cour-constitutionnelle-allemande-relative-au-droit-de-l-union> accessed 23 November 2025

183 M Blanquet, *Droit Général de l'Union Européenne* (Sirey 2018) 524

184 BVerfGE, 271 ff / 1974 *Internationale Handelsgesellschaft* [1974]

185 BVerfGE, Az: 2 BvR 197/83 *Wünsche Handelsgesellschaft* [1986]

186 BVerfGE, 2 BvR 2134/92 & 2159/92 *Brunner* [1993]

187 BVerfGE, 2 BvL 1/97 [2000]

188 BVerfGE, 271 ff / 1974 *Internationale Handelsgesellschaft* [1974]

189 ibid

190 BVerfGE, 271 ff / 1974 *Internationale Handelsgesellschaft* [1974]; BVerfGE, Az: 2 BvR 197/83 *Wünsche Handelsgesellschaft* [1986]

191 BVerfGE, 2 be 2/08 *Lisbonne* [2009]

stitution that cannot be revised in any case and it would stop any European integration process on these aspects. Such declaration must be put in relation with the material conception of the constitution. The democratic and essential elements of the constitution that have been put in place by the original constituent power (as the first generation) cannot be revised in any case. The only possibility is a revolution that would entirely change the current German constitutional system. Thus, the dispositions affected by article 79(3) of the German fundamental law constitute inalienable elements of the constitutional identity of Germany.[192]

Third, in the same decision, the Court of Karlsruhe nonetheless created the concept of *Europarechtsfreundlichkeit*, which means legal friendliness for the EU.[193] This concept is applied to the ultra vires acts of the EU.[194] These acts are the acts where the EU exceeds its attribution of competences according to the German constitution. It is another counter-limit. According to this concept, such counter-limit applies only when there is a serious violation (manifest, significant).[195] Actually, the serious violation especially concerns the German constitutional identity.[196] The act would be, from the German Court's point of view, a serious breach in the structural construction of the EU and of its fundamental competences.[197] However, the German constitutional judge admits that the CJEU can have a constructive interpretation of its competences and even a 'right to make mistakes'.[198] The German Court, similar to the French one and despite being uncompromising, still favourizes dialogue with the CJEU (through *Europarechtsfreundlichkeit* (legal friendliness for the EU)).[199] Nevertheless, it keeps the last word, even if subsidiarily and secondarily.[200] Thus, the CJEU must ensure the required level of protection at the European level and, once it has rendered its judgment or can no longer act, the German Federal Constitutional Court operates its control in the last resort.[201]

192 BVerfGE, 2 be 2/08 *Lisbonne* [2009]: articles 1 and 20 of the German Fundamental Law cannot be revised due to the material interdiction of article 79(3) of the same law

193 See BVerfGE, 2 be 2/08 *Lisbonne* [2009]; M Blanquet, *Droit Général de l'Union Européenne* (Sirey 2018) 526

194 M Blanquet, *Droit Général de l'Union Européenne* (Sirey 2018) 526

195 ibid

196 ibid

197 ibid

198 BVerfGE, 2 BvR 2661/06 *Honeywell* [2010]

199 M Blanquet, *Droit Général de l'Union Européenne* (Sirey 2018) 526

200 ibid

201 BVerfGE, 2 BvR 2661/06 *Honeywell* [2010]

This is what happened with the *Gauweiler* case.[202] The Court of Karlsruhe considered that the European Central Bank (ECB) exceeded the European monetary competence (ultra vires act) and asked for a preliminary ruling before applying its own control. In this case, the CJEU ruled itself that the ECB did not exceed its competence.[203] As such, in the end, the German constitutional judge avoided any confrontation in the name of the *Europarechtsfreundlichkeit* (legal friendliness for the EU).[204] The German Court tried to favourize the dialogue but, still, it conserves its reserve on the democratic level of the EU by always keeping the possibility to perform a control of constitutionality in the last resort. Furthermore, here, democracy is deeply linked to the constituent sovereignty by the necessity to protect constitutional fundamental rights. This idea emerged also when the German Court asked for an assembly elected by direct universal suffrage to determine European fundamental rights. Such aspects can be linked to popular sovereignty as the constituent sovereignty to put in place democratic constitutional principles. Also, democracy would then need a permanent representation of the people through the Parliament to preserve the constitutional democracy. These aspects are sometimes blurred or not even present at the EU level, and that could be a way to understand the tensions that can exist between the German federal constitutional judge and the EU. Indeed, it is important to understand the level of protection of the German State that the German Federal Constitutional Court wants to preserve. There is on one side involvement in the process of European integration and on the other side a strict limit when it comes to Germany as a democratic and constitutional State. Hence, the recent tensions between the CJEU and the national constitutional courts can be highlighted with the German situation. In similar cases from the same years as the *Gauweiler* case, the German Federal Constitutional Court still favourized the dialogue, but it seems that another level of tension has been reached since the 2020s, as illustrated by the aftermath of the *Gauweiler* saga.

A first case, relating to the European arrest warrant, is *Melloni*. In this case, the CJEU insisted on the primacy of EU law.[205] It was a Spanish case on the European arrest warrant and it is in this context that the German federal constitutional judge said that the execution of a European arrest warrant must be refused by the German authorities when such execution is against human dignity.[206] It must be emphasized that the judgment was given without a request

---

202 Case C-62/14 *Gauweiler e.a.* [2015] ECLI:EU:C:2015:400

203 ibid

204 BVerfGE, 2 BvE 13/13 [2016]

205 Case C-399/11 *Melloni* [2013] ECLI:EU:C:2012:600

206 BVerfGE, 2 BvR 2735/14 [2015]

for any preliminary ruling.[207] Thus, this time, it is the CJEU that altered its position by admitting that, in exceptional cases and especially when there is a systemic failure in the judicial system of the State of destination – concerning human dignity, for instance – it is possible to not execute the European arrest warrant.[208] Then, in a second step, the Court of Karlsruhe specified that such warrant should not be executed only when there is a direct threat to the essential characteristics of this right.[209] Both courts here avoided a deadlock by easing their positions. However, another case from 2020 illustrates an opposite position to the dialogue of the judges. Once again, the Court of Karlsruhe judged that the ECB exceeded its competences with the 'Public Sector Purchase Programme'.[210] There, the issue was that the CJEU had already validated the programme in 2018 after a preliminary ruling from the Court of Karlsruhe[211] and, this time, the Constitutional Court did not accept the European judgment. The German Court criticized the actions of the ECB. As such, there was a breach of the principle of primacy, and an infringement procedure was opened against Germany by the Commission.[212] Therefore, at the end of 2021, Germany officially recognized a breach of the principle of primacy of EU law. It self-committed to avoid any new similar situation and to respect the principle of loyal cooperation.[213] Thus, this unique case between Germany and the EU illustrates the current tensions between the national constitutional courts and the EU, which can be the consequences of constitutional claims or political views. Still, it should not determine a whole new pattern. Such tensions should exist as long as there is a European integration process, which needs to explicitly determine its own limits and get full legitimacy in terms of democratic legitimacy. Hence, from a general point of view, both Germany and the CJEU consider their own legal orders as supreme even if they accept each other with their essential components. In addition, regarding the dialogue of the judges, it should be considered that the constitutional judges of the Member States want to preserve the essential democratic elements of their own legal orders but also that they do not forget one of the main initial reasons for the creation of the EU, which is peace in Europe. In this sense, there is a democratic justification for the acceptance of the European integration process

207 M Blanquet, *Droit Général de l'Union Européenne* (Sirey 2018) 527

208 Joined Cases C-404/15 and C-659/15 *Aranyosi-Caldararu* [2016] ECLI:EU:C:2016:198

209 BVerfGE, 2 BvR 890/16 [2016]

210 BVerfGE, 2 BvR 859/15 [2020]

211 Case C-493/17 *Weiss e.a.* [2018] ECLI:EU:C:2018:1000

212 European Commission, 'June Infringement Package: Key Decisions' [2001] INF/21/2743, 15

213 ibid 10

(in its own limits) even if, recently, some tensions have emerged between the constitutional courts of the Member States and the CJEU. Such general relations between the EU and the Member States have sometimes been justified through the theory of constitutional pluralism.

5.3.1.2 About constitutional pluralism

Constitutional pluralism is based on a heterarchical view, by opposition to a hierarchical view, of the combination between the two different orders, that is, the European order and the Member States' orders.[214] The heterarchical view accepts that both orders, the EU level and the Member State level, are supreme from their own point of view.[215] For the Member States it is because of their constitutional organization with their constitutions and for the EU it is due to the principle of primacy of EU law.

However, such view as the doctrine of constitutional pluralism is not always accepted. For instance, Pescatore has a purely hierarchical view characterized by the subordination of the law of the Member States to the law of the EU.[216] It was his vision of the European Community at its beginning. Similarly, for Lagrange, who had a federalist view at the beginning of the Communities, the Member States lost their power to legislate in the field of the transferred competences to the EU.[217] European law takes precedence and if the Member States still act in the field of their lost competences, they would act ultra vires.[218] EU law must prevail. However, such views do not seem entirely adequate. Nowadays, article 4(2) TEU claims, even from a European point of view, respect for the national identities of the Member States ('inherent in their fundamental structures, political and constitutional'). In this sense, the EU cannot entirely prevail on all aspects over the Member States and there can be intertwined constitutional interests even if the fields of transferred competences. Then, according to international law, another perspective can be taken from the principle *pacta sunt servanda* (treaties must be respected).[219] However, it would be a denial of the sui generis character of the EU. Technically, the

---

214 See E Mendez-Pinedo, 'Constitutional Pluralism and Legal Perspectivism in European Union Law' (2020) 10 [5] Juridical Tribune

215 N Walker, *Sovereignty in Transition* (Hart Publishing 2006) 4

216 P Pescatore, *The Law of Integration* (Sijthoff 1974) 94

217 Lagrange's view can be found in: D Piqani, 'Supremacy of EU Law and the Jurisprudence of Constitutional Reservations' in *Central Eastern Europe and the Western Balkans: Towards a 'Holistic' Constitutionalism* (DPhil thesis, European University Institute 2010) 97

218 ibid

219 E Mendez-Pinedo, 'Constitutional Pluralism and Legal Perspectivism in European Union Law' (2020) 10 [5] Juridical Tribune 13

European treaties are international treaties subordinated to the constitutions of the Member States.[220] Yet, constitutionally, the Member States themselves recognized the specificity of the EU and its autonomy. As such, this point of view cannot be entirely correct. However, it remains the point of view of the Member States' national constitutional courts. The Member States needed a constitutional revision to accept the specificities of the EU and, lately, tensions have arisen regarding the principle of primacy of EU law.

Finally, concerning the opposing views on constitutional pluralism, mention must be made of the primacy–supremacy debate from a hierarchical point of view. Some authors make a distinction between both and argue that the principle of primacy of EU law should not be confused with a supremacy claim.[221] The enactment of the primacy of EU law was necessary as a consequence of the doctrine of direct effect and for the effectiveness of the law of the European order.[222] However, according to them, this rule should be seen as a rule made in order to solve conflicts when EU law is applicable and it should not been seen as an institutional claim against the Member States as constitutional States.[223] Yet, the definition of the concept of sovereignty that has been given cannot accept a separation between the effects of primacy and supremacy because both work together. Indeed, the concept of sovereignty is a concept of absolute unity and the law is the act of sovereignty. The latter is important. When a law is put aside and loses effectiveness by being unapplicable, it loses the supreme character of sovereignty. This is the example of the constitution as act of sovereignty that cannot be changed in its essential elements by the constituted powers. In this sense, when a law is discarded, it cannot be defined as an act of sovereignty any longer and its author is not sovereign any longer. Consequently, in its field of competence defined by its legal order, when the EU discards a national law in the name of the principle of primacy of EU law, this means that the EU has the power to discard an act of sovereignty. But why does it discard an act of sovereignty? Similar to the Member States when they apply their own constitutions, it is due to its own sovereignty. The constitutional identity of the Member States contained in the national constitutions cannot be discarded. In this sense, the act of sovereignty of the Member States (their constitutions in their essential elements) is preserved and they remain sovereign through the power of the constituent sovereign of each Member State in order to enact such act. However, the national

220 ibid

221 See T Tuominen, 'Reconceptualizing the Primacy-Supremacy Debate in EU Law' (2020) 47 [3] Legal Issues of Economic Integration 245–65

222 ibid 249

223 L Besselink, *A Composite European Constitution* (Europa Law Publishing 2007) 7–12

constitutions have also been modified to accept the competences of the EU and such changes were constituent actions. It means that the act of sovereignty that is the constitution of a Member State has been changed to accept another power that is not subordinated to such constitution. This other power appeared and has been recognized by a constituent power: the public power of the EU that first manifests itself through the EU treaties. In this sense, the EU also has its own act of sovereignty as a consequence of the apparition of its sovereignty. Thus, the consequence of this European act of sovereignty, which would be the EU treaties as modified by the treaty of Maastricht, is that the EU can discard laws against this act of sovereignty and its interpretation. In this sense, in the whole European integration process, when the EU proclaims the principle of primacy of EU law, which is the primacy of the EU treaties as constitution, it also proclaims its sovereignty as author of an act of sovereignty. Finally, as the EU first acquired sovereignty as public power in its own legal order before progressively reaching sovereignty in a constitutional order through the constituent sovereignty and so through a direct relation with the European people (as a consequence of the doctrine of direct effect), the political process for the appearance of sovereignty at the EU level worked together with legal integration. In this view, primacy and supremacy work together: the act of sovereignty is the essential consequence of sovereignty. Yet, it could be said that there is a circular argument here that could also concern the sovereignty of the EU itself: it is because the EU is sovereign due to the CJEU, which proclaimed the principle of primacy of EU law, that the EU treaties are an act of sovereignty, and it is because the CJEU proclaimed the principle of primacy of EU law that the EU treaties are an act of sovereignty and so that the EU is sovereign. However, sovereignty needs recognition.[224] It is an essential element for the construction of the legal system. Indeed, recognition helps to highlight that what has been proclaimed by a sovereign is really sovereignty because it is a recognition of the essential elements of the concept of sovereignty, and especially its supremacy (with which come the other attributes of sovereignty). Consequently, when the EU proclaims the principle of primacy of EU law, with a direct relation with the European populations, the acceptance of this proclamation is also the acceptance of the conditions for such a proclamation. Such conditions are the essential elements of the concept of sovereignty. As such, in the EU context, the appearance of sovereignty at the same time constituted the EU treaties as act of sovereignty.

---

224 ch 3, section 3.3

Neil MacCormick founded the movement concerning the doctrine in favour of constitutional pluralism.[225] For him, the internal validity of EU law in each Member State depends on the domestic constitutional laws.[226] On the other side, the European order is not dependent from the Member States' constitutions.[227] In his view, 'relations between States inter se and between States and Community are interactive rather than hierarchical'.[228] His theory is a theory of 'overlapping and interacting non-hierarchical legal systems without serious mutual conflict in areas of overlap'.[229] He relies on the interpretative power of the highest decision-making authority in each system as actually being supreme in its own system, and the difficulty lies in the combination of different systems working together.[230] MacCormick leaves the question of sovereignty (as who has the *Kompetenz-Kompetenz*) unresolved.[231] However, there is an evolution in his writings at the end of his life. At the beginning, he argued for radical pluralism, and then he switched to pluralism under international law.[232] Radical pluralism is based on the point of view of each system that can consider itself supreme without having to make any compromise in its decisions.[233] There is no method for the elimination of the conflict. On the other hand, with pluralism under international law, conflicts can be resolved through international arbitration or adjudication.[234]

Another important theorist of constitutional pluralism is Walker. For him, EU law goes beyond international law and has its own independent constitutional claims.[235] The EU constructed its own legal order from an epistemological

---

225 E Mendez-Pinedo, 'Constitutional Pluralism and Legal Perspectivism in European Union Law' (2020) 10 [5] Juridical Tribune 16

226 N MacCormick, *Questioning Sovereignty: Law, State and Nation in the European Commonwealth* (Oxford University Press 1999) 117–18

227 ibid

228 ibid 118

229 E Mendez-Pinedo, 'Constitutional Pluralism and Legal Perspectivism in European Union Law' (2020) 10 [5] Juridical Tribune 17, making reference to N MacCormick, 'Beyond the Sovereign State' (1993) 56 [1] Modern Law Review 1–18

230 N MacCormick, *Questioning Sovereignty: Law, State and Nation in the European Commonwealth* (Oxford University Press 1999) 118

231 E Mendez-Pinedo, 'Constitutional Pluralism and Legal Perspectivism in European Union Law' (2020) 10 [5] Juridical Tribune 17

232 ibid

233 N MacCormick, *Questioning Sovereignty: Law, State and Nation in the European Commonwealth* (Oxford University Press 1999) 120

234 ibid 121

235 N Walker, 'The Idea of Constitutional Pluralism' (2002) 65 [3] Modern Law Review 317–59

point of view.[236] Each constitutional order is valid from its own perspective and the relation between EU law and national law is horizontal.[237] It is necessary, in order to avoid any deadlock, to put in place respect and mutual recognition between the different constitutional legal orders.[238] For him, a solution would not be international law but rather a meta-constitutional law for a higher structure than the actual orders.[239] He would not let the *Kompetenz-Kompetenz* issue remain unresolved.[240] In his observations of the post-Westphalian world, he considers that a shift of authority, and so of sovereignty, can be observed from the State to supra-States, infra-States and even non-State entities.[241] He refers to concepts such as sovereignty in transition and post-sovereignty.[242] Such inputs are interesting for the structure of the shared sovereignty between the EU and the Member States.

Different from Walker but similar to MacCormick, Poiares Maduro chooses to leave the question of *Kompetenz-Kompetenz* unresolved.[243] Through a moderate and balanced approach, he rather proposes a practical way of resolving conflicts that are the consequence of constitutional pluralism.[244] Once again, this idea is based on mutual respect, and he uses a metaphor from musicology (harmony and the technique of contrapunct in baroque music) from which he derives the notion of contrapunctual law (or contrapuntal law).[245] Poiares Maduro argues that it is possible to 'listen to the musical melodies played by different constitutional actors as variations of the same European musical

[236] E Mendez-Pinedo, 'Constitutional Pluralism and Legal Perspectivism in European Union Law' (2020) 10 [5] Juridical Tribune 18
[237] N Walker, 'The Idea of Constitutional Pluralism' (2002) 65 [3] Modern Law Review 317–59
[238] ibid
[239] ibid 359
[240] E Mendez-Pinedo, 'Constitutional Pluralism and Legal Perspectivism in European Union Law' (2020) 10 [5] Juridical Tribune 18
[241] ibid 23
[242] See N Walker, *Sovereignty in Transition* (Hart Publishing 2006)
[243] M Poiares Maduro, 'Contrapunctual Law: Europe's Constitutional Pluralism' in N Walker (ed), *Action in Sovereignty in Transition* (Hart Publishing 2006) 522
[244] E Mendez-Pinedo, 'Constitutional Pluralism and Legal Perspectivism in European Union Law' (2020) 10 [5] Juridical Tribune 19
[245] E Mendez-Pinedo, 'Constitutional Pluralism and Legal Perspectivism in European Union Law' (2020) 10 [5] Juridical Tribune 19. Also, Komarek explained that, as a term of musicology, contrapuntal law would be more exact: J Komarek, 'Institutional Dimension of Constitutional Pluralism' in M Avbelj and J Komarek (eds), *Constitutional Pluralism in Europe and Beyond* (Hart Publishing 2012) 6, footnote 38

theme'.[246] In this sense, constitutional national actors should not act on their own but rather on a broader perspective for a harmonized 'European constitutional orchestra'.[247] Practically, it would be possible to find valid common principles between the different legal orders.[248] It would give a common basis of contrapunctual law[249] or, as a parallel, a general, common and essential identity for all European Member States. Thus, all legal orders should follow the harmony of this common system. Furthermore, some common normative principles should nonetheless be followed in each constitutional system: 'pluralism, consistency, vertical and horizontal coherence, universality and institutional choice.'[250] Yet, Somek analysed this theory of contrapunctual law and found a different result by using another term from musicology: dissonance.[251] For him, the current practice in the EU is more based on 'legal dissonance when judicial rulings are methodologically weak'.[252] A legal inter-

246 E Mendez-Pinedo, 'Constitutional Pluralism and Legal Perspectivism in European Union Law' (2020) 10 [5] Juridical Tribune 19, by reference to M Poiares Maduro, 'Contrapunctual Law: Europe's Constitutional Pluralism' in N Walker (ed), *Action in Sovereignty in Transition* (Hart Publishing 2006) 501–37. Mendez-Pinedo also explains in footnote 70 the nature of this Baroque technique: 'It is difficult to understand Poiares Maduro's metaphor without referring to the art of Baroque music, contrapunct and J.S. Bach. Although the first impression we hear is of diversity, when listening to the music of this European orchestra we realize that variations on the theme do not alter the substance and internal harmony of the musical themes (motives) but only its musical texture, timbre, tone or pitch. Like the special blend of music instruments and timbres in a counterpoint or two or more melodic motives or lines. It is based on a sophisticated use of polyphonic texture where at least two melodies play at the same time, each melody being equally important': E Mendez-Pinedo, 'Constitutional Pluralism and Legal Perspectivism in European Union Law' (2020) 10 [5] Juridical Tribune 19

247 E Mendez-Pinedo, 'Constitutional Pluralism and Legal Perspectivism in European Union Law' (2020) 10 [5] Juridical Tribune 20

248 ibid

249 ibid

250 ibid

251 A Somek, 'The Emancipation of Legal Dissonance' (2009) University of Iowa Legal Studies Research Paper n 09-02 <https://papers.ssrn.com/sol3/papers.cfm?abstract_id=1333194> accessed 23 November 2025

252 E Mendez-Pinedo, 'Constitutional Pluralism and Legal Perspectivism in European Union Law' (2020) 10 [5] Juridical Tribune 20, making a reference to A Somek, 'The Emancipation of Legal Dissonance' (2009) University of Iowa Legal Studies Research Paper n 09-02 <https://papers.ssrn.com/sol3/papers.cfm?abstract_id=1333194> accessed 23 November 2025. In footnote 74, Mendez-Pinedo also explains what dissonance means by reference to Somek's work: 'For Somek the term "dissonance", also a musical metaphor, describes better the

pretation that is not based on an already sufficiently strong legal basis and legal reasoning would be a dissonance. In other words, for legal harmony, sufficiently strong legal bases and legal reasonings are needed in all constitutional orders. Interpretation of principles understood as common to all the institutional actors would not be enough.

Thereafter, Kumm argues for radical pluralism without compromise.[253] He recognizes the European integration process with a strong *telos* (objective) but he rejects the monist understanding of the EU based on the CJEU case-law.[254] Similar to the Member States' defence of their constitutional identities, he argues that when there are contradictory claims, in exceptional cases, the Member States can have constitutional reservations regarding fundamental issues and not compromise on them.[255] The Member States, when in this situation, could derogate from EU law if it is valid from the point of view of their own constitutional system.

There are many other conceptions of constitutional pluralism, such as holistic constitutionalism based on the works of Besselink and Piqani.[256] The main idea is that, under a full commitment of the Member States and of the EU institutions to respect and fulfil their own obligations as previously determined (within the EU treaties in respect of all engagements and so in respect also of the national constitutions), there would be loyalty to all constitutional basic

---

situation of legality in the European Union. He refers to music history and to the "emancipation of dissonance" done by Arnold Schönberg in 1908 which amounted to putting consonant and dissonant sonorities on an equal footing in the composition of music. Somek argues, in the first place, "interesting" or reasoning are to be considered the legal equivalent of dissonance in music. He claims, in the second place, the ECJ has become the chief purveyor of the emancipation of legal dissonance': E Mendez-Pinedo, 'Constitutional Pluralism and Legal Perspectivism in European Union Law' (2020) 10 [5] Juridical Tribune 20

253 M Kumm, 'Who is the Final Arbiter of Constitutionality in Europe? Three Conceptions of the Relationship between the German Federal Constitutional Court and the European Court of Justice' (1999) 36 Common Market Law Review 351–86; M Kumm, 'The Jurisprudence of Constitutional Conflict: Constitutional Supremacy in Europe before and after the Constitutional Treaty' (2005) 11 [3] European Law Journal 262–307

254 See E Mendez-Pinedo, 'Constitutional Pluralism and Legal Perspectivism in European Union Law' (2020) 10 [5] Juridical Tribune 21

255 ibid

256 L Besselink, *A Composite European Constitution* (Europa Law Publishing 2007) 7–12; D Piqani, 'Supremacy of EU Law and the Jurisprudence of Constitutional Reservations' in *Central Eastern Europe and the Western Balkans: Towards a 'Holistic' Constitutionalism* (DPhil thesis, European University Institute 2010) 4

legal orders and so a duty of loyal cooperation.[257] In addition, Pernice proposes a multi-level constitutionalism[258] that should be understood as a unitary position for Walker and not as a constitutional pluralism (hierarchic and not heterarchical).[259] The EU is a sui generis unity made of different legal orders.[260] Thus, under a concept of functional supremacy, there is a complex EU constitution forming a unique legal system composed of complementary constitutional layers and EU law takes precedence in case of conflict.[261] That would be functionally justified for the protection of the European citizens under the rule of law and also for the functionality of the European legal order.[262]

Finally, Weiler and Wind underlined that there is truth in constitutional pluralism.[263] On one side, EU law does not incorporate national constitutional perspectives, which are themselves artificially built and cannot impose their views on other constitutional orders, and, in addition, it is ultimately not possible to derogate from EU law as a matter of unity and integrity.[264] However, on the other side, the CJEU's constitutionalism theory must be deconstructed as it does not take into account the national constitutional perspectives.[265] They call for open constitutionalism where the question of *Kompetenz-Kompetenz* is left unresolved.[266] Thus, the idea of constitutional pluralism is interesting from the perspective of the theory of shared sovereignty but how the latter is different from such idea must be explained through Leibniz's monad.

---

257 D Piqani, 'Supremacy of EU Law and the Jurisprudence of Constitutional Reservations' in *Central Eastern Europe and the Western Balkans: Towards a 'Holistic' Constitutionalism* (DPhil thesis, European University Institute 2010) 7

258 L Pernice, 'Multilevel Constitutionalism in the European Union' (2002) 27 [5] European Law Review 511–29; L Pernice, 'European v. National Constitutions' (2005) 1 European Constitutional Law Review 99–103

259 N Walker, *Sovereignty in Transition* (Hart Publishing 2006) 11–12

260 L Pernice, 'Multilevel Constitutionalism in the European Union' (2002) 27 [5] European Law Review 514

261 Ibid 520

262 See E Mendez-Pinedo, 'Constitutional Pluralism and Legal Perspectivism in European Union Law' (2020) 10 [5] Juridical Tribune 29

263 JHH Weiler, M Wind, *European Constitutionalism Beyond the State* (Cambridge University Press 2003) 99

264 ibid 95 and 101

265 ibid 75

266 ibid 95

5.3.2 The Theory of Shared Sovereignty as a Theory of Unity and Relations between the European Union and the Member States

5.3.2.1 The philosophy of Leibniz as a basis for unity in the theory of shared sovereignty

To explain the notion of unity and the organization of the legal system in the theory of shared sovereignty, Leibniz's theory of the monad as substantial unity is used as a starting point. This theory must aid in the demonstration of the articulation of the concept of sovereignty that encompasses the two legal orders of the EU and of the Member States. Thus, it must help to deduce normative principles to organize the relations between the two orders and, finally, a comparison must be made with constitutional pluralism.

Therefore, as the philosophy of Leibniz is not defined in one or several books but in all of his writings, published or not, a focus is made on the monad as simple substance, with some inputs on his law of dynamics and on the notion of 'the best of all possible worlds'.[267]

Hence, the term monad comes from the Greek word *monas,* which means unity.[268] Monads are units from which the world is formed, but they are not themselves the components of the world.[269] They inform the components of the world without being parts of it.[270] They are units in the sense of unity (as concept) but it is a different kind of unity than the arithmetical kind.[271] In arithmetic, a unity can be divided as a fraction and there is a homogeneity between the different ways of writing a number.[272] Contrarily, what is important to understand about the monad as unit (in the sense of the concept of unity) is that it is indivisible and absolutely different from the components of the nature (or of the world) even if they are the basis of the essence and existence of these components.[273] They inform them but they are not them. They do not have a material existence but they inform the components as material existence.[274] The monads are the true units that founded the nature in all of its

---

267 This formula is Leibniz's answer to the existence of evil in the world: GW Leibniz, *Essais de Théodicée sur la Bonté de Dieu, la Liberté de l'Homme et l'Origine du Mal* (1710)

268 C Angleraux, 'La Simplicité Monadique chez Leibniz' (2018) 12 Philonsorbonne 9 <https://journals.openedition.org/philonsorbonne/945> accessed 23 November 2025

269 ibid

270 ibid

271 ibid

272 ibid

273 ibid 10

274 ibid 9

components.[275] They are units of substance that give their ontological form to the components of the world.[276] Thus, they form these components from above and from below.[277] From above, it is the idea of an integrative model and this aspect must be seen with the notion of 'the best of all possible worlds'.[278] Then, from below, it is the elementary model of the monads as constituent units of the components of the world.[279] They give its substance and its form to the visible world.[280] It is the latter that must be seen first through the notion of simplicity. Indeed, according to Leibniz, simplicity is the essential quality of the monadic unity. It distinguishes it from the components of the world.[281]

Hence, it is important to define what simplicity means for the monad as substantial unit. The most frequent definition that Leibniz gives for monadic simplicity is that it is the quality of being without any parts.[282] It underlines the heterogeneity between the monad and the material world (as the components that the monad informs). While the components can be divided, the monad is indivisible and different from numbers (as in arithmetic, as said before) and atoms.[283] Consequently, the monad is also immaterial.[284] What is material can

---

[275] ibid 10

[276] GW Leibniz, 'Système Nouveau de la Nature et de la Communication des Substances, aussi bien que l'Union qu'il y a entre l'Âme et le Corps' in CI Gerhardt (ed), *Die Philosophischen Schriften von Gottfried Wilhem Leibniz,* vol 4 (Weidmann 1875–90) 482

[277] C Angleraux, 'La Simplicité Monadique chez Leibniz' (2018) 12 Philonsorbonne 10 <https://journals.openedition.org/philonsorbonne/945> accessed 23 November 2025

[278] See GW Leibniz, *Essais de Théodicée sur la Bonté de Dieu, la Liberté de l'Homme et l'Origine du Mal* (1710)

[279] It is the basic idea that is explained in this paragraph about the simplicity of the monad.

[280] C Angleraux, 'La Simplicité Monadique chez Leibniz' (2018) 12 Philonsorbonne 11 <https://journals.openedition.org/philonsorbonne/945> accessed 23 November 2025; GW Leibniz, 'Monadologie' in CI Gerhardt (ed), *Die Philosophischen Schriften von Gottfried Wilhem Leibniz,* vol 6 (Weidmann 1875–90) 607

[281] GW Leibniz, 'Système Nouveau de la Nature et de la Communication des Substances, aussi bien que l'Union qu'il y a entre l'Âme et le Corps' in CI Gerhardt (ed), *Die Philosophischen Schriften von Gottfried Wilhem Leibniz,* vol 4 (Weidmann 1875–90) 482

[282] ibid

[283] C Angleraux, 'La Simplicité Monadique chez Leibniz' (2018) 12 Philonsorbonne 11 <https://journals.openedition.org/philonsorbonne/945> accessed 23 November 2025

[284] ibid 12

be indefinitely divided, so what does not have any part is immaterial by opposition, according to Leibniz.[285] Similarly, the monad cannot perish, as what can perish is material.[286] In this sense, the main qualities of the monad are that it is indivisible, immaterial and unperishable.[287] These attributes constitute the monad as a real unit.[288] Thus, a monad which is simple is a real monad. It depends on these essential qualities and, as it is real, the monad is substantial (it has a substance).[289]

Another characteristic of the simple monad is to have perception and appetition. These aspects will be linked later to Leibniz's law of dynamics. Actually, the philosopher gives another definition of monadic simplicity.[290] He says that the nature of the simple monad is to have perception, meaning being able to harmoniously organize the diversity.[291] Indeed, perception transforms collected data into a representative unit.[292] It is a system of relations and it means that the monads are active and mobile.[293] Moreover, there is an *impetus*,[294] a movement of force, that fills in this system of relations between the different

---

285 ibid

286 C Angleraux, 'La Simplicité Monadique chez Leibniz' (2018) 12 Philonsorbonne 12 <https://journals.openedition.org/philonsorbonne/945> accessed 23 November 2025; GW Leibniz, 'Considérations sur les Principes de Vie, et sur les Natures Plastiques, par l'Auteur du Système de l'Harmonie Préétablie' in CI Gerhardt (ed), *Die Philosophischen Schriften von Gottfried Wilhem Leibniz,* vol 6 (Weidmann 1875–90) 542

287 C Angleraux, 'La Simplicité Monadique chez Leibniz' (2018) 12 Philonsorbonne 12 <https://journals.openedition.org/philonsorbonne/945> accessed 23 November 2025

288 ibid

289 ibid

290 ibid 14

291 See eg C Angleraux, 'La Simplicité Monadique chez Leibniz' (2018) 12 Philonsorbonne 14 <https://journals.openedition.org/philonsorbonne/945> accessed 23 November 2025; GW Leibniz, 'Leibniz à Sophie' in CI Gerhardt (ed), *Die Philosophischen Schriften von Gottfried Wilhem Leibniz,* vol 7 (Weidmann 1875–90) 566

292 C Angleraux, 'La Simplicité Monadique chez Leibniz' (2018) 12 Philonsorbonne 14 <https://journals.openedition.org/philonsorbonne/945> accessed 23 November 2025

293 ibid 14–15

294 C Angleraux, 'La Simplicité Monadique chez Leibniz' (2018) 12 Philonsorbonne 15 <https://journals.openedition.org/philonsorbonne/945> accessed 23 November 2025; P Phemister, *Leibniz and the Natural World* (Springer 2005) 138

perceptions and making monads able to change and adapt.[295] This is appetition, which can be understood as desire in movement (as a philosophical notion). Thus, the evolution of the world and its transformations are the consequence of these flows of appetition.[296] The simple monads contain a power of change and so a power of perception and a power of appetition.[297] Hence, it can be asserted that the simple monad has a substance by being active in the material world. It is the substantive core and the guarantor of the substance as a whole.[298] Furthermore, the activity of the simple monad is defined by Leibniz through the notion of active primitive force, which acts on the passive primitive force.[299] The active primitive force is the power to act of the simple monad as the simplest element of the world (for the quality of being primitive). This force is the active core of the simple substance while the passive primitive force has a role of limitation.[300] For Leibniz, the simple monad is the authentic place of activity (for which the material world would be the consequence as the latter is shaped by this activity) as a consequence of perceptions.[301] Thus, the monad is simple but complex because there are multiple possibilities of change due to an indefinite number of perceptions even if it does not change its unity as essential quality.[302] There is a cohesion (harmony) between the different perceptions and they form altogether only one entity through this cohesion.[303] There is diversity within unity and, for Leibniz, each monad is a mirror of the universe from its own point of view.[304]

---

295 C Angleraux, 'La Simplicité Monadique chez Leibniz' (2018) 12 Philonsorbonne 15 <https://journals.openedition.org/philonsorbonne/945> accessed 23 November 2025

296 C Angleraux, 'La Simplicité Monadique chez Leibniz' (2018) 12 Philonsorbonne 15 <https://journals.openedition.org/philonsorbonne/945> accessed 23 November 2025; GW Leibniz, 'Principes de la Nature et de la Grâce, Fondés en Raison' in CI Gerhardt (ed), *Die Philosophischen Schriften von Gottfried Wilhem Leibniz,* vol 6 (Weidmann 1875–90) 598

297 C Angleraux, 'La Simplicité Monadique chez Leibniz' (2018) 12 Philonsorbonne 15 <https://journals.openedition.org/philonsorbonne/945> accessed 23 November 2025

298 ibid 22

299 ibid 16

300 P Phemister, *Leibniz and the Natural World* (Springer 2005) 242

301 C Angleraux, 'La Simplicité Monadique chez Leibniz' (2018) 12 Philonsorbonne 16 <https://journals.openedition.org/philonsorbonne/945> accessed 23 November 2025

302 ibid 17

303 ibid

304 ibid 17–18

Thus, it can be deduced from what has been said that the simple monad must be associated to an organic body.[305] Indeed, the simple monads, in their multiplicity, shape nature as the visible world. Consequently, each monad as unit shapes its own organic body, and the association between both, the simple monad and the organic body, must form a complete substance.[306] Then, the composite substance is formed of several complete substances.[307] Each simple monad creates its own organic body with its own complexity, and the totality of the simple monads shape the material world with their organic bodies.[308] The simple monad must be understood as the soul of the organic body by giving it its shape.[309]

As such, the different relations between the simple monad and its organic body as well as between the simple monad and the composite monad must now be highlighted. All simple monads have a perception that can take multiple forms and they need an organic body in order to express these perceptions within the material world.[310] This organic body is also unperishable and

---

305 C Angleraux, 'La Simplicité Monadique chez Leibniz' (2018) 12 Philonsorbonne 19 <https://journals.openedition.org/philonsorbonne/945> accessed 23 November 2025; GW Leibniz, 'Leibniz à De Volder 1703' in CI Gerhardt (ed), *Die Philosophischen Schriften von Gottfried Wilhem Leibniz,* vol 2 (Weidmann 1875–90) 251

306 GW Leibniz, 'Leibniz à Des Maizeaux' in CI Gerhardt (ed), *Die Philosophischen Schriften von Gottfried Wilhem Leibniz,* vol 7 (Weidmann 1875–90) 535. On this view, Leibniz is in opposition with Pascal and follows an Aristotelician understanding of the substance. For Pascal, spirit (substance) and matter are the two elements that can be united. The matter or corpse is the form (as a visible form). However, for Aristotle, the spirit is already the element that gives the form to the matter. The substance shapes the matter.

307 C Angleraux, 'La Simplicité Monadique chez Leibniz' (2018) 12 Philonsorbonne 19 <https://journals.openedition.org/philonsorbonne/945> accessed 23 November 2025

308 ibid

309 See C Angleraux, 'La Simplicité Monadique chez Leibniz' (2018) 12 Philonsorbonne 22 <https://journals.openedition.org/philonsorbonne/945> accessed 23 November 2025; GW Leibniz, 'Leibniz à Rémond' in CI Gerhardt (ed), *Die Philosophischen Schriften von Gottfried Wilhem Leibniz,* vol 3 (Weidmann 1875–90) 657

310 C Angleraux, 'La Simplicité Monadique chez Leibniz' (2018) 12 Philonsorbonne 17 <https://journals.openedition.org/philonsorbonne/945> accessed 23 November 2025

lives with the simple monad.[311] The organic body changes through perception.[312] The composite monad is composed of multiple simple monads and there is a regression to the infinity: 'the living bodies are still machines in each of their parts to the infinity.'[313] Simple monads do not change but the organic bodies adapt themselves to their perceptions and the living bodies, as people are composite substances that consequently adapt themselves too.[314] People or animals, for instance, are composite substances or composite monads, and their evolution in the process of life is the consequence of the transformation of the simple monads through their perceptions.

However, there is one simple monad that does not have an organic body, and for Leibniz it is God.[315] This is where the notion of 'the best of all possible worlds' returns. When Leibniz writes on his understanding of the world as the best of all possible worlds, there is an entire reflection on what is necessary and what is possible, and about determination against free will.[316] However, only the elements necessary to understand the parallel with the concept of shared sovereignty must be provided. Hence, Leibniz explains that there are multiple possible worlds where each individual (for instance) makes different choices.[317] For instance, there is a world where Caesar does not cross the Rubicon and another world where Judas does not betray Jesus.[318] Hence, it is for God to choose which world must be the real world in which human beings

311 C Angleraux, 'La Simplicité Monadique chez Leibniz' (2018) 12 Philonsorbonne 21 <https://journals.openedition.org/philonsorbonne/945> accessed 23 November 2025; GW Leibniz, 'Leibniz à Lady Masham' in CI Gerhardt (ed), *Die Philosophischen Schriften von Gottfried Wilhem Leibniz,* vol 3 (Weidmann 1875–90) 340

312 C Angleraux, 'La Simplicité Monadique chez Leibniz' (2018) 12 Philonsorbonne 21 <https://journals.openedition.org/philonsorbonne/945> accessed 23 November 2025

313 GW Leibniz, 'Monadologie' in CI Gerhardt (ed), *Die Philosophischen Schriften von Gottfried Wilhem Leibniz,* vol 6 (Weidmann 1875–90) 618

314 C Angleraux, 'La Simplicité Monadique chez Leibniz' (2018) 12 Philonsorbonne 21 <https://journals.openedition.org/philonsorbonne/945> accessed 23 November 2025; GW Leibniz, 'Leibniz à Lady Masham' in CI Gerhardt (ed), *Die Philosophischen Schriften von Gottfried Wilhem Leibniz,* vol 3 (Weidmann 1875–90) 340

315 C Angleraux, 'La Simplicité Monadique chez Leibniz' (2018) 12 Philonsorbonne 19 <https://journals.openedition.org/philonsorbonne/945> accessed 23 November 2025

316 See GW Leibniz, *Essais de Théodicée sur la Bonté de Dieu, la Liberté de l'Homme et l'Origine du Mal* (1710)

317 ibid

318 ibid

are living. God, as the only simple monad without an organic body, can be considered as the ultimate metaphysical point, and its perception of the world defines the integrative model.[319] It is the ultimate simple monad that organizes the whole world and it does it harmoniously (for the best). Thus, there is harmony within each composite monad but also between the different composite monads. Then, in terms of the best of all possible worlds, God did not choose the best world for each individual on its own but for all individuals as a whole.[320] In this sense, each individual kept its free will on its own decisions, creating all the possible worlds, and God created (knowing already all the possibilities) the best possible world knowing all the different combinations between the free choices of each individual.[321] It is a decision on the world as a whole in order to preserve its harmony.[322]

Finally, the law of dynamics as defined by Leibniz must be mentioned. It has been seen that the simple monads are active and so have activity. For Leibniz, this aspect is essential to understand the monad. His law of dynamics, where he defines mv^2 (part of the formula of kinetic energy) in physics, cannot be separated from the definition of the monad.[323] Again, the purpose here is not to delve into all of the aspects of Leibniz's physics, but it must be understood that the active primitive force of the simple monad is one of its essential elements as characterizing its substance like its other qualities.[324] Also, it is important because, in addition to the two primitive forces, there are two derivative forces, which are the active derivative force and the passive derivative force. These derivative forces are the consequence of the primitive forces and their manifestation among the phenomena.[325] Concretely, the simple monad acts through the active primitive force and then, when it comes to its organic body and the material world, the derivative forces report at the phenomenal level on what

319 See C Angleraux, 'La Simplicité Monadique chez Leibniz' (2018) 12 Philonsorbonne <https://journals.openedition.org/philonsorbonne/945> accessed 23 November 2025

320 See GW Leibniz, *Essais de Théodicée sur la Bonté de Dieu, la Liberté de l'Homme et l'Origine du Mal* (1710)

321 ibid

322 ibid

323 See GW Leibniz, *Dynamica de Potentia et Legibus Naturae Corporeae* (1689)

324 C Angleraux, 'La Simplicité Monadique chez Leibniz' (2018) 12 Philonsorbonne 16 <https://journals.openedition.org/philonsorbonne/945> accessed 23 November 2025

325 P Phemister, *Monads and Machines in Machines of Nature and Corporeal Substances in Leibniz* (JEH Smith and O Nachtomy eds, Springer 2011) 47–48

happens at the primitive level of the simple monad.[326] Thus, the active derivative force is the result of the conflicts between organic bodies in the composite substances, and it accidentally limits the primitive forces.[327] Hence, the active primitive force is the metaphysical basis of the law of dynamics while the active derivative force is the modification of the active primitive force on a mechanical level (and so material) due to the shocks between substances. In conclusion, the roles of the passive primitive force and of the passive derivative force must be explained. The first is the source material while the second is the secondary material as accounting for the different interactions that result in composite substances.[328] The passive primitive force is the mass that must be complementary to the form given by the active primitive force in each substance.[329] It can be assimilated to the organic body of the simple substance. Next, the passive derivative force is the mass of several substances as constituting a composite substance, or a body as a phenomenon (meaning as it appears to our own eyes), and with the possibility to be constantly modified.[330] Passive forces are material supports on which active forces can act to shape the visible world. They have a power of enduring shocks while active forces have the power to act. In that respect, it must now be explained how Leibniz's theory can help to demonstrate the theory of shared sovereignty.

5.3.2.2 The application of Leibniz's philosophy to the relations between the European Union and the Member States

Two important elements in Leibniz's theory seeking to understand the concept of shared sovereignty between the EU and the Member States have been mentioned. The first is God, which chooses the best of all possible worlds with the application of harmony as a principle, and the second is the concept of the monad with simple substance and an organic body. Still, concerning the latter, there is an infinite regression and they are moved by the active primitive force. It is the consequences of this concept that must be applied to the concept of shared sovereignty. Infinite regression means that there are monads within monads. Leibniz uses the example of the herd of sheep.[331] Everything is an

---

326 See P Phemister, *Monads and Machines in Machines of Nature and Corporeal Substances in Leibniz* (JEH Smith and O Nachtomy eds, Springer 2011)

327 See GW Leibniz, 'Leibniz à De Volder 1703' in CI Gerhardt (ed), *Die Philosophischen Schriften von Gottfried Wilhem Leibniz,* vol 2 (Weidmann 1875–90) 252

328 ibid

329 ibid

330 ibid

331 GW Leibniz, *Remarques aux Objections de M. Foucher à mon Système Nouveau* (1695)

assembly.[332] A sheep is a monad with its own soul or simple substance that makes its unity but there are subdivided unities that also are monads within the sheep, and this is infinite.[333] Leibniz makes a distinction between dominant monads and subordinated monads.[334] Dominant monads are constituted of subordinated monads. Still, what is important is that each level has its own unity with its own simple substance.[335] The constituted monads (or dominant monads) are body substance in the sense of a unified diversity.[336] The derivative forces act at the level of the constituted monads (or dominant monads) and build organic machines.[337] Leibniz talks especially of the animal or the body substance that the monad in the machine makes one.[338] This means a soul for each animal. This can be the sheep, but also the herd of sheep as a monad constituted of sheep.[339]

Hence, the relation between Leibniz's theory of the monad and the theory of shared sovereignty can now be explained. First, it has been explained that each level of monads constitutes a unity with its own simple substance that forms the monad through its organic body and that the activity of the simple substance is expressed through the notion of force or power, primitive or derivative. Furthermore, it has also been said that Leibniz's system can be understood from above (God organizing the world) or from below. Thus, here, the explanation is made from above, for explaining both the unity of the system and the principles that regulate it.

Hence, for the concept of shared sovereignty in a legal system, God as the original simple substance must be compared to the concept of sovereignty in itself. As a reminder, the civil society self-organizes in the legal world through the State.[340] Then, the State and its internal sovereignty through public power comes before the international relations and so international law that results from the notion of external sovereignty. Also, the form of the State depends on the choice of a specific civil society and, in modern States, the form is usually

---

332 ibid

333 ibid

334 See AL Rey, 'L'Ambivalence de la Notion d'Action dans la Dynamique de Leibniz. La Correspondance entre Leibniz et De Volder (IIe Partie)' (2009) [Band XLI (Heft 1)] Studia Leibnitiana 157–82

335 GW Leibniz, 'Leibniz à De Volder 1703' in CI Gerhardt (ed), *Die Philosophischen Schriften von Gottfried Wilhem Leibniz,* vol 2 (Weidmann 1875–90) 252

336 ibid

337 ibid

338 ibid

339 ibid

340 Pt 1, ch 3

a democracy as a constitutional State. Accordingly, the concept of sovereignty is the first element of organization of the society in the legal world, as God is the simple substance organizing the world for Leibniz. Similarly, a simple substance is active through its active primitive force and has qualities as being indivisible, immaterial and unperishable. These qualities are similar to those of the concept of sovereignty, which is also indivisible (unity of the power), immaterial (non-written concept in its definition with applications or manifestations in the legal world) and unperishable (permanency of the State). In addition, the notion of force in Leibniz's monad is also similar to the notion of power as authority in the concept of sovereignty. The authority in the concept of sovereignty is what creates the hierarchical relations within the State with the notion of supremacy. Then, within the constitutional State, the constituent sovereignty has the primitive force to create the State through an act of sovereignty which is the constitution, and, then, through the constitution, sovereignty can express itself through derivative powers (as sovereignty as public force as well as constituent sovereignty through the constituent act).

Concretely, this comparison is applied to the Member States and the EU knowing that sovereignty is the first element of organization of the legal world and that simple substances are permanently acting and transforming the visible world through perception and appetition. Thus, a Member State is a constitutional State organized around the concept of sovereignty and around the concept of constituent sovereignty for its constitution as a legal system and for its specific legal and political form. Sovereignty, as the original simple substance, organizes the Member States as legal systems. At the same time, it is the constituent sovereignty that organizes the Member States around their constitutions to make them constitutional States. There is no distinction to make between political and constituent sovereignty but, in the constitutional State, it can be said that it is a specific kind of perception that gives to the State its constitutional form. In addition, authority as power is the first *impetus* (movement of force), as characteristic element of the concept of sovereignty, that creates the State. It is the active primitive force as quality of the concept of sovereignty, which has no organic body (like God for Leibniz). Then, in constitutional States like the Member States, the act of sovereignty is the constitution, but this act is considered as sovereign after the constituent moment. In this situation, as the constitution as act of sovereignty is already within the legal world, the understood sovereignty of the constitution within the legal sphere as constitutional system is the simple substance. The constitutional legal system it creates is its organic body and each Member State as constitutional State is a monad. However, this monad is a dominant monad, like Leibnitz's herd of sheep. Indeed, within the legal systems of the Member States, the constitution organizes the constituted powers and their competences. The active primitive force of the constitution, which is the quality of authority of the concept of sovereignty, acts to create derivative forces (or derivative powers), which are the constituted powers.

Thus, it must now be carefully explained in what way each constituted power and each competence constitute a monad at their own level, still respecting the legal hierarchy and the consequences of the concept of sovereignty as being absolute and supreme. Therefore, the authority of the concept of sovereignty is the force that acts at each level of each monad (monad or complete substance/composite monad or body substance). However, the concept of sovereignty keeps its qualities as being supreme and absolute. The monads can be indefinitely divided but not the ultimate substance that is the concept of sovereignty (that is expressed through the constitution within the constitutional State). Consequently, the system of hierarchy and the legal consequences of the concept of sovereignty are preserved. Then, within the dominant monads that are the legal systems of the Member States shaped by sovereignty as original simple substance, there are different levels of constituted powers, which are other composite monads. The latter are themselves the subordinated monads of the legal systems as dominant monads. Moreover, within the constituted powers, there are then the different material competences that can also be divided between subcategories according to the different delegated powers. There is a hierarchy that begins with the legal system, then the constituted powers, then their different competences, and so on, each level having its own unity as composite and constituted monad. Each level is active through the authority of the concept of sovereignty as the original monad or original simple substance. It is a hierarchy from above. Also, at each level, the constituted powers are equivalent and so equal. The hierarchy works with the different levels of unity but at each level there is no hierarchy. In the herd of sheep, there is no sheep higher than another. Similarly, a competence is equal to another competence. The hierarchy works from the constitution to the competences, and so on.

Furthermore, a hierarchy from below can also be found even if its origin is also in the concept of sovereignty. Indeed, there is authority in each monad, from the smallest to the biggest. For instance, there is the authority of the legal system with sovereignty as simple substance but there is also the authority of the tax inspector with its simple substance that is also authority, even if delegated (as the essence of authority comes from the concept of sovereignty, like God with the world), with a different perception, which is shaped by its context which is the tax administration as delegated body within the Ministry of Finance and under the competence of the power to tax that finds its origin within the constitution. Each level finds its authority within the concept of sovereignty that created the legal system as a whole, but the hierarchy is kept between the different levels under the definition of the concept of sovereignty itself. It is similar to God that can be found in the detail and that organizes the world as a whole. Finally, concerning the Member States as organized as constituted monads, the parallel with Leibniz's theory in terms of legal principle must be highlighted. Indeed, God chooses the best of all possible worlds, and it created the world harmoniously. The concept of sovereignty must be similar. Harmony must be translated as the general principle organizing the Member States as constitutional systems. It consists in a general principle of coherence to avoid inconsistencies within their legal systems. Also, from the definition of harmony and its inherent application through the notion of God can be deduced a fundamental principle for the notion of peace it entails, as God created the best of all possible worlds. Within the legal systems, it is the fundamental legal principle of coherence that must ensure a peaceable organization of the society as initial objective of the idea of organization of the civil society through law (the social contract, for instance). Still, it is important to underline that harmony is inherent to God as concept. Indeed, the idea of God is to organize the society for the greater good ('best of all possible worlds'). Similarly, as the concept of sovereignty creates the State as legal organization, the principle of coherence must be inherent to this creation.

Thus, the EU can now be integrated within this system. Its emergence as a sovereign order comes from transformations that are the consequences of the multiple perceptions of the EU as a whole and so as a legal order as constituted monad. Indeed, simple substances have a multiplicity of perceptions as the origin of the substantial transformations in the world. Concerning the EU and the Member States, the concept of sovereignty did not change but the substance of the EU changed and, consequently, the substance of the Member States also changed. All these transformations have been legally explained.[341] However, the emergence of the EU did not create a heterarchical order in the sense of constitutional pluralism or an idea of divided sovereignty with two distinct sovereignties and two distinct legal systems. The EU and the Member States must rather be understood as a legal system as a whole (and the EU comes from the Member States, it is not another system with a different origin). The concept of sovereignty remains the concept that first organizes the legal world and the legal systems. It manifests itself within the legal world but it is not a written norm in its definition. It creates the hierarchy that gives its value to the norm without being limited to the State. In this sense, a hierarchy must be preserved within the system. Thus, the Member States and the EU create together *one composite monad* shaped by sovereignty as original simple substance, and they form a legal system altogether. There is one dominant monad where the concept of sovereignty manifests itself. The EU and the Member States are equal in this monad and they shape it together through the concept of sovereignty. The hierarchy is then observed within the dominant monad. There is only one

---

[341] Pt 2, ch 4

sovereignty for the EU and the Member States, which form a complete unity. However, concerning the notion of the constitutional State, there are still two constitutions for two orders with the constitutions of the Member States and the EU treaties considered as constitution. Nonetheless, the constitutions are acts of sovereignty considered as sovereigns but not as original sovereigns. The real sovereign of the constitutional State is the constituent people, and there is a common people between the EU and the Member States. Thus, it confirms that both orders constitute together a composite monad with sovereignty as its original simple substance. Accordingly, there are then subordinated monads with, for each of them, the constitution being the manifestation of sovereignty in each legal order as subordinated monads within the united general legal system. As such, the last aspect that is at stake here is the concrete relations between the EU and the Member States as forming one legal system encompassing their respective constitutional orders.

Indeed, even if the legal system constituted by the EU and the Member States remains a hierarchical order in its application with one people, there is still a necessity to organize the relations between them on an equal footing. Thus, parallel to the 'best possible world' with Leibniz, it is the principle of harmony or of general coherence that must be applied as being inherent to the concept of sovereignty organizing the legal system. The application of such principle, which must be understood as a legal principle as organizing a legal system, can be compared to the meta-constitution of Walker[342] and its application could follow a theory of contrapunctual law as elaborated by Poiares Maduro. However, the comparison with the meta-constitution must not be understood as creating another order higher than the unity between the EU and the Member States. The principle of general coherence is inherent to the concept of sovereignty and, as such, inherent to the EU and the Member States. They must apply it as a logical consequence of their organization as one legal system with two orders on an equal footing, as Leibniz organizes the world through the monad. Such ideas already have a legal implementation in article 4 TEU with the recognition of the national identities of the Member States and with the principle of loyal cooperation (in accordance with article 13 TEU for the EU). However, it must be stressed that harmony and coherence based on the concept of sovereignty itself must be followed from the constitution to the smallest possible level of authority. It is an application of the imbrication of the monads. What is meant is that, within the general dominant monad of the legal

342 Indeed, as a manifestation of the concept of sovereignty, the legal system encompassing the EU and the Member States needs its own expression of constitution, which would be the legal expression of harmony through a principle of coherence. The idea of harmony that comes from the parallel with Leibniz is inherent to the idea of organization of the legal system.

system, there is a monad for each Member State and for the EU as legal orders, then a monad for their different competences, and so on. Thus, each monad being part of another monad must respect its delimitation as being part of a bigger monad. It is where the derivative powers (according to Leibniz's definition) play a role. The monads limit themselves at each level. For instance, when it is said that the EU does not have a power to tax,[343] it is limited by this categorization and it cannot put in place a European tax through a non-generally coherent means in the sense of coherence of the whole legal system. Similarly, the distribution and the application of competences between the EU and the Member States must follow a coherent pattern in the sense of coherence of the whole system. This is why it can be considered that the EU is not yet always constitutionally coherent.[344] However, it is also why the EU has the legitimacy to get a competence to tax in coherence with its own objectives.[345] The subordinated monad of the competence to tax is one of the monads that compose the dominant monad of the European legal order.

Finally, the concept of shared sovereignty is itself a shortcut in its wording. There is unity of sovereignty for one general legal system, which is symbolized by the simple substance. Then, there is a cascade effect in each order through the delegation of competences and as subordinated monads.

5.4 CONCLUSION

This chapter has analysed how, with the treaty of Maastricht, the constitutional referendums that happened at that time in the Member States gave the EU an institutional democratic legitimacy, and that consequently, through its democratic material dispositions, the EU must be understood as a constitutional order. Still, subsequent treaty modifications must remain in this constitutional framework and the EU, constitutionally speaking, must regulate its actions by considering this aspect. Then, the chapter analysed the constitutional relations between the EU and the Member States to find a way to ensure a peaceful coexistence of both constitutional orders. As such, the theory of shared sovereignty provides for a solution to protect the perennity of the unity, and so of the sovereignty, of the legal system that encompasses both legal orders. Inspired by Leibniz's works on the monad, the sovereign legal system that contains the EU and the Member States must be governed by a principle of general coherence to preserve its organization and the inherent qualities and objectives of both the EU and the Member States as legal orders. Thus, the consequences

[343] See pt 3, ch 6, para 6.4
[344] See pt 3 on the inadequacy of the EU objectives and the current means to achieve them in the field of direct taxation of businesses.
[345] See pt 3

of the model of the monad for the theory of shared sovereignty must ensure a coherent attribution of the competences between the EU and the Member States according to their own sovereignty and so, also, their own constitutional sovereignty. In this sense, the EU has the legitimacy to get the competences that correspond to the achievement of its constitutional principles and objectives. Its actions must correspond to its value pattern.[346]

346 See ch 1, para 1.2

PART III

Assessing the Sovereignty of the European Union: The Example of the Field of Direct Taxation of Businesses

6. The concept of sovereignty and the legitimacy of the European Union's taxing powers in the field of direct taxation

6.1 INTRODUCTION

The concept of sovereignty and the idea of shared sovereignty that has been derived from it must now be confronted with the current application of the taxing powers of the Member States within the internal market to highlight why the European Union (EU) does not have currently a competence to tax in the field of direct taxation of businesses and why it should have one. As such, it must be explained why the idea of a concept of tax sovereignty is conceptually not possible and why this concept is just the association of several taxing powers, which are the competence to tax and the power to tax. Then, the paradox that exists between the reserved taxing powers of the Member States in the field of direct taxation and the EU's objective to achieve the internal market through its own competences must be highlighted. This paradox can be understood as an application of the flawed concept of tax sovereignty. Thus, the Member States, even if they keep reserved competences in a field (such as the field of direct taxation, notably through the protection of their own tax policy), must respect the principle of primacy of EU law. Such supremacy encompasses especially the main objective of achieving the internal market under the concept of shared sovereignty. Therefore, the paradox that exists between the current application of the competence to tax of the Member States in the field of direct taxation of businesses and the EU objectives must be highlighted. On the other side, it must be explained that the EU does not currently have a power to tax[1] due to the inherent democratic implications of such power.

[1] See F Barreau, 'The Legitimacy of the EU's Tax-Based Own Resources' in A Hultqvist and J Lindholm (eds), *The Power to Tax in Europe* (Hart Publishing 2023) 37–58: elements of the power to tax that can be found in the introduction and section 6.3.1 of this chapter are presented in this article

Thus, in his thesis on the competence to tax,[2] Andreas Kallergis points out the common confusion between the taxing powers and the concept of sovereignty from which has consequently derived a different concept of tax sovereignty. In his work, he mainly concentrates on the French law to demonstrate that the concept of 'tax sovereignty' was widely used until it finally got its own definition.[3] Consequently, the common use of the expression 'tax sovereignty' has been defined in the doctrine. This work of definition has been performed by Chrétien, who seems to be also at the origin of the propagation of the term.[4] For him, 'the tax sovereignty is a territorial sovereignty of a specific kind'.[5] In order to give this definition, Chrétien used Udina's book on international tax law.[6] However, and following Kallergis' interpretation,[7] the reference made to Udina's book is a reference to a passage where the Italian author writes about the spatial delimitation of the taxing power (*potestà tributaria*) but not of tax sovereignty.[8] A shortcut has been made from a territorial conception of the exercise of the taxing power (which is an objective consequence of the power of the State as constituted as a State)[9] to a territorial concept of tax sovereignty. This shortcut, and so this territorial concept of tax sovereignty as a spatially delimited taxing power, remains a dominant concept in the contemporaneous doctrine.[10] For Gest and Tixier, 'the territorial sovereignty, from which the tax sovereignty is just a specific form, is an attribute of the State'[11] and the State, which is 'politically and fiscally sovereign',[12] can exercise an absolute taxing power within its territory but not outside of it.[13]

This concept of tax sovereignty as defined in the doctrine takes into account the normative power to make the law in addition to the operational power to execute the law.[14] This precision is necessary because of a distinction that is specific to the French language by opposition to the English language.[15] In

---

2 A Kallergis, *La Compétence Fiscale* (LGDJ 2018)
3 Ibid 10–13
4 ibid 11
5 M Chrétien, *A la Recherche du Droit International Fiscal Commun* (Sirey 1955) 2
6 M Udina, *Il Diritto Internazionale Tributario* (CEDAM 1949) 57ff
7 A Kallergis, *La Compétence Fiscale* (LGDJ 2018) 11
8 ibid
9 ibid
10 ibid
11 G Gest, G Tixier, *Droit Fiscal International* (2nd edn, PUF 1990) para 4
12 ibid
13 ibid
14 A Kallergis, *La Compétence Fiscale* (LGDJ 2018) 12
15 ibid

French tax law, the word *compétence* is a reference to the normative power in the widest sense possible while the word *pouvoir* is a reference to the executing power.[16] What must be understood here is that while the English law uses the term power for both the normative power and the executing power, the French law uses the term *compétence* for the normative power and the term *pouvoir* for the executing power. In French tax law, the concept of tax sovereignty is the gathering of the 'competence to tax' and the 'power to tax' (this translation is used for a purpose of clarity) for the same tax.[17] The competence to tax is the right to enact the tax law while the power to tax is the right to levy the tax (even without deciding the norms that will regulate this levy).[18] As such, the final consequence of this definition in the tax doctrine is that a distinction is made between the political sovereignty and the tax sovereignty.[19] It gives an idea of dual sovereignty where it is possible to be fiscally sovereign but not politically sovereign.[20] This dual definition assumes a vertical repartition of the power:[21] 'a territorially determined entity, having or not the political sovereignty, has the tax sovereignty as long as it has a tax system which presents two essential characteristics, on one side a technical autonomy, and on the other side an exclusivity of application in such territory.'[22]

Such definition of the concept of tax sovereignty must be discarded. The concept of sovereignty is an absolute concept which appears in order to form the legal sphere.[23] One of its inherent criteria is the indetermination of its power, which is the indetermination of the missions of the State.[24] Moreover, the concept of tax sovereignty has been defined through its powers: the tax sovereignty is the gathering of two elements, which are the competence to tax and the power to tax. In this sense, this concept is a material concept, and so a material sovereignty, because its definition is the consequence of the powers that are contained in the concept. By opposition, the concept of sovereignty is a formal concept because it has been defined through its inherent criteria, which are its inherent qualities, and not through its operational consequences.

---

16 ibid

17 A Maitrot de la Motte, *Droit Fiscal de l'Union Européenne* (2nd edn, Bruylant ed, LGDJ 2016) 2

18 ibid

19 A Kallergis, *La Compétence Fiscale* (LGDJ 2018) 12

20 ibid

21 ibid

22 G Gest, G Tixier, *Droit Fiscal International* (2nd edn, PUF 1990) 15

23 And it appears with its characteristics, which are the absolute (and so independent) supreme authority.

24 A Kallergis, *La Compétence Fiscale* (LGDJ 2018) 15

The latter has been self-defined while the concept of tax sovereignty has been defined as an accumulation of operational consequences.

Furthermore, the two sovereignties, meaning the political sovereignty and the tax sovereignty, are not compatible. Indeed, sovereignty must be absolute and cannot be divided. The first consequence is that it is not possible to have two sovereigns at the same time and on the same territory when it comes to the application of the concept of sovereignty. The second consequence is that there must be indeterminacy as the characterization of the absoluteness of the concept of sovereignty. Yet, tax sovereignty is a limited concept. It is limited because it is defined only by two specific powers. It is in this sense that the second definition given by Carré de Malberg cannot define the concept of sovereignty because an accumulation of powers remains a limited amount of powers.[25] As such, other powers at the same level or at a higher level can coexist and the concept would not be absolute any more. Furthermore, it would not be supreme either, as other equivalent concepts could co-exist. This can be observed with the different concepts of tax sovereignty, economic sovereignty, monetary sovereignty, and so on. Such coexistence is not compatible with the definition of the concept of sovereignty. There is only one concept of sovereignty that is possible, and it is the concept of a formal sovereignty. What should be said instead of 'tax sovereignty' is 'the exercise of the sovereignty of the entity through its taxing powers'. Powers are the attributes of the sovereign and the manifestation of the concept of sovereignty, but they come at a second step and they cannot be the origin of the concept. The concept of tax sovereignty can only be understood as a shortcut to understand the association of the competence to tax with the power to tax. It is not a concept of sovereignty and even less so a different concept that could be compared to the concept of political sovereignty.

Then, concerning the competence to tax and the power to tax that together constitute the concept of tax sovereignty, the latter must be understood as a tax autonomy and not as a tax sovereignty. Indeed, the gathering of these two powers together, even if it does not confer a sovereignty, still confers an autonomy (in the sense of a technical independence) to define a tax system. The main subtlety is that these two powers can be separated. In the doctrine, there are scholars who can consider that there is no distinction between the competence to tax and the power to tax and that both mean the exercise of the taxing power.[26] However, the subtlety that exists between the two terms has an important consequence in EU law. Thus, first, the legal distinction between these two kinds of powers must be explained.

---

25 See ch 3, section 3.2.2.2 about the *summa potestas*.

26 See eg JM Cotteret, L Trotabas, *Droit Fiscal* (4th edn, Dalloz 1980) 122–23

According to Kallergis, among others,[27] the competence is a quality of the entity (here the State as a public entity).[28] The competence helps to determine the functions of the sovereign entity and it is inherently associated with the power (by distinction with the competence).[29] The competence is the legitimization of the power.[30] Concretely, the competence is the power that determines the legal sphere of action of the sovereign entity while the power is the power that determines the content on which sovereignty can be exercised within this legal sphere.[31] As such, the competence can be considered as the title and the power as the content, meaning the concrete exercise of the power in accordance with this title.

Such precisions are particularly important in the EU context. The attribution of competences between the EU and the Member States is initially supposed to follow the subsidiarity principle. In this sense, there would have been a delegation. However, the EU self-revealed as sharing sovereignty with the Member States. The competences of the EU are the consequence of this sovereignty and they get their legitimacy through it. This seems to be a better understanding of the EU situation as it can solve current paradoxes between the EU competences and the Member States' competences. Indeed, the initial understanding of an attribution of competences between the EU and the Member States is sometimes paradoxical because there are some general competences attributed to the EU that overlap on specific competences that have been retained by the Member States as a consequence of the principle of primacy of EU law. Similarly, some EU competences did not exist before the Union.

Furthermore, in EU law, the notion of policy – and so the decisions on how to use an attributed competence (the power to decide) – is not distinct from the notion of competence, in the sense that the dialogue that leads to decisions on how to use the competence is exclusively limited to the entity that received the competence. In other words, when there is a shared competence between the EU and the Member States, the policy dialogue must exist between the different entities but, when there is an exclusive or a direct competence attributed to one of the entities, the latter exercises it on its side without any dialogue and without taking into account the legitimate expectations of the other entity, which should be taken into account as the inherent consequences of their shared sovereignty. This is why, when the EU has a general competence

[27] See eg M Udina, *Il Diritto Internazionale Tributario* (CEDAM 1949) 58ff, 112, 126, 132, 135, 249, 254, 264, 279, 286, 289: a distinction seems to be made between *potestà tributaria* or *potere tributario* and *competenza tributaria*.

[28] A Kallergis, *La Compétence Fiscale* (LGDJ 2018) 16

[29] ibid 15

[30] ibid

[31] ibid 16

that overlaps with a specific competence of the Member States, thanks to the principle of primacy of EU law it can use indirect means to achieve the EU policy goals, doing it on its own side. There is an initial paradox to solve but also paradoxical consequences.

Thus, it should be solved by considering the concept of sovereignty at the EU level. Through an indirect competence the EU applies indirect policy objectives while, through a direct competence, the Member States apply direct policy objectives. They do this alone, without any dialogue. However, having the power to decide on a policy, as an inherent consequence of the power of the State under the meaning of the concept of sovereignty, must follow the concept of shared sovereignty in such context. Then, in terms of legitimacy, having the legitimacy to attain a competence in a field expresses the sovereignty of the entity in this field. Thus, the competence is the concrete and technical expression of the sovereignty of the entity in such field. For a State alone, through the indetermination of its powers, its limits are the State itself (population, territory, the other State, fundamental rights in the constitutional State, etc); but it is different for a Member State because of the EU and its sovereign objectives. As such, in shared sovereign fields between the EU and the Member States, the policy must be shared too. The application of a technical competence should not have the possibility to redefine the sovereign objectives of the entities. The competences must follow sovereignty as being its consequence. In the same sense, policy does not depend on the competence but on the sovereignty and it must give guidance on how to use the competence.

Then comes the technical distinction between the competence to tax and the power to tax. As such, defining that the EU has the legitimacy to get a competence to tax under its sovereignty and as a consequence of the latter means that the EU has the corresponding power to decide as being its own tax policy corresponding to its inherent sovereignty. Whether the competence is general or direct does not change the sovereignty of an entity in a field but only the technical application of the competence. The legal procedure for the application of the competence (in a technical way) can be inadequate.[32] On the other side, concerning the power to tax, as Maitrot de la Motte states, the EU has a competence to tax but not a power to tax.[33] Indeed, the EU can have a power

[32] This is what must be explained in this chapter: the limits of negative integration or, in the next chapter, article 115 TFEU, are indeed legal limits depending on the technical writing of the EU treaties. It can lead to inadequacies between some provisions of the Treaties (EU objectives that cannot be achieved because of unanimity voting in some situations for instance) and so demonstrate the incoherence of a whole system in terms of legitimacy.

[33] A Maitrot de la Motte, 'La Souveraineté Fiscale et les Organisations Internationales à Vocation Economique' in N Baccouche (ed), *Les Implications*

to decide on the rules that must apply to a specific tax but it cannot levy its own taxes.[34] The power to tax must be analysed from a democratic perspective within the constitutional State.

Hence, the EU's power to tax in the field of direct taxation is analysed through the prism of the consent to tax and then through the prism of the constitutional legitimacy of the EU.[35] Thus, the power to tax of the EU, so the EU's power to levy taxes, must be understood as the possibility for the EU to get its tax-based own resources. In this perspective, a new article 311 has been introduced in the treaty on the functioning of the European Union (TFEU) with the Lisbon Treaty:

> The Council, acting in accordance with a special legislative procedure, shall unanimously and after consulting the European Parliament adopt a decision laying down the provisions relating to the system of own resources of the Union. In this context it may establish new categories of own resources or abolish an existing category. That decision shall not enter into force until it is approved by the Member States in accordance with their respective constitutional requirements.[36]

With this new article, the EU envisages putting in place new tax-based own resources.[37] However, this possibility raises the question of the consent to tax. Indeed, in modern democracies, the right to levy taxes for a State is understood as having the consent of the taxpayer-citizens to do so. The question, then, is whether the EU has this consent to tax to put in place its tax-based own resources.

To answer this question, first, a distinction must be made between different possible designs of European taxes. There are three possibilities.[38] The first is a revenue-sharing system.[39] In this system, a tax is fully harmonized in the

---

Financières, Fiscales et Douanières de l'Union Euro-Méditerranéenne (Revue Tunisienne de Fiscalité 2009) 188 footnote 20

34 ibid

35 About the constitutional legitimacy of the EU, see ch 5, section 5.2.2.2

36 TFEU, art 311

37 See Council Decision (EU, Euratom) 2020/2053 on the System of Own Resources of the European Union and Repealing Decision 2014/335/EU [2020] OJ L 424/1; European Commission, 'Proposal for a Council Decision on the System of Own Resources of the European Union and Repealing Decision (EU, Euratom) 2020/2053' COM (2025) 574 final 2

38 M Schratzenstaller, A Krenek, 'Tax-Based Own Resources to Finance the EU Budget – Potential Revenues, Summary Evaluation, from a Sustainability Perspective, and Implementation Aspects' (2019) [581] WIFO Working Papers 24 <www.econstor.eu/bitstream/10419/207154/1/1668604884.pdf> accessed 24 November 2025

39 ibid

EU (tax base and tax rate) and implemented at the national level. Then, the Member States transfer a partial share of the revenues to the EU. This is known as a transfer system.[40] The second one is the surcharge system; there is only a harmonization of the tax base.[41] The EU 'levies a surcharge in addition to the national tax rate'.[42] This system is similar to the transfer system and is also based on a revenue-sharing arrangement. There is no direct tax claim from the EU. An example is Value-Added Tax (VAT). Finally, with a separation system, there is the introduction of a European tax completely distinct from the national systems.[43] Thus, the consequence of this distinction is that the different kinds of systems do not have the same relation with the consent to tax at the EU level. Only the separation system implies a direct relation between the EU and the taxpayers. This means that only this system can be used to put in place the EU's tax-based own resources. The other two systems are indirect for the EU. The power to tax remains with the Member States, which then allocate a contribution to the EU. It is again the example of VAT. Consequently, only the separation system is at stake here as being the adequate system for a European power to tax. Only with this system can the EU have direct tax claims towards the European taxpayers, which would necessitate their consent to tax. Currently, the EU has non-tax claims over the Member States, which have direct-tax claims over the taxpayers.[44] Thus, new propositions such as the proposal for a Corporate Resource for Europe (CORE)[45] are understood as being within this general framework where the tax claim remains within the hands of the Member States or where the EU has a direct-tax claim for its own ressources. However, the second possibility is, for the moment, deemed here impossible due to the constitutional context of the EU.[46]

---

40 ibid

41 ibid

42 ibid

43 ibid 25

44 A Maitrot de la Motte, *Droit Fiscal de l'Union Européenne* (2nd edn, Bruylant ed, LGDJ 2016) 41

45 European Commission, 'Proposal for a Council Decision on the System of Own Resources of the European Union and Repealing Decision (EU, Euratom) 2020/2053' COM (2025) 574 final 2

46 Also, it does not seem possible to consider that the power to tax could give a power to decide like the competence to tax in terms of tax policy. Indeed, this power to decide depends on the concept of sovereignty and not on the taxing powers. However, there is a technical articulation between the competence which determines the sphere of application and the power which is the executing power. As such, it does not seem possible to have a power to tax in an area where the entity having this power does not already have the competence to tax. Thus, the power to decide should not rely on the power to tax and the European integration process

Second, another distinction must be made concerning the consent to tax in itself. There is a legal consent to tax and a political consent to tax.[47] Even though this linguistic distinction might exist in other languages, it is a translation of the *consentement à l'impôt* (legal consent to tax) and the *consentement de l'impôt* (political consent to tax) in the French language.[48] The legal consent to tax is the application of the principle of legality.[49] As long as the legal procedure is respected, there is a consent to tax. On the other hand, the political consent to tax is a social acceptance by citizens that they must pay taxes as being part of the society.[50] For instance, in the French Constitution, article 14 of the Declaration of the Rights of Man and of the Citizen expresses the political consent to tax: 'all citizens have the right to ascertain, by themselves, or through their representatives, the need for a public tax, to consent to it freely, to watch over its use, and to determine its proportion, basis, collection and duration.'[51] By comparison, article 34 of the French Constitution defines the legal consent to tax: 'statutes shall determine the rules concerning: [...] Finance Act shall determine the revenue and expenditure of the State in the conditions and with the reservations provided for by an Institutional Act.'[52] Both articles are found in the Constitution but the second article is the legal basis and a clear explanation of the procedure to enact the tax rule (by the Parliament) while the first contains the consent to be taxed by the citizens and cannot be invoked in a legal procedure.[53] This distinction highlights the difference between legal and political understandings of the consent to tax. Both are of equal importance and an analysis from one side should not neglect the importance of the other side.[54] Thus, what must be analysed is whether the EU has the legitimacy to put in place tax-based own resources and so whether a European consent to tax is democratically possible. Here, legitimacy would

---

gives a complex example of the interaction between both, and of the limits that should be respected.

47 M Bouvier, *Introduction au Droit Fiscal Général et à la Théorie de l'Impôt* (LGDJ 2020) 34; A Maitrot de la Motte, 'Le Consentement à l'impôt et les Autorités Européennes' (2020) [150] RFFP 67

48 ibid

49 ibid

50 ibid

51 Declaration of the Rights of Man and of the Citizen [1789] art 14

52 Constitution of France [1958] art 34

53 French Constitutional Council, *SNC Kimberly Clark*, 2010-5 QPC, 18 June 2010: the French Constitutional Court considers that the article 14 of the Declaration of the Rights of Man and of the Citizen is put in application by the article 34 of the French Constitution and cannot be invoked by the taxpayer.

54 See JHH Weiler, 'The Transformation of Europe' (1991) 100 Yale Law Journal

mean that the EU has a sufficient democratic level. Concerning the legal consent to tax, it is a question of the formal legitimacy of the EU: whether the principle of legality is applied through a democratic process and so whether there is a formal validity with a sufficient democratic foundation.[55] Then, concerning the political consent to tax, it is the question of the social legitimacy of the EU: whether there is a 'social acceptance of the system'.[56] There is social legitimacy when a government preserves and enhances values being part of the current political culture, such as justice, freedom and general welfare.[57] In modern European States, this culture is a democratic culture. That said, democracy here is essentially a question of representation in a State respecting the rule of law: the link between the citizen and the decisive bodies of the institution, with the preservation of the citizens' rights.[58]

Furthermore, the question should be answered whether a simple treaty revision is possible for the EU to have both a competence to tax and a power to tax in the field of direct taxation of businesses, considering that the latter involves a fundamental right such as the consent to tax.

6.2 NATIONAL TAX SOVEREIGNTY IN THE FIELD OF DIRECT TAXATION

6.2.1 Fundamental Freedoms and Tax Disparities

6.2.1.1 The limits of the European Union's legal system

In a first step, consideration must be given to the practical impacts of the material concept of tax sovereignty on the EU's internal market, which amounts to delimiting policy decisions as the consequence of the exercise of competences according to the strict distribution of competences as written in the EU treaties.

When competences have been attributed to the EU, the Member States kept a direct competence in the field of direct taxation,[59] which meant on the facts a reserved tax policy for the Member States in this field. It means that on one side, the EU has the general objective of achieving the internal market, and on the other side, to achieve this objective it does not have any specific competence in the field of direct taxation. However, even if, because of the pure initial economic purpose of the internal market, it can be thought that the EU's shared competence in the field of indirect taxation is more justified than a competence in the field of direct taxation, the impact of the latter on

55 ibid 2468
56 ibid 2469
57 ibid
58 ibid
59 Such attribution of competence does not exist in the TFEU

the internal market is not innocuous.[60] Indeed, it can be factually proven that, concerning businesses, the field of direct taxation impacts the internal market in a comparative way to the field of indirect taxation. The consequence, for instance, is the numerous directives enacted in the field of direct taxation of businesses compared to the amount of secondary law concerning personal taxes. Furthermore, in the EU context, policies follow competences. In this sense, the Member States have the exclusivity of their tax policies in the field of direct taxation.[61] This is understood as national tax sovereignty in the field of direct taxation according to the concept of tax sovereignty. Consequently, there is here a focus on the current inadequacies that result from the actual attribution of competences between the EU and the Member States in the field of direct taxation. The EU has a general competence to achieve the internal market, which is mainly translated through the fundamental freedoms,[62] and the Member States have their direct competence in the field of direct taxation. There are overlaps as the direct taxation of the Member States interacts with the internal market. Also, there is the principle of primacy of EU law to allow the EU to achieve the internal market. However, due to only having a general competence, the EU does not have direct means to solve the inconsistencies and it must go with the reserved policies of the Member States as the consequence of their direct competence. The EU has an indirect (general) competence while the Member States have a direct (specific) competence, which is the competence to tax.[63] Thus, in relation to the sovereignty of the EU, it

60 See eg B de la Cuesta and others, 'Do Indirect Taxes Bite? How Hiding Taxes Erases Accountability Demands from Citizens' [2021] Princeton School of Public and International Affairs Working Paper <https://hvmilner.scholar.princeton.edu/sites/g/files/toruqf2801/files/documents/VAT_manuscript_final.pdf> accessed 24 November 2025: the common perception by the citizen of indirect taxes and direct taxes plays a role when it comes to politics. In this way, in the step-by-step harmonization of the internal market, it has been easier to give an economic role to the EU in the field of indirect taxation than it could be in the field of direct taxation

61 Here is the distinction with the field of indirect taxation where writing the competence to tax in the EU treaties gave to the EU a power in terms of tax policy

62 TFEU, art 26 para 2

63 The competence to tax is the right to enact the tax law, which is now exclusive to the Member States who have a tax autonomy as being the accumulation of the competence to tax and the power to tax. The term 'competence' used here for the EU is the term as defined in the EU treaties. In this situation, the EU does not have a right to enact the tax law but powers in a certain area; this is why the terms 'general competence' or 'indirect competence' are used in order to be clear. A direct competence would consequently be a right to enact the tax law, so the competence to tax. Article 115 TFEU is not considered as giving a competence to tax to the EU because the Member States retained their power to decide in terms

must be understood that the current taxing powers of the Member States must respect the field of competence of the EU. Therefore, there are two issues: the first is when the Member States exercise their competence to tax within a field of competence of the EU, and the second is when the EU should be able (has the legitimacy) to exercise the related competence to tax. Thus, to assess the legitimacy of a European competence to tax under its own tax policy, there must be analysis of the situation where the Member States should not exercise their own competence to respect the EU order and so the EU's sovereignty through the principle of primacy of EU law. Then, through this interaction can be observed the legitimacy of an own competence to tax of the EU with its own tax policy (indeed, it is considered that a rightful competence to tax follows its attribution under the concept of sovereignty and so with the adequate power to decide in terms of tax policy) in this field to regulate it. Hence, the subtleties of the inadequacies between the general competence of the EU and the competence to tax of the Member States must be highlighted before asserting any EU legitimacy in the field of direct taxation. This must be demonstrated through the Court of Justice of the European Union's (CJEU) case law. Indeed, the general competence of the EU in the field of direct taxation through the primacy of the European objective of achieving the single market only lets the Union use legal tools that are mainly applied by the CJEU in this field.[64] Through the exercise of the fundamental freedoms (article 26 TFEU), the CJEU can assess when the Member States should not exercise their competence in order to respect the European order. However, respect of the principle of non-discrimination through the exercise of the fundamental freedoms, if it avoids any discriminatory application of the competence to tax of the Member States within the internal market, does not help to fill gaps when necessary. Therefore, through fundamental freedoms, the CJEU can determine the limits of the Member States' competence to tax, and so determine the general field of competence of the EU, but also the limits of the EU to achieve its objectives by not having any competence to tax as the consequence of the actual technical writing and understanding of the EU treaties. Thus, in a second step, through State aid rules or even through fundamental rights, it must be found how the EU can try to positively compensate its lack of competence to tax. However, there is no adequate solution for the CJEU to compensate in such a situation.

---

of tax policy, technically speaking through the unanimity voting requirement (see ch 7). Logically, they retained the exercise of sovereignty in this situation. As such, a rightful competence to tax is not conferred to the EU: herein lies the inadequacy regarding its sovereign objectives

64 The general competence, as a consequence of the EU treaties, is applied through negative integration by the CJEU

As such, the absence of an EU direct competence in the field of direct taxation means that there are discrete national tax systems that exist in the internal market. The difference between these tax systems results in variations or disparities between the Member States.[65] For instance, the Corporate Income Tax (CIT) rates are different between the Member States and they are not regulated by the EU. This is a mere disparity. However, as explained by Douma, 'the existence of these disparities has inevitable distorting effects on investment, employment and, for companies and self-employed persons, establishment decisions'.[66] Consequently, a mere disparity that is the result of the repartition of competences between the EU and the Member States is not a problem in itself, but it can become one when it creates a distortion to the detriment of the internal market. Here, a distortion must be understood as a bad disparity that is important for the effective achievement of the higher objective of achieving the internal market.[67] The main issue is that disparities, and so distortions resulting from bad disparities, do not fall within the scope of the non-discrimination principle, which is the main tool that the EU can use in order to protect the internal market under its general competence when it comes to direct taxation (negative integration).[68] It is the first consequence of the attribution of competences between the EU and the Member States. The CJEU said:

> That, in prohibiting every Member State from applying its law differently on the ground of nationality, within the field of application of the Treaty, Articles [12, 43 and 49 EC] are not concerned with any disparities in treatment which may result, between Member States, from differences existing between the laws of the various Member States, so long as they affect all persons subject to them in accordance with objective criteria and without regard to their nationality.[69]

---

[65] S Douma, 'The Three Ds of Direct Tax Jurisdiction: Disparity, Discrimination and Double Taxation' (2006) 46 [11] European Taxation 524

[66] ibid

[67] To conceptually clarify this point: the objective of achieving the internal market is higher than the reserved competence of the Member States in the field of direct taxation because it is the main and sovereign objective of the EU, as sharing sovereignty with the Member States, and it is contained in its constitutive treaties. A competence is a consequence of the sovereignty as its manifestation. It exists to achieve the sovereign unity and so, here, the objective of achieving the internal market. Furthermore, due to the shared sovereignty between the EU and the Member States, the objective of achieving the internal market is a common objective to them both and not only a specific objective of the EU alone

[68] S Douma, 'The Three Ds of Direct Tax Jurisdiction: Disparity, Discrimination and Double Taxation' (2006) 46 [11] European Taxation 524

[69] Case C-177/94 *Gianfranco Perfili* [1996] ECR I-00161

Accordingly, disparities that result in distortions to the detriment of the internal market are inherent obstacles without any given solution. Furthermore, they must be distinguished from non-inherent obstacles that result from discrimination as there is a given solution for the latter (the principle of non-discrimination).[70] Wattel provides for a tool to make the distinction.[71] When there is a disadvantageous tax effect of doing business or working abroad, it should be imagined that both States involved have exactly the same legal system. Then, if the disadvantage disappears, it is a disparity. If not, it is a discrimination, a restriction or a dislocation caused by a lack of jurisdictional competence of the Member State involved.

Some examples must be given to illustrate disparities within the internal market. First, in the *Gilly* case,[72] a married couple was living in France next to the German border and the wife was working in Germany as a teacher. According to the double tax treaty between France and Germany, she was paying taxes on her salary in Germany, benefiting from a French tax credit. However, the tax scale for Personal Income Tax (PIT) was more progressive in Germany than in France and, consequently, the French tax credit was not able to compensate for the total taxes paid in Germany. For Mrs Gilly there was a discrimination because she was carrying a heavier tax burden than the other French tax residents. Nevertheless, the CJEU answered that, while the abolition of double taxation is one of the objectives of the EU treaties, there were no unifying or harmonizing measures for the elimination of double taxation at the EU level.[73] In this situation, the non-discrimination principle was not applicable because double taxation was the result of a disparity. This disparity, which is the result of a different progression for the PIT in the two Member States, can be considered as a distortion to the detriment of the internal market as it could prevent individuals from being resident in one Member State and working in another Member State because of this inherent disadvantage that has not been considered as a discrimination by the CJEU because of the reserved competence of the Member States in the field of direct taxation. However, it can be noted that there was a double tax treaty between the two Member States and that tax coordination is a proposed solution when the EU is not competent. This is shown in the next example.

---

70 S Douma, 'The Three Ds of Direct Tax Jurisdiction: Disparity, Discrimination and Double Taxation' (2006) 46 [11] European Taxation 524

71 BJM Terra and PJ Wattel, *European Tax Law* (4th edn, Kluwer 2005) 58

72 Case C-336/96 *Gilly* [1998] ECR I-02793; for a similar case see Case C-513/03 *Van Hilten* [2006] ECR I-01957

73 Case C-336/96 *Gilly* [1998] ECR I-02793, para 23

Second, in the *D* case,[74] Mr D wanted to benefit from the double tax treaty between the Netherlands and Belgium despite being resident in Germany. For him, he was in a comparable situation to the Belgian residents. In the case at hand, there was an allowance on wealth tax in the Netherlands for its residents and, thanks to the double tax treaty between the Netherlands and Belgium, in the non-discrimination clause the allowance was extended to Belgian residents. Mr D wanted to benefit also from the extended scope for this allowance as a resident of another Member State. However, the CJEU ruled that he was not in a comparable situation.[75] There was an advantage that had been negotiated between the Netherlands and Belgium but not between the Netherlands and Germany. Thus, the Member States can bilaterally negotiate their conventions in order to avoid double taxation and this depends on their reserved competence in the field of direct taxation. This case illustrates the distinction between harmonization and unification. The EU has a general competence of harmonization to achieve the internal market. Also, even if there are overlaps between its general competence and the reserved competence of the Member States in the field of direct taxation, the latter remains with the Member States. It must be exercised by taking into account the internal market but the EU must also respect the limits of its own competences. The Member States are free to negotiate their tax treaties as long as double taxation is relieved. There was no obligation to extend the advantage to Mr D.

Such issue can also be illustrated by the *Kerckhaert-Morres* case.[76] In this case there was a tax advantage (deduction of a fixed percentage) in Belgium on dividends already taxed abroad and paid to a resident. However, this advantage had been repealed by the Belgian legislator in the Belgian tax code, even if it was still mentioned in the France–Belgium double tax convention. The Kerckhaert-Morres spouses wanted to still benefit from this advantage as, without it, they would have supported a heavier tax burden because of investing abroad. For them, there was a discrimination and the Court recognized that 'it is true that discrimination may consist not only in the application of different rules to comparable situations but also in the application of the same rule to different situations'.[77] Indeed, in this case, France, as the source country, applied the same withholding tax to residents and non-residents while Belgium, as the residence country, applied the same tax rate on foreign and domestic dividends. Yet, the Court continued:

---

74 Case C-376/03 *D* [2005] ECR I-05821

75 ibid para 61

76 C-513/04 *Kerckhaert-Morres* [2006] ECR I-10967

77 ibid para 19

> However, in respect of the tax legislation of his State of residence, the position of a shareholder receiving dividends is not necessarily altered, in terms of that case-law, merely by the fact that he receives those dividends from a company established in another Member State, which, in exercising its fiscal sovereignty, makes those dividends subject to a deduction at source by way of income tax. In circumstances such as those of the present case, the adverse consequences which might arise from the application of an income tax system such as the Belgian system at issue in the main proceedings result from the exercise in parallel by two Member States of their fiscal sovereignty.[78]

Once again, there is only a disparity according to the CJEU in this case. What it is interesting to point out here is that there is even no discrimination from the point of view of the source country (France) and no discrimination from the point of view of the residence country (Belgium) even if the general situation resulted in a disadvantage for Belgian residents investing outside of Belgium. Indeed, the CJEU underlined once again that tax coordination through double tax treaties is a solution in such situations, which are the result of the reserved competence of the Member States in direct taxation. However, a double tax burden, as in the situation evoked, which, in this case, is the consequence of a repealed tax measure of a Member State and so of a new national tax policy measure at a moment when the internal market already exists, could be considered as a distortion regarding the objective of achieving the internal market.[79] Indeed, according to this objective, fair competition, and so competitive neutrality, should be ensured within the internal market; and in tax terms it means ensuring tax neutrality within the internal market.[80] In legal terms, it is the objective of the non-discrimination principle.[81]

Thus, reaching complete tax neutrality means making a choice. In international taxation, neutrality can be Capital Import Neutrality (CIN) or Capital Export Neutrality (CEN). CIN is when there is 'tax neutrality between the profits of domestic economic agents and foreign economic agents doing business within the same country'.[82] It is neutrality from the perspective of the source state. CEN is when there is 'tax neutrality between the profits from business carried on abroad by domestic economic agents and the profits of domestic

---

78 ibid paras 19–20

79 F Vanistendael, 'The Functioning of Fundamental Freedoms and Tax Neutrality in the Internal Market' in CHJI Panayi, W Haslehner and E Traversa (eds) *Research Handbook on European Union Taxation Law* (Edward Elgar Publishing 2020) 149

80 ibid 147

81 ibid

82 ibid

economic agents doing business in their own country'.[83] It is neutrality from the perspective of the residence country. Both cannot be achieved at the same time in one single tax system.[84] There is always a policy choice to make. In the EU, this policy choice is consequently made at the level of the Member States in the field of direct taxation as the consequence of their national tax sovereignty. There are two consequences. First, the Member States are free to make different policy choices, choosing independently between CIN and CEN depending on the consequences, which is incoherent with the internal market. Second, this incoherence is translated in the *Kerckhaert-Morres* case and it is the reason why it is quoted here in order to demonstrate the inadequacy between the general competence of the EU and the direct competence of the Member States in the field of direct taxation. In this case, France chose to apply CIN by imposing the same withholding tax on residents and non-residents while Belgium chose to apply CEN by imposing the same tax rates on domestic and foreign dividends. There is a national tax coherence at the level of each country, in accordance with their competence to tax, and no discrimination from the perspective of each country. However, there is an inadequacy at the EU level, which can be considered as a distortion in terms of tax neutrality according to the general objective of achieving the single market, and it cannot be solved by the application of the non-discrimination principle by the CJEU while this principle necessitates a full neutrality. In this sense, in the CJEU cases, both CIN and CEN are alternatively applied to avoid both discriminations and restrictions depending on the facts of the case at hand. A policy choice should be made but it does not depend on the CJEU, which has the legal responsibility to apply the non-discrimination principle as it exists.

Finally, one last case that can be related to tax neutrality must be quoted. It is the *Block* case.[85] In this case, on an inheritance tax, Mrs Block had to pay two inheritance taxes, one in Spain and one in Germany, because there was no double tax treaty between the two Member States concerning such direct tax. The nexus for both countries was different (tax residence of the deceased in Germany and location of the estate in Spain) and the CJEU considered that it was only a disparity. Here, there is a lack of tax neutrality in the internal market because of a lack of coordination. However, the distortion is so obvious that, as already mentioned, a fundamental right's perspective could be applied to avoid such kind of distortion. Indeed, fundamental freedoms can help to avoid discrimination, but it is mainly an obligation not to do. They help to suppress existing discrimination, but they cannot help the EU to fill in the

---

[83] ibid

[84] ibid 148

[85] Case C-67/08 *Block* [2009] ECR I-00883

gaps when there are disparities, first, and, second, when there is a necessity to legislate. Thus, following the *Block* case, the Commission gave an impetus for tax coordination in the field of inheritance tax, highlighting the potential confiscatory effect of double taxation in this field.[86] Indeed, confiscatory taxation is generally considered to arise when the State takes more than 50 per cent of the income.[87] Here, the point of reference is not one State but the EU, encompassing the two involved States, and, consequently, article 17 of the Charter of Fundamental Rights (CFR) applies as the prohibition of confiscatory taxation, which can be derived from the protection of private property in European tax systems.[88] In this sense, even if it is on a case-by-case analysis and with the necessity of going in front of the CJEU, fundamental rights should be able to ensure a coherent application of their competence to tax by the Member States by respecting their European obligations. Also, keeping in mind that the fundamental rights should be able to ensure the coherent cohabitation of the European legal order and of the Member States' legal orders, when the fundamental freedoms are ineffective, the State aid rules can apply. The main issue with them is their scope but when a distortion is within their scope, they apply in addition to the fundamental freedoms (as long as their scope is also concerned) in order to avoid distortions in the EU in the field of direct taxation. Thus, depending on their scope of application, fundamental freedoms and State aid rules can apply independently or together to the same tax in addition to fundamental rights that must encompass the whole European system. Therefore, negative integration helps to erase distortions in the field of direct taxation, but it also has limits that are in breach of the consistency between the EU objectives and its current competences in order to achieve them.

Thus, there are other aspects of the non-discrimination principle that must illustrate the paradoxical current application of the general competence of the EU and of the direct competence of the Member States in the field of direct taxation.

6.2.1.2 Justifications in the discrimination test: another form of disparity?

The absence of a European competence to tax in the field of direct taxation left the European legislator unable to achieve a coherent internal market except for the limited possibilities of article 115 TFEU.[89] It is only through negative

[86] European Commission, 'Tackling Cross-Border Inheritance Tax Obstacles within the EU' COM (2011) 864 final 5

[87] CM Lopez Espadafor, 'Extra-Taxation and Property Right in the European Union Law' (2019) [12] The Age of Human Rights Journal 91

[88] ibid

[89] See ch 7

integration and so on a case-by-case basis that, still nowadays, the internal market can be achieved when it comes to direct taxation. Distortions due to tax disparities cannot be resolved at the EU level. Also, even when the principle of non-discrimination applies, there are still situations where breaches into the single market are preserved. The objective must not be achieving a complete unity within the internal market but to achieve a coherent market where both the objectives of the EU and of the Member States, common and personal, can be pursued coherently (respecting the concept of shared sovereignty). In this sense, the justification stage in the discrimination test also illustrates the inadequacies between the EU's general policy of achieving the internal market and national tax sovereignty.

Hence, in the history of negative integration, the CJEU rendered a judgment in the field of direct taxation for the first time in 1986 with the *Avoir fiscal* case.[90] Then, already in 1992, a first justification to a discrimination by a Member State arose in the same field. Possible justifications to a cross-border discrimination have been initially recognized in the *Cassis de Dijon* case with the rule of reason test.[91] This became a reality in the field of direct taxation with the *Bachmann* and *Commission v Belgium* cases in 1992.[92] These two cases concerned a same provision in the Belgian tax law: a deduction of insurance contributions was possible when the insurance company was located on the Belgian territory. Consequently, if the insurance company was located abroad, it was not possible to benefit from this deduction. The Court ruled, for instance in the *Bachmann* case, that:

> Legislation of a Member State which makes the deductibility of sickness and invalidity insurance contributions and pensions and life assurance contributions conditional on those contributions being paid in that State is contrary to Articles 48 and 59 of the EEC Treaty. However, that condition may be justified by the need to preserve the cohesion of the applicable tax system. Such legislation is not contrary to Articles 67 and 106 of the EEC Treaty.[93]

The justification accepted in these cases, and so the first justification accepted in the field of direct taxation, is the principle of cohesion of the tax system. Under this principle, there must be a nexus between the tax advantage that has been granted by a State and the future levy of tax that counterbalances

---

[90] Case 270/83 *Avoir Fiscal* [1986] ECR 273

[91] Case 120/78 *Cassis de Dijon* [1979] ECR 649

[92] Case C-204/90 *Bachmann* [1992] ECR I-00249; Case C-300/90 *Commission v Belgium* [1992] ECR I-00305

[93] Case C-204/90 *Bachmann* [1992] ECR I-00249

it.[94] Thus, this kind of justification is understandable when it comes to the distinction between the competence to tax and the power to tax. Even if the two together must not design a concept of sovereignty but a technical autonomy, as only the Member States have a power to tax,[95] the exercise of the competence to tax must consider this limit.[96] It can be related to the principle of territoriality. If only a said Member State has the right to levy taxes on a said territory, the competence to tax that enacts the tax law in relation to this specific tax levy must not render it impossible or grotesque. Nonetheless, this logical relation does not prevent the EU from having a competence to tax in the field of direct taxation as EU law applies on the territory of the Member States and it does not prevent the EU from also having a power to tax if the conditions for it are reunited.[97] Still, in the current situation where the Member States have a reserved competence, the limits of their territories as the limits of the exercise of their tax autonomy must be considered. It can be compared to what has been said on tax neutrality: tax neutrality can be preserved and so be coherent at the level where the tax policy is exercised, here the Member States' level. Similarly, the cohesion principle is the consequence of the tax autonomy of the Member States in the field of direct taxation: they can fully decide on the design of their direct tax system in the limits of their territory.

Then, concerning the justifications recognized by the CJEU, the latter did not rule in favour of a Member State on this ground until 2005.[98] This year, in the *Marks and Spencer* case,[99] the Court recognized three different types of justifications:

> Nonetheless, as the United Kingdom rightly observes, the preservation of the allocation of the power to impose taxes between Member States might make it

---

[94] I Lazarov, 'The Relevance of the Fundamental Freedoms for Direct Taxation' in M Lang and others (eds), *Introduction to European Tax Law on Direct Taxation* (7th edn, Linde 2022) 92

[95] As already said, only the Member States can levy taxes: see ch 6, section 6.3

[96] Shared sovereignty between the EU and the Member States implies a dialogue between both, which is manifested through the notion of tax policy (see ch 7). Shared sovereignty, through this dialogue, expresses itself through the power to tax and the competence to tax that must work together even if both are not shared by the EU and the Member States. This is the consequence of the unity of the system through the concept of sovereignty.

[97] See section 6.3.1

[98] See eg I Lazarov, 'The Relevance of the Fundamental Freedoms for Direct Taxation' in M Lang and others (eds), *Introduction to European Tax Law on Direct Taxation* (7th edn, Linde 2022) 92–93

[99] Case C-446/03 *Marks and Spencer* [2005] ECR I-10837

> necessary to apply to the economic activities of companies established in one of those States only the tax rules of that State in respect of both profits and losses. [...]
> As regards the second justification, relating to the danger that losses would be used twice, it must be accepted that Member States must be able to prevent that from occurring. [...]
> As regards, last, the third justification, relating to the risk of tax avoidance, it must be accepted that the possibility of transferring the losses incurred by a non-resident company entails the risk that within a group of companies losses will be transferred to companies established in the Member States which apply the highest rates of taxation and in which the tax value of the losses is therefore the highest.[100]

First, on the need to ensure that losses are not taken into account twice, it is a specific justification related to the facts of the case. In this judgment, the UK refused to allow the possibility to take into account domestically the losses that incurred in another Member State's subsidiary of a UK resident's parent company. The CJEU recognized the justifications brought by the UK except when the losses are final, and that 'the non-resident subsidiary has exhausted the possibilities available in its State of residence of having the losses taken into account'.[101] Second, the balanced allocation of taxing rights became a persistent justification alongside the cohesion principle.[102] At first, in the *Marks and Spencer* case, other justifications, in combination with this one, were necessary.[103] Then, in the *Oy AA* case,[104] only the balanced allocation of taxing rights and the need to combat tax avoidance have been necessary together as a justification;[105] finally, the balanced allocation of taxing rights became a justification on its own in the *X Holding* case.[106] Similarly, after the *Bachmann* case and the *Commission v Belgium* case, the cohesion principle was accepted again only in 2008 in the *Krankenheim* case.[107] Since then, this

[100] ibid paras 45, 47 and 49

[101] Case C-446/03 *Marks and Spencer* [2005] ECR I-10837

[102] See eg I Lazarov, 'The Relevance of the Fundamental Freedoms for Direct Taxation' in M Lang and others (eds), *Introduction to European Tax Law on Direct Taxation* (7th edn, Linde 2022) 92–94

[103] I Lazarov, 'The Relevance of the Fundamental Freedoms for Direct Taxation' in M Lang and others (eds), *Introduction to European Tax Law on Direct Taxation* (7th edn, Linde 2022) 93

[104] Case C-231/05 *Oy AA* [2007] ECR I-06373

[105] I Lazarov, 'The Relevance of the Fundamental Freedoms for Direct Taxation' in M Lang and others (eds), *Introduction to European Tax Law on Direct Taxation* (7th edn, Linde 2022) 93

[106] Case C-337/08 *X Holding* [2010] ECR I-01215; I Lazarov, 'The Relevance of the Fundamental Freedoms for Direct Taxation' in M Lang and others (eds), *Introduction to European Tax Law on Direct Taxation* (7th edn, Linde 2022) 93

[107] Case C-157/07 *Krankenheim* [2008] ECR I-08061

principle and the need to safeguard the balanced allocation of taxing rights have been used together in the *K.* case.[108] Depending on the case, both are merged ('the requirements of the balanced allocation of powers of taxation and coherence of the tax system coincide'[109]) or used separately.[110] The guiding line of the Court can still evolve. Yet, as for the cohesion principle, it can be considered that the justification of balanced allocation of taxing rights is 'a manifestation of the idea of territoriality'[111] but still concerning different situations. While the cohesion principle is about the preservation of a domestic measure and concerns an independent domestic tax system, the balanced allocation of taxing rights concerns a cross-border situation with two national tax systems and so usually when a double tax treaty applies. However, in both cases, it is about the coherent preservation of the tax autonomy at the Member State level. Third, the last justification that has been evoked in the *Marks and Spencer* case is the need to combat tax avoidance. Concerning this justification, it has been used at the justification stage in the discrimination test, but it has also been recognized as a general principle by the CJEU.[112] Combatting tax avoidance is a common purpose for the EU and the Member States. Due to the reserved competence of the Member States in the field of direct taxation, it is understandable that this justification appeared to preserve their independent tax systems. However, depending on the situation, the EU can be better placed to combat tax avoidance as EU law will apply on the totality of the territories of the Member States and put in place harmonization within the internal market, therefore preventing tax avoidance within its boundaries. Debate as to whether the anti-abuse principle can also be a justification[113] is the consequence of this reserved competence in the field of direct taxation that can lead to inadequacies between the Member State level and the EU level. As such, it might be the case that the necessity to combat tax avoidance should be resolved at a higher level.

A final justification has been accepted by the CJEU. It is the effectiveness of fiscal supervision and tax collection. This justification barely stands within the

108 Case C-322/11 *K* [2013] ECLI:EU:C:2013:716

109 Case C-388/14 *Timac Agro Deutschland* [2015] ECLI:EU:C:2015:829, para 47

110 Case C-650/16 *Bevola* [2018] ECLI:EU:C:2018:424, paras 44–51

111 I Lazarov, 'The Relevance of the Fundamental Freedoms for Direct Taxation' in M Lang and others (eds), *Introduction to European Tax Law on Direct Taxation* (7th edn, Linde 2022) 94

112 See eg I Lazarov, 'The Relevance of the Fundamental Freedoms for Direct Taxation' in M Lang and others (eds), *Introduction to European Tax Law on Direct Taxation* (7th edn, Linde 2022) 94–96

113 ibid

internal market because of the several possibilities granted by administrative assistance,[114] even if some cases exist.[115] Consequently, this justification is of particular relevance especially in the relation with third countries.[116]

Thus, as already mentioned previously with a fundamental rights perspective, there might be general principles of EU law that could come into opposition with the Member States' positions. If justifications as entailed in the discrimination test have their arguments to protect the Member States' competences in the field of direct taxation, they might not always be justified under the general principles of EU law. The rule of reason became an inherent part of the discrimination test when the CJEU examines a case from the perspective of the fundamental freedoms, but the development of its case law could benefit from an emphasis on the general principles of EU law that should constantly be considered.[117] They could help to preserve the internal market from distortions. Moreover, from a policy perspective, a duty of loyal cooperation, for instance, should be imposed upon the Member States to exercise their competence to tax in due regard of the internal market. Such duty, as well as the necessity of general coherence between the EU level and the Member State level, should be inherently deduced from the theory of shared sovereignty.

The EU has an indirect competence in the field of direct taxation. Through the case law of the CJEU, the European judge has been able to solve discrimination cases in the field of direct taxation by its work of interpretation. However, there are limits to this work of interpretation. There are distortions within the internal market which are the direct consequence of the attribution of a reserved competence to the Member States in the field of direct taxation. These distortions cannot always be solved by the application of the non-discrimination principle because it is not legally tailored specifically to the field of direct taxation. It is the consequence of the disparities between the different

---

114 ibid 97

115 See eg Case C-250/95 *Futura Participations* [1997] ECR I-02471; Case C-522/14 *Sparkasse Allgäu* [2016] ECLI:EU:C:2016:253

116 See eg I Lazarov, 'The Relevance of the Fundamental Freedoms for Direct Taxation' in M Lang and others (eds), *Introduction to European Tax Law on Direct Taxation* (7th edn, Linde 2022) 97

117 General principles of EU law, like the fundamental freedoms, are primary EU law. Among them, some principles, through the primacy of EU law, would overcome justifications at the Member State level to justify the achievement of the EU order through its objectives and the preservation of the internal market. They would be European justifications having priority over the Member States' justifications in coherence with the European integration process. It would be, generally speaking, the principles of coherence and of sincere cooperation. The protection of abuse at the EU level could also be such an inevitable principle

national tax systems, for instance the impossibility to achieve tax neutrality at the EU level, of the justifications in the discrimination test which are the consequence of the national tax sovereignty (as understood under the concept of tax sovereignty but which is, in reality, a tax autonomy), and of a case-by-case analysis.

Then, to clarify the indirect competence of the EU, article 4 TFEU must be remembered. Under article 26 TFEU, there is the objective of achieving the internal market that cannot be overridden. Then, in article 4 TFEU, it is said that the EU shares competences in the area of the internal market. In this sense, when direct taxation involves issues concerning the internal market, the EU has a shared competence in the field of direct taxation (knowing that the internal market has an economic perspective, which encompasses the field of direct taxation of businesses). It is also a justification of the fact that the tax sovereignty of the Member States is just a tax autonomy as their direct competence can be legitimately limited by the general competence of the EU for the internal market and so by the principle of primacy of EU law. However, even if the legitimacy of the EU in the field of direct taxation exists, the legal means to achieve the EU objectives, which is mainly the non-discrimination principle, has a limited impact.

Consequently, the legitimate solution would be for the EU to have a direct competence in the field of direct taxation and not only an indirect competence, as inadequacies cannot be solved through an indirect competence. A direct competence must be understood as a competence to tax and so as the right to enact the tax law. In this sense, the attribution of competences between the EU and the Member States would legitimately follow their shared sovereignty. As the EU has the general and main objective of achieving the internal market, it should sovereignly have the adequate competences to achieve this objective as the consequence of its shared sovereignty. The EU has a right to a competence to tax in the field of direct taxation of businesses. As a direct competence, it would still follow the shared competence in the area of the internal market as this right must fit within the general objective of achieving the internal market. It is not justified to give an exclusive competence to the EU which would outreach this objective. However, in the current state of the EU treaties, the legitimacy of the EU to exercise a competence to tax in the field of direct taxation of businesses is justified by the concept of sovereignty but the legal tools to exercise this direct competence do not currently exist.

Thus, for the purpose of clarification, it must be understood that the application of the discrimination test is the application of one legal technique as permitted by the EU treaties. The application of the State aid rules would be the application of another legal technique. Furthermore, in the same way, unanimity voting concerning the adoption of secondary law in the field of direct taxation is a legal procedure. Also, as already observed, the technical competences as enacted in the EU treaties currently attract the attribution of the power to decide of the tax policy, here at the national level. However, the application of the concept of shared sovereignty requires that the attribution of the power to decide on tax policy does not depend on a technical competence or on a legal technique but on sovereignty itself. As such, the competence to tax that should be attributed to the EU to enact secondary law to necessarily eliminate bad disparities in the field of direct taxation of businesses must be the consequence of the sovereignty of the EU in order to preserve or achieve the internal market. Similarly, tax policy must follow sovereignty and not the technical competence. The power to decide must be understood as an inevitable consequence of the concept of sovereignty, as a rightful competence to tax must also follow sovereignty. In this situation, under the concept of shared sovereignty, there should be a shared tax policy between the EU and the Member States. The competences follow sovereignty and not the opposite. The technical distribution of powers cannot decide on the attribution of the power to decide (and so of the attribution of the tax policy); it depends on sovereignty, as the ultimate authority must remain as such. In this reversal of the construction of the system lies an inadequacy. Solving such inadequacy requires an evolution of the European integration process.

Finally, other current legal possibilities offered by the EU treaties to achieve the internal market, and so to solve current inadequacies due to the field of direct taxation of businesses, must be explored. It must be considered first whether the EU can get its legitimate, and so coherent, competence to tax without any treaty modification.

6.2.2 State Aid Rules and the Objective of Achieving the Internal Market

6.2.2.1 The necessity of a selective advantage

Similar to the use of the fundamental freedoms in the field of direct taxation, another means that the CJEU uses in order to protect the internal market is the EU prohibition of State aid. Such rule has been put in place in the EU treaties to ensure fair competition within the internal market and to preserve a competitive economy.[118] Consequently, State aid rules are initially part of the EU rules on competition.[119] Article 107 paragraph 1 TFEU explains:

---

[118] A Miladinovic, 'The State Aid Provisions of the TFEU in Tax Matters' in M Lang and others (eds), *Introduction to European Tax Law on Direct Taxation* (7th edn, Linde 2022) 110

[119] ibid

> Save as otherwise provided in the Treaties, any aid granted by a Member State or through State resources in any form whatsoever which distorts or threatens to distort competition by favouring certain undertakings or the production of certain goods shall, in so far as it affects trade between Member States, be incompatible with the internal market.[120]

In this paragraph are contained the four cumulative criteria to qualify a prohibited State aid. First, there must be an advantage which can confer a more favourable position. This can be done by subsidizing or by relief of a charge. Second, it must be a public aid in the sense that it has a State's origin. Third, the advantage must be a selective advantage and so not favourize a system as a whole. Fourth, there must be a distortion which affects competition and trade within the internal market. Finally, State aid targets undertakings in the sense of economic activity and not non-profit organizations, public enterprises or individuals when staying outside of economic life.[121]

State aid cases in the field of direct taxation of businesses are not new but they have exploded recently, especially since the LuxLeaks affairs in 2014.[122] Recent cases concern many tax rulings that have been issued by different Member States with a specific interest in transfer pricing rules or double non-taxation issues.[123] However, here, the focus is on the application of the State aid rules by the CJEU in order to protect the internal market from the excesses caused by national tax sovereignty in the field of direct taxation of businesses. In this sense, the focus is on the selectivity criterion to qualify as prohibited State aid and on the distortions this kind of aid can provoke. Indeed, while the fundamental freedoms are limited to cross-border situations, State aid rules can apply in purely domestic situations.

Thus, selectivity is the main criterion for the application of article 107 paragraph 1 TFEU. General measures are outside the scope of the State aid rules. In this sense, these rules do not seem perfectly adequate to achieve the internal market as their only objective is to prevent a distortion of competition with a public origin; it is a distortion which is specific to a delimited area by definition and not to the general market. Nevertheless, the CJEU took advantage of the State aid rules to protect the internal market and to harmonize it, the latter of which could become a problem as it is not the objective of the State aid rules. Ideally, these rules complement the application of the

---

120 TFEU, art 107 para 1

121 A Miladinovic, 'The State Aid Provisions of the TFEU in Tax Matters' in M Lang and others (eds), *Introduction to European Tax Law on Direct Taxation* (7th edn, Linde 2022) 120

122 ibid 113

123 ibid 114

fundamental freedoms; when State aid rules apply, they can consistently plug some of the flaws of the fundamental freedoms (domestic application, neutrality from the perspective of only one State).

Thus, there are two kinds of selective measures: material and regional.[124] While regional selectivity emphasizes the distinction between different regions of a Member State, material selectivity differentiates between certain undertakings within a Member State as a whole.[125] It is the latter that is interesting here. To determine whether a measure is selective or not, the CJEU performs a selectivity test.[126] This test consists in a derogation test in three steps.[127] First, the common tax system of the Member State must be identified. It is the point of comparison. Second, the tax measure at stake must be identified too as deviating from the common tax system while the economic operators are still comparable. Third, it must be verified whether the deviation (or derogation) can be justified by 'the nature or general scheme of the tax system'[128] and so whether it 'results directly from the basic or guiding principles of the tax system in the member state concerned'.[129] It can be complicated to find a point of comparison in this test as the deviation can take many forms.

For instance, in the *Gibraltar* case,[130] the general CIT system applicable to all companies was amended in Gibraltar. Nonetheless, the CJEU considered that three aspects of the new system were selective. First, a company was supposed to make a profit before becoming liable to payroll tax and business property occupation tax. Second, the cap limiting liability to both taxes was 15 per cent of the profits. The third reason was the inherent nature of both taxes. Actually, in practice, the intention was to favour offshore companies, which had no real physical presence in Gibraltar. Domestic companies and offshore companies were in a comparable situation according to State aid rules.[131] However, the nature of a payroll tax and of a business property occupation tax, when applied, would mean they were paid only by domestic companies. The Court ruled that there was a prohibited State aid even if there was no deviation within the law in itself and that the system concerned was the full CIT system as a whole. Here is another distinction between de facto selectivity, where it is the application of apparently objective legal provisions that reveals

---

124 ibid 125

125 ibid

126 ibid

127 ibid

128 Case C-88/03 *Portugal v Commission* [2006] ECR I-07115, para 81

129 ibid

130 Joined Cases C-106/09 P and C-107/09 P *Commission v Gibraltar* [2011] ECR I-11113

131 ibid

the selective advantage, as in the *Gibraltar* case, and de jure selectivity, where it is the legal provision in itself, as a formal criterion, that provides for a selective advantage.[132] Thus, it is interesting to note that the derogation test did not work in the *Gibraltar* case as there was no formal point of comparison. This raises a question. In its practical application, Gibraltar's CIT system provided for a de facto selectivity. However, initially and so formally, there was only a disparity. Indeed, the full CIT system was involved, and its rules were defined by the Member State without the EU having the possibility to rule on it. In this sense, through de facto selectivity, the EU found a way to combat tax disparities and protect the internal market. Thus, here, through State aid rules, the CJEU could bring neutrality within the internal market through a means other than the fundamental freedoms. As such, from a general perspective of coherence, the solution in the *Gibraltar* case is understandable. It can be said that the CJEU tries to put in place a consistent dialogue between the different provisions of primary EU law to preserve its general objectives.

Furthermore, the notion of selectivity keeps evolving.[133] The CJEU seems to widen the scope of the State aid rules. For instance, in the *World Duty Free* case,[134] there was an advantage given to Spanish resident companies if they were investing in a foreign company. For an investment of at least 5 per cent in one year, the goodwill which was the result of the shareholding was deductible. This deduction was not possible if the investment was in a domestic company. This specific tax provision did not apply to a certain category of undertaking but to a specific kind of operation. The selective advantage has been qualified by the CJEU on a comparison between foreign and domestic companies: 'whether the situation of operators benefiting from the measure is comparable with that of operators excluded from it.'[135] The category was the particular kind of transaction. After an appeal of the General Court (GC), the CJEU confirmed its decision in 2021.[136] A selective advantage can result from the possibility of a more advantageous transaction and so of a more advantageous situation for the undertakings that choose to carry out this transaction.[137] Once again, when fundamental freedoms cannot apply because of the lack of a direct cross-border element, State aid rules can compensate. Reverse discrimination

132 A Miladinovic, 'The State Aid Provisions of the TFEU in Tax Matters' in M Lang and others (eds), *Introduction to European Tax Law on Direct Taxation* (7th edn, Linde 2022) 125

133 ibid 131

134 Case C-20/15 *World Duty Free Group SA* [2016] ECLI:EU:C:2016:981

135 ibid para 94

136 Joined Cases C-51/19 and C-64/19 P *World Duty Free Group v Commission* [2021] ECLI:EU:C:2021:793

137 ibid

to the detriment of domestic situations is outside the scope of the fundamental freedoms[138] but such kinds of distortions can be within the scope of the State aid rules, as long as article 107 TFEU applies.

Therefore, this case and the *Gibraltar* case are examples showing that the CJEU can use the State aid rules when the fundamental freedoms cannot apply to protect the internal market. However, it happens that the CJEU goes beyond the protection of the internal market and uses these rules to harmonize when it is not their initial role. This can be an issue. The balance between the prerogatives of the Member States and of the EU must not go beyond the work of interpretation of the CJEU. In addition, it remains a case-by-case approach even if, with the State aid rules, a prohibited State aid can be qualified ex ante by the Commission. The latter emphasizes the role of protection and not of harmonization of these rules. Similarly, as has been pointed out in the *Gibraltar* case for instance,[139] the application of the State aid rules by the CJEU in the field of direct taxation remains similar to the application of the fundamental freedoms through the process of comparability when an entire system (or not a specific category of undertakings) is at stake. It emphasizes the necessity to avoid diverting from the objective of a European treaty provision. Also from a European perspective, a technical competence must remain within its defined limits. Such aspect will be dealt with in what follows.

As a temporary conclusion, a word should be said on distortion as a criterion. To have a prohibited State aid, there must be a distortion of competition that affects trade. What is important to emphasize is that not every deviation and not every disparity lead to distortions. In the EU, the idea of a harmonized internal market preserves free competition but also the sovereignty of the Member States.[140] Finding the limits to qualify a distortion can be a complicated exercise and depends on the balanced exercise of their shared sovereignty by the EU and the Member States through their competences.

6.2.2.2 A non-adequate rule

The fact that the application of State aid rules can look similar to the application of fundamental freedoms is a sign of a potential drift. The complexity of the State aid rules is that, while the Member States have a reserved competence in the field of direct taxation, the EU has an exclusive competence to establish 'the competition rules necessary for the functioning of the internal

---

138 See eg Case C-11/92 *Gallaher* [1993] ECR I-03545, para 22

139 Joined Cases C-106/09 P and C-107/09 P *Commission v Gibraltar* [2011] ECR I-11113, para 65

140 Here, it is the concept of sovereignty, and so of shared sovereignty, that is mentioned, not the concept of tax sovereignty that is only a material sovereignty and a conceptual impossibility

market' according to article 3 TFEU. In this sense, the State aid rules are limited by this competence, as being part of the block on competition rules in the TFEU (chapter 1, title VII, TFEU), while the fundamental freedoms depend directly on the objective of achieving the internal market (article 26 TFEU). They are different rules with different direct objectives. The final objective is always article 26 paragraph 1 TFEU but the direct objective of the State aid rules is to ensure fair competition through the specific rules that are defined for it. Even if it is the general objective of article 26 TFEU that justifies the application of State aid rules in the field of direct taxation of businesses, these rules are part of a different block and of a different competence of the EU than the fundamental freedoms. They cannot be confused with them. State aid rules must remain State aid rules even if it is necessary to solve the inadequacies that are due to the overlap between the opposite exercise of their competences between the Member States and the EU.

Thus, to describe this potential drift, the three basic goals of a tax must be remembered:

- Revenue collection;
- Regulatory functions;
- Redistribution of wealth.[141]

The goal of article 107 TFEU is also explained, for instance, in the State Aid Action Plan 2005–2009:

> State aid control comes from the need to maintain a level playing field for all undertakings active in the Single European Market, no matter in which Member State they are established. There is a particular need to be concerned with those state aid measures, which provide unwarranted selective advantages to some firms, preventing or delaying the market forces from rewarding the most competitive firms, thereby decreasing overall European competitiveness. It may also lead to a build-up of market power in the hands of some firms, for instance when companies that do not receive state aid (e.g. non-domestic firms) have to cut down on their market presence, or where state aid is used to erect entry barriers. As a result of such distortions of competition, customers may be faced with higher prices, lower quality goods and less innovation.[142]

---

[141] AM Jiménez, 'Level Playing Field versus Member States' Direct Tax Policies: the State Aid Revolution' in P Pistone (ed), *European Tax Integration: Law, Policy and Politics* (IBFD 2018) 294

[142] European Commission, 'State Aid Action Plan – Less and Better Targeted State Aid: a Roadmap for State Aid Reform 2005-2009' COM (2005) 107 final, para 7

This plan was supposed to bring certainty on the application of the State aid rules, which have the objective to protect the overall free competition within the internal market.[143] However, an evolution towards budget discipline instead of sticking to internal market protection has been observed.[144] It can be seen, for instance, in paragraphs 7 and 14 of the State Aid Modernization Communication:

> Some of that public spending will take the form of State aid, be it in the form of direct expenditure, tax incentives, State guarantees or other. Stronger and better targeted State aid control can encourage the design of more effective growth-enhancing policies and it can ensure that competition distortions remain limited so that the internal market remains open and contestable. It can also contribute to improving the quality of public finances. A more focused framework will allow Member States to better contribute both to the implementation of the Europe 2020 strategy for sustainable growth as well as to budgetary consolidation. [...]
>
> State aid control can also help Member States to strengthen budgetary discipline and improve the quality of public finances – resulting in a better use of taxpayer's money. It is particularly important in order to achieve smart fiscal consolidation, reconciling the role of targeted public spending in generating growth with the need to bring budgets under control.[145]

This orientation towards fiscal discipline does not correspond to the initial goal of State aid rules[146] and the CJEU cases show that it limits insidiously the Member States' competence to tax and, consequently, their tax policy in the field of direct taxation of businesses. While, on one side, State aid rules can be an efficient tool to eliminate some distortions in the field of direct taxation, on the other side, a diversion towards goals not intended by the EU treaties should not happen because of excessive use of the same rules.

Thus, concretely, if this communication is broadly interpreted, according to Jiménez:

> The Commission's control of the Member States' tax policies with the tool of article 107(1) of the TFEU may be going beyond the supervision of the efficiency of state measures and moving towards a more pervasive limitation of tax policy (especially

---

143 AM Jiménez, 'Level Playing Field versus Member States' Direct Tax Policies: the State Aid Revolution' in P Pistone (ed), *European Tax Integration: Law, Policy and Politics* (IBFD 2018) 296

144 ibid

145 European Commission, 'EU State Aid Modernization' COM (2012) 209 final

146 AM Jiménez, 'Level Playing Field versus Member States' Direct Tax Policies: the State Aid Revolution' in P Pistone (ed), *European Tax Integration: Law, Policy and Politics* (IBFD 2018) 297

in connection with corporate taxes) in at least three aspects, with severe effects on the Member States' autonomy:

(1) The Commission may control the (corporate) tax policy goal of the Member States;
(2) The Commission may define how to implement these goals in the Member States (proportionality); and
(3) The Commission may define what 'harmful tax competition' is and how to eradicate it within the European Union [...].[147]

In order to target this aspect, the *British Aggregates* case must be recalled.[148] A UK environmental tax was at stake and it was finally considered as a prohibited State aid because it was not affecting all the producers of a certain good. However, there were specific environmental and commercial reasons.[149] In this case, the CJEU confirmed that a non-tax goal was irrelevant when it comes to an appreciation in the light of the State aid rules.[150] The UK could not decide on its environmental tax policy because the Commission had a different view. There are two lessons from this case. First, the exception of the nature of the tax system does not hold any longer[151] and, second, the Member States cannot

---

147 ibid 298

148 Case C-487/06 *P British Aggregates Association v Commission of the European Communities* [2008] ECR I-10515

149 See Case T-210/02 *P British Aggregates Association v Commission of the European Communities* [2006] ECLI:EU:C:2006:253, para 123ff

150 AM Jiménez, 'Level Playing Field versus Member States' Direct Tax Policies: the State Aid Revolution' in P Pistone (ed), *European Tax Integration: Law, Policy and Politics* (IBFD 2018) 300

151 The exception of the nature of the tax system was recognized in Case 173/73 *Italy v Commission* [1974] ECR 709, para 15: 'It must be concluded that the partial reduction of social charges pertaining to family allowances devolving upon employers in the textile sector is a measure intended partially to exempt undertakings of a particular industrial sector from the financial charges arising from the normal application of the general social security system, without there being any justification for this exemption on the basis of the nature or general scheme of this system.' The Commission then shed some light on this exception: Commission Decision 96/369/EC [1996] OJ L 146/92, 46: 'In terms of taxation the Commission takes the view that measures derogating from the general rule do not qualify as State aid where they are economically justified in respect of the efficiency of the system. This is usually reflected in the fact that such measures are not applied solely to specific sectors, are based on objective and horizontal criteria or sectorial provisions, have indefinite temporal scope since they are periodically carried over for a number of years'

rely on external elements when defining their tax system,[152] limiting de facto their tax policy choices and the regulatory function of taxes.

In parallel, this idea of the limitation of the taxes' regulatory function can also be observed when it comes to the assimilation of the State aid rules with a kind of non-discrimination principle. Indeed, the fundamental freedoms apply only in cross-border situations, but to avoid domestic tax rules applying to the detriment of the residents of other Member States. By doing that, the CJEU limits the regulatory function of the domestic taxes of the Member States, or rather extends this regulatory function to the borders of the internal market by preserving equality between the EU residents. To achieve a similar role, an extension of the perception of the State aid rules has been observed through a kind of assimilation of the selective advantage to the non-discrimination principle.[153] Indeed, the State aid rules have a broader field of application[154] and can be more effective in this sense. They apply in purely domestic situations and in cases of reverse discrimination, which are outside the scope of the fundamental freedoms.[155]

This is why the *Regione Sardegna* case[156] must be presented now. In this case, a Sardinian tax was found contrary to the free provision of services and the State aid rules. It was a tax on specific flight and ship stopovers. Only the residents of Sardinia were exempted and so the tax had to be paid by non-residents from other Member States but also from other regions of Italy. The most important aspect in this case is not the application of both the State aid rules and the non-discrimination principle in the same case, even if an arbitration on their combined application is always necessary as both concepts lead to different legal solutions (an extension of the advantage for the fundamental freedoms and a refund with interests for a prohibited State aid),[157] but the

---

152 See eg AM Jiménez, 'Level Playing Field versus Member States' Direct Tax Policies: the State Aid Revolution' in P Pistone (ed), *European Tax Integration: Law, Policy and Politics* (IBFD 2018) 300–01

153 ibid 302

154 A Miladinovic, 'The State Aid Provisions of the TFEU in Tax Matters' in M Lang and others (eds), *Introduction to European Tax Law on Direct Taxation* (7th edn, Linde 2022) 117

155 AM Jiménez, 'Level Playing Field versus Member States' Direct Tax Policies: the State Aid Revolution' in P Pistone (ed), *European Tax Integration: Law, Policy and Politics* (IBFD 2018) 304

156 Case C-169/08 *Presidente del Consiglio dei Ministri v Regione Sardegna* [2009] ECR I-10821

157 A Miladinovic, 'The State Aid Provisions of the TFEU in Tax Matters' in M Lang and others (eds), *Introduction to European Tax Law on Direct Taxation* (7th edn, Linde 2022) 118

use of a non-discrimination test in order to qualify a selective advantage.[158] Indeed, for the purpose of this tax, it has been considered that residents and non-residents were in a comparable situation, therefore qualifying as selective advantage.[159] Advocate General Kokott defended this solution by saying that there was a well-defined group of non-residents that represented a specific group for the application of article 107 TFEU in this case.[160] There was a true competition between the residents of Sardinia and these non-residents.[161] The idea was to say that it was, indeed, a specific situation, as was necessary for the application of State aid rules, and that the solution could be different with provisions of a more general nature.[162] Furthermore, this specific group was composed of residents and non-residents of Italy. However, Jiménez underlines that another interpretation was possible and that paragraphs 59–66 of the case could have been interpreted in a more general way.[163] This was a serious step towards a broad non-discrimination analysis to apply the State aid rules with a merger between the criteria of selectivity and advantage.[164]

The same happened with the *Gibraltar* case and the *World Duty Free* case. In the *Gibraltar* case, it was the general CIT system that was at stake and the analysis was performed between residents and non-residents. To define a selective advantage, the CJEU made a comparison between both. The specific group was the offshore companies and so all non-resident companies. Such selectivity was englobing the whole notion of tax policy by applying to all non-residents. On the facts, it was not possible to apply the derogation test.[165] The deviation found was from an ideal CIT system, which was the proper view of the CJEU at that moment.[166] This decision might have been necessary,

---

158 AM Jiménez, 'Level Playing Field versus Member States' Direct Tax Policies: the State Aid Revolution' in P Pistone (ed), *European Tax Integration: Law, Policy and Politics* (IBFD 2018) 302–03

159 Case C-169/08 *Presidente del Consiglio dei Ministri v Regione Sardegna* [2009] ECR I-10821

160 Case C-66/14 *IFN Holding AG and IFN Beteiligungs GmbH* [2015] ECLI:EU:C:2015:66, Opinion of AG Kokott, para 106

161 See AM Jiménez, 'Level Playing Field versus Member States' Direct Tax Policies: the State Aid Revolution' in P Pistone (ed), *European Tax Integration: Law, Policy and Politics* (IBFD 2018) 303

162 See Case C-66/14 *IFN Holding AG and IFN Beteiligungs GmbH* [2015] ECLI:EU:C:2015:66, Opinion of AG Kokott

163 AM Jiménez, 'Level Playing Field versus Member States' Direct Tax Policies: the State Aid Revolution' in P Pistone (ed), *European Tax Integration: Law, Policy and Politics* (IBFD 2018) 304

164 ibid

165 ibid 305–06

166 ibid

but the State aid rules applied with a purpose other than their initial goal. Furthermore, the CJEU decided on tax policy measures, which overcame its role of interpretation in this situation. Then, in the *World Duty Free* case, the selective advantage was also defined after a comparable analysis between residents and non-residents. There was a selective advantage because there was discrimination between domestic and foreign investments.[167] Finally, this identification between the two instruments (State aid rules and the non-discrimination principle) has even been clearly expressed in the *Lübeck* case:

> The examination of whether such a measure is selective is thus, in essence, coextensive with the examination of whether it applies to that set of economic operators in a non-discriminatory manner (see, to that effect, judgment of 14 January 2015, *Eventech*, C-518/13, EU:C:2015:9, paragraph 53). The concept of selectivity, as the Advocate General states in point 75 of his Opinion, is thus linked to that of discrimination.[168]

For Jiménez, this merger between selectivity, advantage and the non-discrimination principle is 'a serious setback for the Member States'.[169] For him, corporate taxes would become only revenue-raising tools.[170] Indeed, the EU tried to apply its exclusive competence to set the competition rules in a field which does not directly depend on these rules. Through the general objective of achieving the internal market, it seems that it became possible to make an assimilation with the fundamental freedoms; but it remains an assimilation that is not purely adequate in legal terms. State aid rules can apply to direct taxation of businesses when it comes to competition policy, but by strictly applying the block of rules on State aid. Only in a second step, through the principle of primacy of EU law, can the exclusive competence of the EU take priority over the reserved competence of the Member States when there is a true overlap.

Similarly, in transfer pricing matters, the CJEU had to rule in a case similar to *Gibraltar* and *World Duty Free*. In the *Magnetrol* case,[171] the excess profit rulings allowed Belgian companies and establishments belonging to a multinational group to exempt from CIT excess profit generated because of the taxpayer's membership of a group. It was a profit that exceeded that which a

---

167 ibid 308

168 Case C-524/14 P *European Commission v Hansestadt Lübeck* [2016] ECLI:EU:C:2016:971

169 AM Jiménez, 'Level Playing Field versus Member States' Direct Tax Policies: the State Aid Revolution' in P Pistone (ed), *European Tax Integration: Law, Policy and Politics* (IBFD 2018) 309

170 ibid 309–10

171 Case C-337/19 P *Commission v Kingdom of Belgium and Magnetrol International* [2021] ECLI:EU:C:2021:741

comparable single company would have generated in Belgium. The reason for this advantage was that such excess profit was generated by economies of scale arising from the membership of a group, but this profit was not attributable to the Belgian company or establishment. It was a transfer pricing measure. The Belgian companies, which were considered as central entrepreneurs, were initially applying the Transactional Net Margin Method (TNMM) in order to determine the profits to allocate to companies of other countries. Then, they were applying the method a second time in order to determine the true profits of the Belgian company. The difference was exempt in Belgium and was not taxed in another country. So, the Commission considered that the excess profit should have been taxed somewhere and that Belgium should have not applied the TNMM twice. In addition, this measure only applied to central entrepreneurs being part of a group. This case had similarities to the *Gibraltar* case as it concerned a general application of an exemption of CIT, but only for multinational companies and not for purely resident companies. Similarly, compared to the *World Duty Free* case, the final distinction was still between two kinds of resident companies. In her conclusions,[172] Advocate General Kokott said that it was the consistent administrative practice that was an aid scheme. Belgium disconnected the excess profit regime from the arm's length principle and the Organization for Economic Co-operation and Development's (OECD) recommendations,[173] and granted it to all companies asking for it (paragraph 76 of the conclusions). The Belgian provision, because of the administrative practice, became an aid regime, which was forbidden. The CJEU followed the opinion of Advocate General Kokott and annulled the judgment of the GC for different errors of law. The CJEU notably noted that it is possible to refer to a consistent administrative practice, and so a systematic approach, and, in order to do that, examine a sample of tax rulings representative of the practice.[174]

Then, in the *Fiat* case,[175] the Commission found that Luxembourg provided for a prohibited State aid through tax rulings. However, the point of reference of the Commission was the arm's length principle as defined by the OECD

---

[172] Case C-337/19 P *Commission v Kingdom of Belgium and Magnetrol International* [2021] ECLI:EU:C:2021:741, Opinion of AG Kokott

[173] See Organization for Economic Co-operation and Development, 'OECD Transfer Pricing Guidelines for Multinational Enterprises and Tax Administrations 2022' < https://www.oecd.org/en/publications/oecd-transfer-pricing-guidelines-for-multinational-enterprises-and-tax-administrations-2022_0c655865-en.html> accessed 28 November 2025

[174] Case C-337/19 P *Commission v Kingdom of Belgium and Magnetrol International* [2021] ECLI:EU:C:2021:741, para 131

[175] Joined Cases C-885/19 P and C-898/19 P *Fiat Chrysler* [2022] ECLI:EU:C:2022:859

and not implemented in Luxembourg. The CJEU annulled the Commission's decision as the reference must be made to general domestic law (or at least an effective domestic law) and not to an ideal or abstract framework. A similar conclusion was reached by Advocate General Kokott in her opinion in the *Engie* case:[176]

> The Advocate General first of all emphasises that tax rulings do not, in themselves, constitute illegal State aid. They are an important instrument for creating legal certainty. Tax rulings are unproblematic in terms of State aid law as long as they are open to all taxpayers and are in line with the relevant national tax law, which forms the sole reference framework.[177]

The conclusions of the Advocate General have, then, been confirmed by the CJEU.[178] In this case, as in the *Amazon* case,[179] the CJEU reiterated that there must be a reference system, which must not be abstract but be adequately determined according to the applicable domestic law.

There is one exception, with the *Apple* case.[180] In this case, the CJEU confirmed the Commission's decision that Ireland provided illegal State aid to Apple. The CJEU accepted the reference to the OECD approach in terms of transfer pricing, adhering to the GC's statement, saying that the Irish domestic provision at stake 'corresponded in essence to the functional and factual analysis conducted as part of the first step of the Authorised OECD Approach'.[181] The CJEU accepted the use of a reference that was exterior and so not incorporated into the Irish domestic law. In addition, the Irish tax rulings at stake were previous to the Authorised OECD Approach as used.[182] It should not have been possible to use it as a legal reference.[183] Such surprising decision, contrary to the *Fiat*, *Engie* and *Amazon* cases, and decided after them, still should not be seen as a landmark decision, for three reasons. First,

---

176 Joined Cases C-451/21 P and C-454/21 P *Engie and Luxembourg v Commission* [2023] ECLI:EU:C:2023:948, Opinion of AG Kokott

177 Court of Justice of the European Union, *Press Release no 73/23* [2023] 1

178 Joined Cases C-451/21 P and C-454/21 P *Engie and Luxembourg v Commission* [2023] ECLI:EU:C:2023:948

179 Case C-457/21 P *Commission v Amazon* [2023] ECLI:EU:C:2023:985

180 Case C-465/20 P *Commission v Ireland* [2024] ECLI:EU:C:2024:724

181 ibid para 123

182 The rulings at stake were from 1991 and 2007 while the OECD Model reference used did not appear before 2010: see S Daly and R Mason, 'What Went Wrong in the Apple State Aid Case: Part 1 – The Case' (2025) 44 Virginia Tax Review 418

183 S Daly, R Mason, 'What went Wrong in the Apple State Aid Case and How to Fix It: Part 2 – Suggested Reforms' (2025) 44 Virginia Tax Law Review 450

some days after this *Apple* case, the CJEU ruled again in line with the other cases.[184] Second, in terms of procedure, there was no direct appeal of Ireland and Apple on this issue concerning the reference system. As such, the CJEU considered that it was a res judicata by the GC.[185] Such solution could be seen as a technical consequence of the legal procedure. Third, there was a political dimension.[186] Thus, it is not said that there was no illegal State aid in this situation but rather that the State aid rules were wrongly applied. There is here again an argument for the necessity of coherence between the fields of competence of the CJEU and of the Member States, and so of the legal tools that such fields encompass. It would reinforce the legitimate expectations between both sides, and so loyal cooperation.[187]

Consequently, in the exception to the *Apple* case, the CJEU limited the possibilities of extension of the use of State aid rules. On one side, this limits the possibility for the EU to limit the Member States' sovereignty in order to protect its own interests, but on the other side, it confirms that State aid rules have a specific scope of application and that it is the same for the sovereignty of the EU. Thus, on one side, being sovereign in its own field of competence does not mean an unlimited right of authority, especially outside of its own legal system (being the field of competence). However, on the other side, such recent developments justify the distinction between tax policy and legal techniques contained in the EU treaties. Indeed, recently, the CJEU annulled different Commission's decisions on the same grounds used in the *Fiat* case in the sphere of transfer pricing.[188] Thus, the Commission proposed a directive on transfer pricing[189] in order to implement the arm's-length principle as defined by the OECD in EU law, which would change the perspective as it would impose a legal point of reference within the Member States in order to apply

[184] Joined Cases C-555/22 P, C-556/22 P and C-564/22 P *United Kingdom of Great Britain and Northern Ireland, ITV, LSEGH and London Stock Exchange Group Holdings v Commission* [2024] ECLI:EU:C:2024:763

[185] S Daly, R Mason, 'What Went Wrong in the Apple State Aid Case and How to Fix It: Part 2 – Suggested Reforms' (2025) 44 Virginia Tax Law Review 468–71

[186] ibid 476

[187] See also S Daly, R Mason, 'What Went Wrong in the Apple State Aid Case and How to Fix It: Part 2 – Suggested Reforms' (2025) 44 Virginia Tax Law Review 474–75

[188] See eg Case C-562/19 P *Commission v Poland* [2021] ECLI:EU:C:2021:201

[189] European Commission, 'Proposal for a Council Directive on Transfer Pricing' COM (2023) 529 final. However, due to a lack of support from the Member States, this proposal has been withdrawn for now: European Commission, 'Commission Work Programme 2026: Europe's Independence Moment' COM (2025) 870 final, Annex IV

the State aid rules. Similarly, several cases can be approached as well under the perspective of the fundamental freedoms as under the perspective of the State aid rules,[190] in the same way that fundamental rights are always applicable whatever the situation is. The final idea remains the same: to remove the bad disparity, by using fundamental freedoms or by using State aid rules. Both are legal techniques in specific spheres of competence that express the higher purpose of the EU treaties as a whole: the objective of achieving the internal market. They are the expression of this objective and its legal application. Consequently, they find their unity in this objective. It is the same with secondary law, which has the same reason of existence and the same objective. Distinctions are practical legal techniques depending on the specific spheres of competence and on the field of application. Here, concretely, this field of application is the field of direct taxation of businesses as demonstrated by the transfer pricing matters and the recent proposals for new directives.[191] Therefore, what must be highlighted here is that there is one EU level where its shared sovereignty must express itself. Here, it would be through its own tax policy as its means of expression and, consequently, through an adequate competence to tax. Negative integration and positive integration should not be divided as being different legal techniques. In terms of legitimacy, there should be a shared tax policy between the EU and the Member States depending on their own specific objectives, and with the adequate powers in order to achieve these specific objectives.

Finally, more so than the *Gibraltar* case and the *World Duty Free* case, the *Magnetrol* case illustrates the necessity to combat certain practices within the internal market. Maybe it is a paradox within a paradox, as State aid rules can help to combat such practices but still must be restricted to its area of application. They cannot palliate the flaws of the non-discrimination principle in the field of direct taxation of businesses. This aspect has been confirmed by the *Fiat* case. Other legal solutions should be proposed in order to solve the inadequacies between the legitimate competences of the EU and those of the Member States.

---

190 See eg Case C-75/18 *Vodafone* [2020] ECLI:EU:C:2020:139

191 European Commission, 'Proposal for a Council Directive establishing a Head Office Tax System for Micro, Small and Medium Size Enterprises, and amending Directive 2011/16/EU' COM (2023) 528 final; European Commission, 'Proposal for a Council Directive on Business in Europe: Framework for Income Taxation (BEFIT)' COM (2023) 532 final

6.3 THE INVESTIGATION OF A POSSIBLE EUROPEAN POWER TO TAX

6.3.1 The Need for European Consent to Tax for a European Power to Tax

6.3.1.1 The legitimacy of the European Union's formal consent to tax

When it comes to the legitimacy of the formal consent to tax and so to a democratic legal basis for the consent to tax, there are two aspects that must be examined. The first is the constitutional basis[192] and the second is the principle 'no taxation without representation', which must be involved within this constitutional basis as the consequence of the democratic design of the legal system's institutional construction.

At the European level, formal legitimacy is indirect,[193] and it is especially important for a separation system. If the EU wants to put in place its own taxes, as there would be a direct link with the taxpayer-citizens, direct democratic requirements would be necessary. Thus, it must be remembered that, under article 311 TFEU, a special legislative procedure (unanimity voting) is required in addition to the approval of the national Parliaments. It only gives an indirect legitimacy and article 311 TFEU, as only giving the possibility for the creation of new categories of taxes, cannot be considered as a basis for the creation of new European taxes. It does not give the *Kompetenz-Kompetenz* to the EU, according to the German Federal Constitutional Court.[194] It would mean that the EU does not have the sovereignty to put in place its own taxes. Thus, another distinction must be made. Here, it is not a question of sovereignty in itself[195] but a question of democratic sovereignty in the sense of whether the EU has the democratic legitimacy to put in place its own taxes through a separation system in the field of direct taxation of businesses.

---

192 Constitution of France, art 34; Constitution of Denmark, art 43; Constitution of Bulgary, art 60, para 1; Constitution of Greece, art 78 para 1; Constitution of Ireland, paras 22.2.1–22.2.6; etc

193 JHH Weiler, 'The Transformation of Europe' (1991) 100 Yale Law Journal 2430

194 C Waldhoof, *Legal Restrictions and Possibilities for Greater Revenue Autonomy of the EU in The Future of EU-Finances* (T Buettner and M Thöne eds, FiFo Institute for Public Economics, University of Cologne 2016) 152; BVerfG, 2 BvE 2/08 [2009]

195 For political sovereignty as such, as a question of absolute supreme authority, if recognized by the people, a sovereign can be legitimate to use the power to tax. It is not a question of democracy as the political and legal system might not be a democracy (monarchy, aristocracy).

It is considered that the EU is a 'community based on the rule of law'[196] and that the EU treaties can be considered as an EU Constitution as judged by the CJEU in the case *Les Verts*.[197] The democratic dimension of the EU has been enshrined in article 6 TEU:

> The Union recognizes the rights, freedoms and principles set out in the Charter of Fundamental Rights of the European Union of 7 December 2000, as adapted at Strasbourg, on 12 December 2007, which shall have the same legal value as the Treaties.
>
> The provisions of the Charter shall not extend in any way the competences of the Union as defined in the Treaties.
>
> The rights, freedom and principles in the Charter shall be interpreted in accordance with the general provision in Title VII of the Charter governing its interpretation and application and with due regard to the explanations referred to in the Charter, that set out the sources of those provisions.
>
> The Union shall accede to the European Convention for the Protection of Human Rights and Fundamental Freedoms. Such accession shall not affect the Union's competences as defined in the Treaties.
>
> Fundamental rights, as guaranteed by the European Convention for the Protection of Human Rights and Fundamental Freedoms and as they result from the constitutional traditions common to the Member States, shall constitute general principles of the Union's law.[198]

Thus, the rule of law, as understood in the light of article 6 TEU, involves different principles such as legal certainty, which is a general principle of EU law. This principle means that a law adopted by the EU and having effect in its legal order must be certain, clear and precise; its legal implications must be foreseeable, especially concerning financial obligations; and there must be a proper legal basis.[199] Then, as an application of the principle of legal certainty, there is the misuse of powers test.[200] This verifies whether or not a lawful power is not exercised for any other purpose than that for which it has been conferred.[201] In the light of this principle, it must be demonstrated that the EU does not have formal legitimacy in terms of consent to tax in the field of direct taxation of businesses. It has already been said that article 311 TFEU cannot be considered as an adequate legal basis. Similarly, article 115 TFEU is not a specific basis for taxation and can only be used as a basis to legislate,

---

196 Case C-294/83, *Les Verts* [1986] ECR 1339

197 ibid

198 TEU, art 6

199 Case T-115/94 *Opel Austria GmbH v Council of the European Union* [1997] ECR II-00039

200 Case 105/75 *Giuffrida v Council of the European Communities* [1976] ECR 1395

201 ibid

meaning for the competence to tax, which is not conditioned by a fundamental right such as the consent to tax.[202] It is the main distinction between the competence to tax and the power to tax. Actually, a parallel can be made with indirect taxes. Article 113 TFEU is also only a basis for the competence to tax and not for the power to tax, as no new categories of indirect taxes can be created. Both articles 113 and 115 TFEU are articles meant for harmonization at the EU level. They apply in the tax field but they only give a right to legislate without giving any consent to tax to the EU, and article 311 TFEU only allows for the creation of new categories of taxes without containing any consent to tax too. The only legal consent to tax that exists in the EU treaties is in articles 192 paragraph 2 and 194 paragraph 3 TFEU concerning the possibility to create environmental taxes. In this specific case, the taxes are explicitly determined within the treaties. However, the question on their formal legitimacy remains vivid (they have a constitutional basis but there is still the requirement of the motto 'no taxation without representation'). Consequently, in the field of direct taxation, there is no constitutional basis in the EU treaties for the consent to tax and so for a European power to tax. Using article 311 TFEU as a basis to create a European tax through a separation system could be considered as a misuse of powers in breach of the principle of legal certainty and so of the rule of law. The indirect legitimacy through unanimity voting and the punctual approval of the national Parliaments should not be considered as sufficient. The taxpayer-citizen, in its direct relation with the EU through the European tax, would not be protected through a constitutional basis any more. The consent to tax must be considered as a fundamental right in a democratic system and there must be a parallel in its exercise in the sense that, if the EU has its own tax and creates a direct relation with the taxpayer, the citizen must directly give its consent to it also (and not indirectly through the executive power of the Member States or through an only punctual approvement by the legislative power). This issue is particularly about the question of the referendum concerning fundamental rights and constitutional issues.[203]

Furthermore, the second aspect of the formal legitimacy of the consent to tax is the motto 'no taxation without representation'. The consent to tax implies that the people give the power to tax to their Parliament by means of representation. Indeed, popular sovereignty implies that, in most European democracies, the people must govern even if they give their consent to be taxed to the power in place. This paradox is achieved through representation in a

[202] See eg JJ Rousseau, *Du Contrat Social* (1762); J Locke, *Two Treatises of Government* (1690): consenting to tax is considered as a basic foundation of the civil society and of the social contract (especially for Rousseau, who considers that the right for property is one of the most fundamental rights).

[203] See pt 2, ch 5, para 5.2

constitutional system. Thus, the importance of the role of the Parliament is covered through a historical approach.

One of the first appearances of the consent to tax can be found in the Magna Carta (Greater Charter of Liberties) of 1215.[204] At that time, the conception of the State was different from that in modern democracies. The monarch often had an absolute power of *vis et voluntas* (force and will).[205] Sovereignty was exercised through a monarchic form. Hence, King John, in old England, abused this power as he was levying high taxes in order to support war expenses even in times of peace.[206] Yet, in the late Middle Ages, when there was no need to unite in order to defend the kingdom, the king was living on his own like his vassals;[207] that is, in times of peace, the king was not imposing taxes or heavy burdens on his vassals and was taking care of his own lands as they did theirs. King John abused his right to levy taxes and this is why the Greater Charter of Liberties (Magna Carta) was signed, after a short civil war between the king and his barons. Clauses 12 and 14 stated:

> No scutage nor aid shall be imposed on our kingdom, unless by common counsel of our kingdom, except for ransoming our person, for making our eldest son a knight, and for once marrying our eldest daughter; and for these there shall not be levied more than a reasonable aid. In like manner it shall be done concerning aids from the city of London.[208]
>
> And in order to have the common counsel of the kingdom for the levying of an aid, other than in the three instances aforesaid, or for the levying of scutage, we are to cause the archbishops, bishops, abbots, earls and greater barons to be summoned individually by our letters; and moreover we are to have a general summons made, through our sheriffs and bailiffs, of all who hold in chief of us; for a fixed day, at least forty days thence, and at a fixed place. And in all the letters of summons we are to set out its cause. And after the summons has thus been made the business is to go forward on the appointed day according to the counsel of those present, even if not all those summoned have come.[209]

The king was no longer able to put in place taxes without the approval of the 'common counsel'.[210] Different from the idea of representation, this was a first appearance of a consent to tax in a system different from modern democracies.

---

[204] Magna Carta Libertatum [1215]

[205] MC Fregni, 'Legitimacy in Decision-Making in Tax Law: Some Remarks on Taxation, Representation and Consent to Imposition' in P Pistone (ed), *European Tax Integration: Law, Policy and Politics* (IBFD 2018) 129

[206] ibid

[207] ibid

[208] Magna Carta Libertatum [1215] clause 12

[209] ibid clause 14

[210] ibid

Thus, it is in the American foundation that consent through representation must be found.

After the Seven Years War, the British government faced a huge national debt[211] and new taxes were imposed on the American colonies.[212] In addition to already existing local taxes, they had to pay high import duties on products coming from Great Britain, among others.[213] However, under the English Bill of Rights,[214] the imposition of taxes without the consent of Parliament was forbidden, and the American colonists did not have any representatives in the British Parliament.[215]

Two theses were in opposition. For James Otis, a Massachusetts lawyer and politician, 'taxation without representation is tyranny'.[216] The act of taxing unrepresented people in the Parliament is a direct attack on the most essential rights of freemen. This was the American position.[217] On the other side, the British position was that there was a virtual representation.[218] George Grenville and Thomas Whateley had previously theorized the idea that members of Parliament could represent the people of a Nation even if some of the people could not vote for them.[219] The American colonies were not the only ones to not be represented in the British Parliament and Samuel Johnson wrote a pamphlet, 'Taxation no tyranny',[220] emphasizing this aspect.[221] The American colonists refused to agree to this position and many tax duties and

211 MC Fregni, 'Legitimacy in Decision-Making in Tax Law: Some Remarks on Taxation, Representation and Consent to Imposition' in P Pistone (ed), *European Tax Integration: Law, Policy and Politics* (IBFD 2018) 130

212 ibid

213 ibid

214 An Act Declaring the Rights and Liberties of the Subject and Settling the Succession of the Crown [1689]

215 MC Fregni, 'Legitimacy in Decision-Making in Tax Law: Some Remarks on Taxation, Representation and Consent to Imposition' in P Pistone (ed), *European Tax Integration: Law, Policy and Politics* (IBFD 2018) 130

216 J Otis Jr, *A Vindication of the Conduct of the House of Representatives* (1762)

217 MC Fregni, 'Legitimacy in Decision-Making in Tax Law: Some Remarks on Taxation, Representation and Consent to Imposition' in P Pistone (ed), *European Tax Integration: Law, Policy and Politics* (IBFD 2018) 131

218 ibid

219 ibid

220 S Johnson, *Taxation No Tyranny* (1775)

221 MC Fregni, 'Legitimacy in Decision-Making in Tax Law: Some Remarks on Taxation, Representation and Consent to Imposition' in P Pistone (ed), *European Tax Integration: Law, Policy and Politics* (IBFD 2018) 131

tax disputes such as the controversial Stamp Act[222] and the Boston Tea Party[223] led to secession and to the American Declaration of Independence of 1776.[224]

Historically, the motto 'no taxation without representation' became the pillar of modern democracies and the American democracy is one of the first democratic models. It seems to be preceded only by the Corsican Republic of 1755, whose constitution already included the consent to tax and its vote by the Parliament.[225] Consequently, the formal legitimacy of the modern democracies implies a constitutional consent to tax embodied by the representation through an elected parliament, which exemplifies the popular sovereignty. The European procedure for the adoption of European tax rules does not follow this process. The European Parliament does not have the legislative power in tax matters and acts as a consultative body.[226] Since 1979, the representatives of the European populations are directly elected by the people, but they still do not have the tax powers that must involve the principle 'no taxation without representation'. Thus, there is a democratic flaw at the EU level.

Nevertheless, there is still a democratic procedure, but it is fulfilled at the national level of the Member States. For Vanistendael,[227] democratic legitimacy cannot be accomplished at both the European and national levels at the same time.[228] With the unanimity procedure and the approval of the national Parliaments, formal legitimacy is accomplished at the Member State level. In this sense, the EU does not have a formal legitimacy in itself; it is only indirect through the Member States. For a European separation system, the taxation powers of the European Parliament should be enhanced.

6.3.1.2 The legitimacy of the European Union's social consent to tax

The concept of virtual representation leads to the analysis of the social legitimacy of the EU in terms of consent to tax to assess whether a separation system could be put in place. There are two aspects. First, the taxpayer as a voter and so as a citizen questions the *demos* (people of a Nation) of the EU in terms of representation through the European Parliament. Second, the idea of a possible fiscal contract to put in place European taxes questions the possibility of a European *ethos* (character).

---

222 Parliament of Great Britain, *Duties in American Colonies Act* (1765)

223 Boston Tea Party [1773] in reaction to the Tea Act [1773]

224 United States Declaration of Independence [1776]

225 Constitution of Corse [1755]

226 See in this chapter, section 6.3.2.1

227 F Vanistendael, 'On Democratic Legitimacy of European Tax Law and the Role of the European Parliament' in P Pistone (ed), *European Tax Integration: Law, Policy and Politics* (IBFD 2018)

228 ibid 104

Before beginning the analysis, the distinction between indirect taxes and direct taxes should be mentioned. The relation between the taxpayer-citizen and the State as well as the fiscal contract concern both indirect taxation and direct taxation. However, this distinction exists at the European level as a consequence of the economic objectives of the EU. The relation between indirect taxes and the objective of achieving the internal market could have given social acceptance to such taxes. Like a kind of application of the benefit principle,[229] harmonization of indirect taxes at the European level seems to be the price to pay to have an internal market, which might be seen as an economic advantage for taxpayers. The same could be said about environmental taxes. They would be the fair price for more effective protection of the environment. On the other side, this social acceptance is not true yet for direct taxes. More than a technical way of financing the State, they have an important social impact, as can be seen in the history of political philosophy.[230]

Thus, the principle of 'no taxation without representation' is a reference to the taxpayer-citizen. The members of a Parliament, who represent the people, are elected by the citizens, who are also taxpayers. The right to be represented in terms of taxation becomes an intrinsic element of belonging to a State as an individual. This implies the notion of the 'Nation State'[231] where the sum of the individuals, as taxpayer-citizens, constitutes the Nation of the State. There are two issues concerning the EU: the first is general and is only mentioned, and the second is inherent to the EU.

First, the theory of virtual representation has been developed because the link between the taxpayer and the citizen does not work in reality. Individuals are taxed as a result of residence and not as citizens. In a State, all the residents must contribute to taxes, but they are not all citizens. Therefore, they do not all have a right to vote. Similarly, there are individuals who can vote but who are not taxed. This is why there is a theory of virtual representation. It is a general representation of a collectivity. In any Nation State, this can be an issue in terms of social acceptance of a fiscal policy.[232] Then, this issue is multiplied at the EU level.

Indeed, the notion of the taxpayer-citizen implies that the taxpayer belongs to a Nation. This thesis is supposed to be an important part of the social acceptance

---

229 M Stewart, 'The Tax State, Benefit and Legitimacy' in PHADDC (ed), *Studies in the History of Tax Law*, vol 7 (Hart Publishing 2015) 22

230 See JJ Rousseau, *Du Contrat Social* (1762); J Locke, *Two Treatises of Government* (1690)

231 E de Crouy Chanel, *La Citoyenneté Fiscale* (2002) [46] Archives de Philosophie du Droit 40

232 It was the case with the American Revolution.

of taxes.[233] Consequently, the question is whether the EU can be understood as a Nation or not, so whether it has a *demos*.[234] For instance, Weiler[235] considers this issue as being part of the 'new constitutional order'[236] that constitutes the EU. Due to the doctrine of direct effect, not only the Member States but also the individuals are subjects of the European order.[237] This should, among others, justify the constitutionalization of the EU.[238] However, it does not mean that the EU is de facto a Nation.[239] European individuals can be subjects of the EU independently of national legislations, but this must not reduce the notion of citizen to the application of a doctrine.[240]

'Citizens constitute the Demos of the polity.'[241] *Demos* is the collective side of citizenship, and a crucial one in terms of democracy.[242] Individuals must be members of the democracy. In Weiler's words, the authority and legitimacy of a majority is justified by the *demos*.[243] The Nation as a sum of individuals being part of the same collectivity must be the place where the rules of the democracy can impose sacrifices. In the example of the political consent to tax of article 14 of the French Declaration of Rights of the Man and of the Citizen, it is the collective consent to tax that gives the right to the State to impose an individual burden.[244] Yet, the issue is that there is no *demos* at the European level[245] and it is a matter of empirical observation.[246] For instance, French and Austrian people are part of two different Nations. There are no French representatives in the Austrian parliament, and vice versa. Now, with a majority rule at the European level and empowering the European parliament (giving formal legitimacy), French representatives could impose their tax views on

---

233 E de Crouy Chanel, *La Citoyenneté Fiscale* (2002) [46] Archives de Philosophie du Droit 40
234 JHH Weiler, 'European Neo-Constitutionalism: in Search of Foundations for the European Constitutional Order' [1996] Political Studies XLIV, 521
235 ibid
236 ibid
237 ibid
238 ibid
239 ibid 522
240 ibid
241 ibid
242 ibid 523
243 ibid 522
244 M Bouvier, *Introduction au Droit Fiscal Général et à la Théorie de l'Impôt* (LGDJ 2020) 34
245 JHH Weiler, 'European Neo-Constitutionalism: in Search of Foundations for the European Constitutional Order' [1996] Political Studies XLIV, 522
246 ibid

the Austrian people. In other words, the Nations represented by the minority would lose their democratic *demos*.

This leads to a simple observation. In terms of formal legitimacy of the European consent to tax, giving more powers to the European Parliament would substantiate the democratic legitimacy of the EU. However, in terms of social legitimacy, it would break the link between the taxpayer-citizens and their cultural backgrounds. It would be difficult to get social acceptance for a tax from the people of a Member State when the representatives of this State voted against it. In this situation, the democracy is separated from the Nation State. However, a European *ethos* (character) is still possible to create a European community and overcome this issue.

Therefore, even if there is no European *demos*, a European *ethos* (character) might exist. This *ethos* (character) could be the foundation of a European fiscal contract. It expresses here the idea that political and social acceptance of the individuals is necessary to put in place European taxes in terms of social legitimacy. From a democratic point of view, this would be the expression of popular sovereignty – where individuals accept an intrusion into their right to property[247] – even if, afterwards, taxes are imposed.

The *ethos* (character) can be understood as a general set of formal and informal values accepted by individuals who become part of a community founded on these values. In the EU, a reference can be made to the already quoted article 6 TEU, but also to article 2 TEU:

> The Union is founded on the values of respect for human dignity, freedom, democracy, equality, the rule of law and respect for human rights, including the rights of persons belonging to minorities. These values are common to the Member States in a society in which pluralism, non-discrimination, tolerance, justice, solidarity and equality between women and men prevail.[248]

These values can be the foundation of a common *ethos* (character) in the EU. They are 'common to the Member States in a society'.[249] This reference to a society requires a European integration which is not legal but social. As there is no European *demos* (people of a Nation), the only way to create this European community is through common values. If the different peoples of the EU recognize themselves in these values, there is a possibility to create a community under EU law. To accomplish this integration in the specific field of taxation, and especially direct taxation, trust seems to be of utmost importance.

---

247 JJ Rousseau, *Discours sur l'Economie Politique* (1755): the real foundation of the civil society is the right to property.

248 TEU, art 2

249 TEU, art 2

In the approach taken here, trust is an important aspect of justice as it could be perceived by individuals. Even if, in a State, there is a theory of a collectively accepted fiscal contract, there is a duty for individuals to pay taxes.[250] In order to help them accept this duty, the administration must demonstrate to the taxpayers that they can trust it. This is a matter of legitimacy, where the effort of the citizens is rewarded by a national benefit (the value pattern of the fiscal contract provides for adequate governmental outputs). This can be done through good management of public resources but also by the capacity of the State to deal with matters such as tax evasion or tax fraud.[251] As an example, on this very last point, the EU has already begun to create the basis for a fiscal contract. Through directives such as the Anti-Tax Avoidance Directives (ATAD)[252] or the Pillar II directive,[253] the Union acts to enhance fair taxation in the entire internal market. Despite the legal bumps that can exist to achieve such objective, the social perception by the European people is what matters here to build this fiscal contract. It is the general application in all the Member States that could bring cohesion between the European peoples to build the social legitimacy of the EU. Thus, the progressive achievement of the internal market, as the economic *telos* (objective) of the EU, could build acceptance of a hypothetical fiscal contract. As such, the economic *telos* (objective) that is the internal market was one of the foundations of the EU. Furthermore, it has been demonstrated that business taxation, especially under the perspective of competitive neutrality, is an inherent part of the economic objective of achieving the internal market. Consequently, depending on the outcomes of directives such as the Pillar II directive and the BEFIT directive proposal,[254] it could be considered that the fiscal contract already exists.[255] The only remain-

---

250 MC Fregni, 'Legitimacy in Decision-Making in Tax Law: Some Remarks on Taxation, Representation and Consent to Imposition' in P Pistone (ed), *European Tax Integration: Law, Policy and Politics* (IBFD 2018) 137

251 ibid

252 Council Directive (EU) 2016/1164 Laying Down Rules Against Tax Avoidance Practices that Directly Affect the Functioning of the Internal Market [2016] OJ L 193/1; Council Directive (EU) 2017/952 Amending Directive (EU) 2016/1164 as regards Hybrid Mismatches with Third Countries

253 Council Directive (EU) 2022/2523 on Ensuring a Global Minimum Level of Taxation for Multinational Enterprise Groups and Large-Scale Domestic Groups in the Union [2022] OJ L 328/1

254 European Commission, 'Proposal for a Council Directive on Business in Europe: Framework for Income Taxation (BEFIT)' COM (2023) 532 final

255 See ch 7 concerning the notion of policy consensus. Reaching a consensus between the EU and the Member States in a specific area within the field of direct taxation of businesses would be a good indication that there is a social fiscal contract at least in such area.

ing obstacles for a European power to tax in this field would be the constitutional requirements.

Finally, the ways in which the legitimacy of the EU may be concretely enhanced in terms of consent to tax and so of power to tax should also be explored.

6.3.2 Improving the Legitimacy of the European Union for a Hypothetical European Power to Tax

6.3.2.1 The European Parliament and the legislative procedure in the field of direct taxation

As previously said, the formal legitimacy of a European consent to tax needs a constitutional provision but also representation by the European Parliament. These two aspects involve an effective power of representation for the EU to have a legitimate legal consent to tax. This means that respect for the principle of legality is also respect for the power of representation of the parliament. In other words, the European Parliament should have a decisive role if European taxes are implemented. However, currently, in the field of taxation, and especially that of direct taxation of businesses, the European legislative procedure only gives a minor role to the European Parliament. Consequently, the legislative procedure at the EU level must be detailed before proposing how the formal legitimacy can be enhanced in terms of consent to tax.

First, article 289 TFEU explains that there is an ordinary legislative procedure alongside a special legislative procedure. The ordinary legislative procedure is detailed at article 294 TFEU, while there is no specific treaty provision for the special legislative procedure.[256] There are, actually, different special legislative procedures that are defined depending on the substantive treaty provision that is involved.[257] Their common point is that they involve the participation of both the Council and the Parliament.[258] Concerning the ordinary legislative procedure, the main elements are that:

- The legislative proposal is made by the Commission, which submits it to the Council and the Parliament;
- Then, the Council and the Parliament jointly adopt the proposal during the first or the second reading;

256 L Del Federico, 'Monitoring Decision-Making, Enforcement and Application of EU Tax Law: The Role of Intermediate Bodies and Lobbies' in P Pistone (ed), *European Tax Integration: Law, Policy and Politics* (IBFD 2018) 184

257 ibid

258 ibid

- If there is no agreement after these two readings, a conciliation committee intervenes to reshape the text and there is a third reading afterwards; the act is consequently adopted or definitely rejected.[259]

In this procedure,[260] the Parliament has a right of initiative and can ask the Commission to submit a proposal by a simple majority. Then, during the first reading, the Parliament can adopt the act or amend it before sending it to the Council by a simple majority. The Council can accept the act or amend it also and will consequently send it back to the Parliament. During the second reading, the Parliament can adopt the amended act, reject it (thus putting an end to the procedure) or amend it again by absolute majority, which means a second reading by the Council. Thus, the Council approves all the new amendments of the Parliament, or the conciliation committee intervenes. This committee is composed of an equal number of members of the Parliament and of the Council, and only if they agree on a new text will there be a third reading. In this committee, the delegation of the Parliament votes by absolute majority while, generally, the Council votes by qualified majority. Finally, during the third reading, the Parliament must approve the proposal by simple majority and, if the Council approves it also, the act is adopted.

Second, there is a special procedure in the field of taxation. In the field of indirect taxation, for instance, article 113 TFEU provides for an adoption of the legislative acts by the Council by unanimity voting after consulting the European Parliament and the European Social Committee (ESC). Similarly, the field of direct taxation is ruled by article 115 TFEU, which also requires adoption by the Council by unanimity voting after consulting the European Parliament and the ESC. In both cases, the right of legislative initiative belongs to the Commission and the Parliament acts as a consultative body.[261] The Council must wait for its opinion, but it does not have to take it into account.[262] Then, concerning the flexibility clause (article 352 TFEU),[263] the Council also adopts the acts by unanimously voting on a Commission's proposal but it must obtain the consent of the Parliament, which has a veto power.[264] Finally, about

[259] European Union, 'The Ordinary Legislative Procedure' <www.consilium.europa.eu/en/council-eu/decision-making/ordinary-legislative-procedure/> accessed 25 November 2025

[260] ibid

[261] ibid

[262] ibid

[263] About the flexibility clause, see ch 7, section 7.2.2.2

[264] L Del Federico, 'Monitoring Decision-Making, Enforcement and Application of EU Tax Law: The Role of Intermediate Bodies and Lobbies' in P Pistone (ed), *European Tax Integration: Law, Policy and Politics* (IBFD 2018) 187

article 116 TFEU,[265] the ordinary legislative procedure applies.[266] It means that the Parliament becomes a co-legislator with the Council and that a simple majority applies (while a qualified majority is required within the Council).

Hence it can be seen that, in the field of direct taxation of businesses, the European Parliament has no decisive role in the legislative procedure. This means that its role of representation of the taxpayer-citizens is ineffective and that, currently, the legal consent to tax, in addition to being nonexistent, could not even be legitimized by the Parliament in terms of representation. The decisional power entirely relies on the executive power embodied by the Commission, which represents the EU, and the Council, which represents the Member States.[267] However, with the ordinary legislative procedure, even if the Parliament is a co-legislator and not the unique legislator, it has, in addition to its right of initiative, a decisive role as it can prevent the adoption of a legislative act and as it is a key institution in the process of adoption of the act with a possibility of amending the proposal. In this sense, if the ordinary legislative procedure applies in the field of direct taxation, as the approval of the European Parliament would be necessary to adopt a legislative act, there would be a formal legitimacy of the consent to tax in terms of representation. Indeed, the importance of the executive power in the adoption of tax acts is a common feature of European countries[268] and, as long as the legislative power has a decisive role, it does not seem to be an obstacle in order to reach formal legitimacy.

However, in the literature, it might be argued that the actual legislative procedure in the field of taxation at the EU level can be legitimized through other means.[269] For instance, Del Federico writes: 'in the context of the European Union, these troubles are attenuated by some stopgaps measures, including the important role of the intermediate bodies and the trend towards developing the bottom-up method.'[270] Thus, different means of democratic legitimization are effective concerning the competence to tax as it does not involve the consent to tax as fundamental principle. However, concerning the power to tax and so the consent to tax, on its legal side, the only democratic legitimacy that

---

[265] About article 116 TFEU, see pt 3, ch 7, para 7.3.2.1

[266] TFEU, art 116

[267] See eg L Del Federico, 'Monitoring Decision-Making, Enforcement and Application of EU Tax Law: The Role of Intermediate Bodies and Lobbies' in P Pistone (ed), *European Tax Integration: Law, Policy and Politics* (IBFD 2018)

[268] See eg AP Dourado (ed), *Separation of Powers in Tax Law* (IBFD 2010)

[269] See eg L Del Federico, 'Monitoring Decision-Making, Enforcement and Application of EU Tax Law: The Role of Intermediate Bodies and Lobbies' in P Pistone (ed), *European Tax Integration: Law, Policy and Politics* (IBFD 2018)

[270] ibid 209

can be reached is through the constitutional basis and the principle 'no taxation without representation'. This means that, in terms of formal legitimacy, if the EU wants to put in place its own taxes, the European Parliament needs to have a decisive role in line with the consent to tax as a fundamental democratic principle. Nonetheless, still concerning this principle, all other means of democratic legitimization can help to improve the social legitimacy of the EU, as this aspect depends on the perception of the people.

6.3.2.2 About sovereignty and the political importance of the Member States for a legitimate European Union power to tax: does size matter?

The purpose here is not to fall back on social legitimacy if the European Parliament gets a decisive role in terms of formal legitimacy. The European *ethos* (character) could easily follow such change if it is supported by an adequate constitutional basis, which should itself be introduced by a referendum. Thus, with direct and explicit consent from the European people, the European *ethos* (character) would get its own legitimacy. On the other side, the question here falls to the co-legislator of the Parliament: the Council, to which can be added the Commission for its right of legislative initiative. In terms of social legitimacy and so of political science, the question is about the importance of a Member State for its voice to be heard. For instance, when the ATAD was voted on, no Member State vetoed it.[271] Small Member States with advantageous tax regimes in order to attract investments could have had an interest in doing so but they did not.[272] Similarly, the Pillar II directive has finally been adopted by unanimity voting and the majority of small Member States never voted against it.[273] Consequently, the question is about the weight of such small Member States in order for their voice to be heard and so about the social legitimacy of the EU concerning the populations of these specific Member States. Indeed, the voices of these Member States need to be considered in the decision-making process at the European level if the EU wants to get full social legitimacy. It is not only about big Member States. Thus, this question is predominant when it comes to unanimity voting but it still exists also with QMV, depending on the repartition of voices for or against when it comes to voting on a proposition. Furthermore, it concerns both the competence to tax

---

271 C Brokelind, 'Smaller versus Bigger Member States: How Can Their Voices and Goals be Harmoniously Reconciled' in P Pistone (ed), *European Tax Integration: Law, Policy and Politics* (IBFD 2018) 155

272 See ibid 171

273 Poland and Hungaria refused to adopt the directive for a moment but they are not among the small Member States at least in terms of population: see Eurostat Communication, 111/2020

and the power to tax in terms of democratic legitimacy in the field of political science due to the decisive role of the Council as co-legislator, but also due to the Commission according to its right of legislative initiative. The distinction between the competence to tax and the power to tax is that the latter specifically needs direct democratic legitimacy and relies exclusively on it as it is a criterion of democracy, as demonstrated through the historical analysis of the motto 'no taxation without representation'.

Hence, it must first be explained what kind of State can be considered as a small Member State. According to Brokelind and based on political science research, a small Member State has significantly less than 40 million inhabitants.[274] In the European Union, 15 Member States have a population of less than 10 million and 8 are even below 5 million.[275] However, this criterion does not correspond with the modern situation where small States can be high economic competitors.[276] Nowadays, six categories of measures can be cited in order to define the size of a State:

- Population and geographic size.
- Sovereignty and State structure (effective sovereignty of a specific territory).
- Political size (military and administrative capacity).
- Economic size (GDP, market size and development success).
- Perceptual size (how domestic and international actors regard that state).
- Preference size (ambitions of the governing elite in terms of international positioning).[277]

Internal and external aspects of each criterion should be taken into account.[278] For instance, France has more personnel in its foreign services than Germany and UK (States of a similar size) and thus may have increased influence

[274] C Brokelind, 'Smaller versus Bigger Member States: How can their Voices and Goals be Harmoniously Reconciled' in P Pistone (ed), *European Tax Integration: Law, Policy and Politics* (IBFD 2018) 157; S Bunse, P Magnette and K Nicolaïdis, 'Is the Commission the Small Member States' Best Friend?' (2005) [9] Swedish Institute for European Policy Studies 8

[275] On 1 January 2020: Eurostat Communication, 111/2020

[276] B Thorhallsson, 'The Size of States in the European Union: Theoretical and Conceptual Perspectives' (2006) 28 [1] European Integration 8

[277] C Brokelind, 'Smaller versus Bigger Member States: How Can Their Voices and Goals be Harmoniously Reconciled' in P Pistone (ed), *European Tax Integration: Law, Policy and Politics* (IBFD 2018) 158

[278] ibid

compared to these States.[279] Nonetheless, there is no consensus on the specific criteria and it depends on the situation of each State. Thus, in the EU, the small Member States could be assimilated to the weak part in the process of European integration.[280] Big Member States will be proactive and shape European policies while small Member States will be reactive and will have difficulty defending their own interests. For instance, the latter have less people and less economic resources. They are consequently not able to compete in terms of diplomatic and technical expertise.[281] Moreover, it is worse at the EU level, as the small States surrendered their autonomy to the European supremacy.[282] Consequently, according to Wivel, these States must adopt a smart State's strategy based on avoiding conflicts.[283] Such soft strategies mainly consist of avoiding conflict with existing initiatives or focusing on specific issues where they have a comparative advantage to big Member States.[284]

Then, institutionally, the opposition between big and small Member States lies in an opposition between sovereignty and democratic representation.[285] Tocqueville describes such opposition in relation to the United States' political system: it is an opposition between federative States and democratic representation.[286] In other words, is it better to respect equality in sovereignty between the States or an equal representation of the people? In the EU, it is the opposition between the States' sovereignty and the *demos* (favouring the number of people). According to Tocqueville, the origin of the democratic deficit lies in this opposition of principles. Indeed, there is a distinction between the State's sovereignty as political sovereignty and democratic sovereignty as a form of government and so as a form of legal and political system. A comparison can be made with virtual representation. Equality in sovereignty gives equal political power to the States independently from the number of people in

---

279 B Thorhallsson, 'The Size of States in the European Union: Theoretical and Conceptual Perspectives' (2006) 28 [1] European Integration 20

280 C Brokelind, 'Smaller versus Bigger Member States: How Can Their Voices and Goals be Harmoniously Reconciled' in P Pistone (ed), *European Tax Integration: Law, Policy and Politics* (IBFD 2018) 160

281 ibid

282 ibid

283 A Wivel, 'From Small State to Smart State: Devising a Strategy for Influence in the European Union' in R Steinmetz and A Wivel (eds), *Small States in Europe: Challenges and Opportunities* (Ashgate 2010) 15–29

284 ibid

285 See C Brokelind, 'Smaller versus Bigger Member States: How Can Their Voices and Goals be Harmoniously Reconciled' in P Pistone (ed), *European Tax Integration: Law, Policy and Politics* (IBFD 2018) 161

286 A de Tocqueville, *Democracy in America* (1835)

each State, while equal representation of the people seems to be a more tangible and democratic way to represent a population as a whole and especially its majority when it comes to a democratic vote. Hence, according to Brokelind, the EU found a balance from this opposition: the Council enacts the law, the Commission represents the EU's interests and the CJEU equally enforces the enacted legislation.[287] The Council represents the sovereignty of the Member States and the CJEU is supposed to take into account each specificity of each case and so of the local populations. Furthermore, QMV as the ordinary legislative procedure is supposed to soften the small Member States' power due to equal sovereignty by impelling the taking into consideration of equal representation of the people.[288] On the facts, the Commission became the best institution to defend small Member States' interests.[289]

Also, in the Council, it is demonstrated in the field of political science that the influence of the small Member States is weak even when they can theoretically apply their veto power: 'due to a lack of equal resources, small States tend to show inadequate preparation of issues for which they wish to push for adoption through their own proposals, which large States use to set the framework for the Council of the European Union's negotiations.'[290] Furthermore, consensus is often sought even with QMV and, now, political science demonstrates that small Member States do not use often their veto power when unanimity voting is required. They know that a proposition can come back on the agenda in time and they keep their veto for issues that are very essential for their countries (such as budgetary concerns).[291] Generally, they do not use it, and the consensus is based on negotiations.[292] Also, seniority, experience and expertise play an important role, to the advantage of the big Member States.[293] Nonetheless, with the Lisbon treaty and the rotating presidency of the Council following the rotating presidency of the Council of the European Union for six months for each Member State (plus 12 months as cooperative president, even if it is not the official one due to the collegial presidency of 3), small Member States got more important influence on the Council, with the possibility to set the agenda during these six months.[294]

[287] C Brokelind, 'Smaller versus Bigger Member States: How Can Their Voices and Goals be Harmoniously Reconciled' in P Pistone (ed), *European Tax Integration: Law, Policy and Politics* (IBFD 2018) 161
[288] ibid
[289] ibid 162
[290] ibid 163
[291] ibid 164
[292] ibid 163
[293] ibid 164
[294] ibid 165

Concerning the Commission, the small Member States won on the issue concerning the number of commissioners. This number was supposed to pass to two-thirds of the Member States in 2014 with the adhesion of Croatia.[295] However, the small Member States were against this change and Ireland vetoed the adoption of the Lisbon treaty.[296] It finally did sign it and the number of commissioners, one for each Member State, did not change. In addition, the Commission, as representing the EU, often helps the small Member States as they both have an interest in the open frontiers of the internal market.[297] Nonetheless, when it comes to protective measures concerning their domestic system, the issue remains the same. They can lack influence due to a lack of resources and so technical expertise. Thus, they need to focus on specific strategies and on their predominant fields of experience.[298]

Yet, in economics, and by extension concerning taxation, the size of a country is incidental[299] and the influence of a State is related to its capacity to change the policy context.[300] For a small Member State to be influential, the policy context needs to be as institutionalized as possible.[301] Institutionalization, thus, depends on the decision-making process, voting rules or the degree of absorption of norms by the international organization.[302] Then, according to Brokelind, the influence of the small State depends on its level of activity in respect of the institutionalized policy.[303] For instance, small Member States

[295] ibid 166

[296] See European Council, 'Conclusions of the Presidency on the European Council of Bruxelles of 18 and 19 June 2009' 11225/2/09, 2

[297] C Brokelind, 'Smaller versus Bigger Member States: How Can Their Voices and Goals be Harmoniously Reconciled' in P Pistone (ed), *European Tax Integration: Law, Policy and Politics* (IBFD 2018) 166

[298] See D Panke, 'Being Small in a Big Union: Structural Disadvantages, Counterbalancing Strategies and the Varying Success of Small States in European Policy Making' [2009] Paper for the Irish Research Council for the Humanities and Social Sciences

[299] C Brokelind, 'Smaller versus Bigger Member States: How Can Their Voices and Goals be Harmoniously Reconciled' in P Pistone (ed), *European Tax Integration: Law, Policy and Politics* (IBFD 2018) 167

[300] ibid 168

[301] B Thorallsson and A Wivel, 'Small States in the European Union: What Do We Know and What Would We Like to Know?' (2006) 19 [4] Cambridge Review of International Affairs 651–58

[302] AS Björkdahl, 'Norm Advocacy: A Small State Strategy to Influence the EU' (2008) 15 [1] Journal of European Public Policy 135–54

[303] C Brokelind, 'Smaller versus Bigger Member States: How Can Their Voices and Goals be Harmoniously Reconciled' in P Pistone (ed), *European Tax Integration: Law, Policy and Politics* (IBFD 2018) 168

are not part of the G20, where important decisions such as BEPS are discussed, and they do not have influence except if they work in a larger environment through cooperation.[304] An example is the Advance Pricing Agreements (APA) in the Netherlands, Luxembourg or Ireland. They could benefit from the support of the US, which considered that the EU decisions could have a wider consequence.[305] Also, the other option for the small Member States to have an influence is to be expert in the field concerned.[306] In any case, in a less institutionalized environment, the voice of a small State is less heard.[307] For instance, it has been demonstrated that the influence of Sweden on the other Member States decreased due to its lack of participation in the Economic and Monetary Union (EMU).[308] Furthermore, it is interesting to note that the same study on Sweden demonstrated that participating in an international organization can weaken domestic influence even if it increases influence on other States.[309] There is a balance to maintain between domestic interests and international interests.

Thus, the consequence for the social legitimacy of the European power to tax in relation to the small Member States' populations should not be neglected, as the Council is a co-legislator in the EU legislative process where the Commission, but not the Parliament, has a right of legislative initiative. On one side, the democratic representation of the people through the Parliament is a decisive aspect of the consent to tax to provide for a European *ethos* (character) but, on the other side, this *ethos* (character) can be undermined in the eyes of the small Member States' populations if their voice is not heard or considered. Therefore, the political balance between the small Member States and the larger ones is especially important in terms of influence for such matter.

6.4 CONCLUSION

It has been explained that the concept of tax sovereignty is not compatible with the concept of sovereignty. The concept of tax sovereignty is a material concept, which is the consequence of the association of the competence to tax and of the power to tax. Therefore, this concept cannot be a concept of sovereignty,

---

304 ibid 169 and 171

305 US Department of the Treasury, 'White Paper on State Aid' [2016]

306 C Brokelind, 'Smaller versus Bigger Member States: How Can Their Voices and Goals be Harmoniously Reconciled' in P Pistone (ed), *European Tax Integration: Law, Policy and Politics* (IBFD 2018) 169

307 ibid 168–70

308 M Jernek, 'Sveriges Inflytande i EU Efter Krisen' [2013] SIEPS series n 10epa

309 ibid

but it designates a tax autonomy. Then, the competence to tax is the power to enact the tax law and the power to tax is the power to levy taxes. These taxing powers must reveal the legitimate application of sovereignty in taxation. They are the concrete manifestation of the concept of sovereignty. However, in the EU, the Member States kept tax autonomy through their own tax policy in the field of direct taxation, while the EU has the objective of achieving the internal market. Direct taxation, especially in the field of business taxation and as demonstrated by the CJEU case law, is not excluded from this objective. The concrete attribution of competences between the EU and the Member States is paradoxical.

The general competences of the EU, being the shared competence of the internal market and the exclusive competence for the competition policy, overlap with the reserved competence of the Member States in the field of direct taxation. In this sense, as the competences of the EU can be only indirect in this field, it is the use of negative integration that was supposed to solve the inadequacies between the two levels. However, the limited effect of the principle of non-discrimination to solve these inadequacies and the limits of State aid rules that must remain in the block of competition rules as being its own legitimate field of application have been demonstrated. Indeed, in the end, through article 26 TFEU, the objective is the functioning of the internal market and it includes fair, so tax neutral, competition. However, the EU treaties are legal instruments and the way they have been written must be respected as it defines the European legal system. In this sense, competences must be limited to their own fields and they can be used in another field only when there are overlaps, which are justified by the attribution of competences as policy choices and the consequence of the general objectives of both the EU and the Member States (in other words, through their sovereignty). This is why, even if used, the concept of tax sovereignty cannot formally exist, and why the demonstration of the EU powers had to begin at its source with the concept of sovereignty. The legitimization of the EU powers (competences, as written in the EU treaties) as governmental outputs is the result of the sovereignty of the EU as defined by its objectives and its own construction, and so as value pattern. Consequently, in terms of legitimacy, there are still inadequacies to solve within the internal market concerning the field of direct taxation and the EU has a right to a shared competence to tax in this field, as negative integration has been deemed insufficient. Indeed, going beyond the technical attribution of competences, tax policies cannot be limited by powers in the sense of the concept of sovereignty. The political power to decide must be attached to political sovereignty and not to the technical attribution of competences. Thus, in its own limits, the shared sovereignty of the EU means also a right to a power to decide in terms of tax policy. Then, the consequence in the field of direct taxation of businesses is that the EU has the legitimacy to get a competence to tax, which will inherently express itself through secondary law.

Concerning the power to tax, the EU must enhance its legal and social legitimacy in order to put in place its very own taxes in the field of direct taxation of businesses, as the fundamental principle of the consent to tax is the democratic basis of such taxing power even if it could already be considered that the EU has a sufficient *ethos* (character) in terms of business taxation. Thus, only the legal requirements of constitutional law would then be required for the EU to have a power to tax in such field. As such, institutionally speaking, a constituent referendum is needed to properly give a power to tax to the EU.[310] The creation of a European tax needs a constitutional basis that would require a treaty modification based on a constituent referendum. Indeed, the consent to tax is a decisive democratic principle within the constitutional State and this principle requires a constitutional basis. For a European tax through a separation system, an action from the constituent sovereign is required in a constitutional democracy.[311] On the other hand, concerning the competence to tax, the legitimacy of the EU to get such taxing power is not directly affected by such a democratic principle. Consequently, a constituent referendum would not be needed to give a competence to tax to the EU and a revision based on the ordinary legislative procedure would be enough (article 48 TFEU). Nevertheless, institutionally, the EU must still embrace the democratic shape of its Member States.[312] It has been seen,[313] with the treaty of Maastricht, that the constitutional referendums of that time gave the EU its institutional

[310] About the constituent referendum, see ch 5, section 5.2

[311] Interestingly, concerning indirect taxes for environmental purposes, it has been previously said that articles 192 paragraph 2 and 194 paragraph 3 TFEU are constitutional bases. Article 192 paragraph 2 TFEU was article 130S paragraph 2 in the treaty of Maastricht and has been approved by constituent referendum. However, article 194 paragraph 3 TFEU did not exist at that time. In this sense, it can be considered that the other theory has been followed: the formal theory. As there was no new referendum that accepted new treaty modification, the formal application of the procedure of revision has been considered sufficient to insert such modification, which does not correspond to the material theory that has been preferred here as a more democratic basis

[312] Here, it is not said that the EU lacks full democratic legitimacy as a whole. It can acquire it through multiple means, depending on what is involved, such as the agreement of the national parliaments. However, with the latter for instance, it is an indirect democratic legitimacy. It is similar with output democratic legitimacy. Here, it is question of an institutional democratic legitimacy of the EU as sovereign legal order, which requires some aspects of direct legitimacy and so direct democratic requirements like a regular constitutional State.

[313] See ch 5, section 5.2.2.2

democratic legitimacy and that consequently, through its democratic material dispositions, the EU can be understood as a constitutional order. However, subsequent treaty modifications must remain in this constitutional framework and the EU, constitutionally speaking, must regulate its actions by considering this aspect.

7. The application of the theory of shared sovereignty in the field of direct taxation of businesses: the European Union's shared competence to tax

7.1 INTRODUCTION

There is a paradox between the current European Union (EU) process of tax integration and its shared sovereignty with the Member States, and so with its legitimate competence to tax. Thus, this chapter will demonstrate the legitimacy of the EU's competence to tax, as being part of its shared competence for the internal market, and its consequences.

Respecting the step-by-step European integration process, it is suggested to limit the European competence to tax to the field of business taxation as being an inherent consequence of the market-based competence of the EU. Also, such competence should find a coherent application within the current agenda of the EU concerning business taxation.

The objective, here, is to demonstrate the current limits of the current context of the EU in terms of positive integration, as has been done with negative integration. Solutions can be found through the concrete application of the theory of shared sovereignty. As such, some treaty solutions are proposed for the EU to apply its legitimate shared competence to tax, before trying to put in place the definitive solution of a treaty revision.

7.2 THE FRUSTRATED LEGITIMACY OF THE EUROPEAN UNION'S COMPETENCE TO TAX BECAUSE OF THE MATERIAL CONCEPT OF TAX SOVEREIGNTY

7.2.1 European Union Objectives and Tax Integration in the Field of Direct Taxation of Businesses

7.2.1.1 Justifying the shared competence to tax of the European Union in the field of direct taxation: about a market-based competence

Before exploring positive integration in the field of direct taxation as the consequence of the notion of competence to tax, the legitimacy of this European competence must be demonstrated. Indeed, negative integration in the field of direct taxation is insufficient to solve the inadequacies between the European objectives and the national tax systems. Also, it has been seen in the precedent chapter that inadequacies in the field of direct taxation, by affecting the achievement of the EU's objectives, demonstrated that this field is in the general field of competence of the EU.

Thus, such inadequacies must be resolved. Concerning the economic dimension of the EU, article 26 of the treaty on the functioning of the European Union (TFEU) is the lead provision, with 'the aim of establishing or ensuring the functioning of the internal market, in accordance with the relevant provisions of the Treaties'.[1] There are two points to highlight from this quote. The first is the objective of achieving (or ensuring by avoiding new distortions) the internal market: the EU is based on objectives. The second is the legal limit of the provisions of the European treaties: to achieve this objective, the legal construction of the Treaties must be respected.

This leads on to a second element. The fundamental freedoms are first quoted, concerning the economic dimension of the European treaties,[2] in paragraph 2 article 26 TFEU. Furthermore, in terms of repartition of competences between the EU and the Member States, they are the application of the shared competence for the internal market in article 4 TFEU.[3] It must also be remembered that competences not attributed to the EU remain with the Member States (article 4 of the treaty on the European Union (TEU)), which is not the case here as there is a shared competence.[4] Shared competence, in general, is

---

[1] TFEU, art 26

[2] P Craig, *The Lisbon Treaty: Law, Politics and Treaty Reform* (revised edn, Oxford University Press 2013) 316

[3] ibid 160

[4] ibid 167

the default position concerning the division of competences that resulted from the Lisbon Treaty.[5] Concerning the fundamental freedoms, in the history of the Lisbon Treaty, the main reason was the will to not preclude a Member State from adopting legislative acts in their field, knowing that such acts could have been acts going in the direction of achieving the internal market.[6] This is why the internal market is a shared competence. Finally, according to article 2 paragraph 6 TFEU, the exercise of its competences by the EU is 'determined by the provisions of the Treaties relating to each area'.[7] It confirms the legal limits according to the Treaties and it confirms that the only aim can be harmonization and not unification. Indeed, the chapter of the TFEU on enacting legislative acts according to article 26 TFEU is named 'approximation of laws'; an appellation that cannot be confused with unification.[8]

These two first elements lead to a third one, which is the limits of the application of the competition rules and so of the State aid rules. There are overlaps between the shared competence of the internal market and the exclusive competence of article 3 paragraph 1 TFEU.[9] Article 3 paragraph 1 b) says 'the establishing of the competition rules necessary for the functioning of the internal market'.[10] The State aid rules, which are legal provisions for the application of this exclusive competence, are part of chapter 1, title VII, part III of the TFEU.[11] This is a different chapter from the general chapter on the approximation of laws (chapter 3) and from the chapter on tax provisions (chapter 2). Furthermore, the latter cannot be confused with chapter 1 as the provisions on indirect taxation apply to Value-Added Tax (VAT), which is a shared competence between the EU and the Member States (while chapter 1 is an exclusive competence). It justifies the application of the State aid rules to its block of competence only (article 3 paragraph 1 TFEU) and so its inherent distinction with the fundamental freedoms. The difficulty here is to determine, when there are overlaps, what can be addressed under article 3 TFEU and what can be addressed under article 4 TFEU.

---

5 ibid

6 ibid 160

7 TFEU, art 6 para 2

8 See eg P Craig, *The Lisbon Treaty: Law, Politics and Treaty Reform* (revised edn, Oxford University Press 2013) 315–18

9 ibid 160: 'The very creation of categories of competence nonetheless inevitably means that there will be problems of demarcating borderlines between the different categories. Such problems can arise in demarcating the line between exclusive and shared competence'

10 TFEU, art 3 para 1, b)

11 P Craig, *The Lisbon Treaty: Law, Politics and Treaty Reform* (revised edn, Oxford University Press 2013) 161

Thus, the consequence of these elements for the field of direct taxation of businesses is that 'the devil is in the details'.[12] The lines between the different competences can be blurred or difficult to draw.[13] Indeed, there are overlaps between the direct competence of the Member States in the field of direct taxation and the two competences of the EU, exclusive or shared, concerning the competition rules and the internal market. It means that the EU is legitimate to act when there is an overlap with the State aid rules in their limits and with the fundamental freedoms in their limits, through negative integration. However, the limits of these provisions also limit a sufficient harmonization in the sense that there are still distortions in contradiction with article 26 TFEU that cannot be eliminated under these provisions. Also, as negative integration has been applied in the field of direct taxation, it means that direct taxation is concerned by article 26 TFEU and impacts the internal market. This field also interacts with competition rules. Consequently, as the rules used for negative integration are not sufficient in order to achieve the EU objectives written within the EU treaties and accepted by the Member States as objectives to attain, here the EU has legitimacy to get a competence to tax and so to act through positive integration in order to fix the inadequacies that cannot be fixed through negative integration. This is a consequence of the sovereignty of the EU. Article 26 TFEU is the sovereign objective that must be achieved in this sense. The competence is the consequence of sovereignty: a sovereign has competences in order to act as a sovereign. Therefore, the EU has sovereign objectives to attain, which come first, through its competences, which come second, within its legal system. However, here too there would be a limit, or a hierarchy: as long as the competence to tax in the field of direct taxation is not explicitly given to the EU and so explicitly written within the European treaties, there would first be a need to apply the current provisions explicitly given in such Treaties before trying to apply palliative provisions that could be used for positive integration. It is only in a second step that a treaty revision should be envisaged. Indeed, this corresponds to the legal limits of sovereignty, which can be inadequate in terms of legitimacy.[14]

---

[12] ibid 188

[13] ibid 160: once again, for the parallel, as the line can be blurred between the own competences of the EU, it can also be blurred between the EU's competences and the Member States' competences.

[14] In a constitutional system, only the constituent power (in the world of facts) is not limited (see ch 5, section 5.2). The constitution is legally self-limited. In this situation, it is the EU treaty provisions. However, it does not mean that there are no inadequacies in terms of legitimacy that must not be solved through revisions for instance.

Finally, this competence to tax of the EU in the field of direct taxation should be legitimate only as a shared competence concerning the internal market and not under the exclusive competence on competition. First, making a parallel, indirect taxation is not an exclusive competence but a shared competence (so it concerns the shared competence for the internal market and not the exclusive competence on competition), and second, the exclusive competence on competition interacts with the field of direct taxation of businesses without targeting it directly.

Then, it must be highlighted why, for now, in the field of direct taxation, the objective must remain harmonization within the field of business taxation. The emphasis must be put on the notion of market-based competence. Indeed, there is a long history with direct taxation from the beginning of the European Communities until today in terms of positive integration. It is a series of mishaps until the first directives of the 1990s and the explosion of the 21st century. Yet, still nowadays, the application of article 115 TFEU for positive integration in the field of direct taxation remains politically sensitive and legally complicated.

Thus, at the beginning of the EU, Georges Vedel, one of the authors of the TFEU, explained on the peculiarities of the harmonization of direct taxation that:

> It was first a question linked to the tax sovereignty of the states. Direct taxation is, more than indirect taxation, an instrument of redistribution and of social intervention. Second, it is certain that tax distortions must be assessed according to the notion of competition and so of cost price. In what measure are the different important direct taxes impacting companies incorporated in the cost price? It is one of the most difficult questions of financial economy and we know that the solution varies depending on the economic structure of each state, following the economic conditions and following the peculiarities of each sector.[15]

Nonetheless, Vedel still insisted on the necessity of a tax fair-play and the elimination of the tax distortions as imperative elements, alongside a will for tax harmonization, to achieve a real internal market.[16] However, in direct taxation, it relied on the good will of the Member States.[17]

Not long after, in 1962, the Neumark Committee[18] also agreed on similar grounds concerning the economic aspect of direct taxation:

---

[15] G Vedel, 'Les Aspects Fiscaux du Marché Commun' (1958) XII Bulletin de Documentation Fiscale Internationale 337–38

[16] ibid 337

[17] ibid 321

[18] *The EEC Reports on Tax Harmonization* (IBFD 1963)

> Rational compromise between the necessity of eliminating or at least strongly reducing, in the interest of optimum functioning of the Common Market, the fiscal or financial disparities hindering the free play of competition between the Member States on the one hand, and the expediency of not interfering in the policy of the Member States anxious to maintain national peculiarities arising from natural conditions and/or historical evolution on the other hand.[19]

Still, the first results were attained only in 1990 with the parent-subsidiary directive,[20] the merger directive[21] and the arbitration convention,[22] which has been decided as a coordination instrument and not as an integration instrument. On this basis, harmonization in the field of direct taxation was concretely able to begin even if it remained bumpy, as a large part of the work has been left to the CJEU through negative integration.

The Code of Conduct was adopted in 1997[23] and the interest-royalty directive in 2003.[24] From the 1990s, with past experience, the Commission progressed step by step and focused on business taxation, similar to what can be observed nowadays.[25] This can be understood as a lesson of the integration process of the EU and so as a first argument for a market-based competence. Indeed, for example, Kofler states:

> In some areas Union action does not seem necessary (for example, with regard to most of personal income taxation) and in others there is a considerable nexus with the functioning of the internal market (for example, VAT and energy taxation); other

19 ibid

20 Council Directive 90/435/EEC on the Common System of Taxation applicable in the case of Parent Companies and Subsidiaries of Different Member States [1990] OJ L 225/6

21 Council Directive 90/434/EEC on the Common System of Taxation applicable to Mergers, Divisions, Transfers of Assets and Exchanges of Shares concerning Companies of Different Member States [1990] OJ L 225/1

22 Convention 90/436/EEC on the Elimination of Double Taxation in Connection with the Adjustment of Profits of Associated Enterprises [1990] OJ L 225/10

23 See Conclusions of the ECOFIN Council Meeting 98/C concerning Taxation Policy [1998] OJ 2/01

24 Council Directive 2003/49/EC on a Common System of Taxation applicable to Interest and Royalty Payments made between Associated Companies of Different Member States [2003] L 157/49

25 See European Commission, 'Commission Work Programme 2026: Europe's Independence Moment' COM (2025) 870 final: the annexes show the numerous proposals from the Commission, the field of direct taxation of businesses not being forgotten.

> areas lie in between those extremes (for example, taxation of business and capital), and a true internal market might require some coordination or harmonization.[26]

Maitrot de la Motte confirms this statement by quoting Teitgen: corporate taxation has a direct influence on the internal market, unlike personal taxation.[27] Both the history of the European integration process through the lesson of the step-by-step approach and these statements on the direct link with the internal market confirm that it must be focused for now on the direct taxation of businesses. These are the arguments for a market-based competence of the EU in the field of direct taxation. The objective of article 26 TFEU and the shared competence for the internal market of article 4 TFEU are both an economic objective and an economic competence. As long as this explicit economic objective for the internal market is not achieved, it is unrealistic to try to achieve further objectives of integration.

Then, this market-based competence must be confirmed and more deeply explained in the light of the recent evolution of positive integration in the field of direct taxation.

7.2.1.2 The current political agenda of the European Union: a dead end to solve tax fragmentation for an enhanced competitive market?

Having assessed the legitimacy of the EU for having competence in the field of direct taxation of businesses, it must be understood how the EU currently tries to attain it. This can be observed through the current political agenda of the EU.

First, the Commission put in place a new project, the 'Business in Europe: Framework for Income Taxation' (BEFIT) project[28] that arose in 2021. The objectives are to enable fair and sustainable growth within the internal market,[29] but also efficient taxation.[30] In order to be attained, these objectives need fair, sustainable and efficient tax frameworks, according to the

---

[26] G Kofler, 'EU Power to Tax: Competences in the Area of Direct Taxation' in CHJI Panayi, W Haslehner, E Traversa (eds) *Research Handbook on European Union Taxation Law* (Edward Elgar Publishing 2020) 13

[27] A Maitrot de la Motte, *Souveraineté Fiscale et Construction Communautaire: Recherche sur les Impôts Directs* (Bibliothèque de Science Financière, tome 44, LGDJ 2005) 311, quoting PH Teitgen, 'Droit Financier et Fiscal Européen' in *Paris: Les Cours de Droit* (1969–1970) 186, where an emphasis is put on the word 'direct'.

[28] European Commission, 'Business Taxation for the 21st Century' COM (2021) 251 final

[29] ibid 2

[30] ibid 3

Commission.[31] Actually, the BEFIT project must be understood as an umbrella providing for different directive proposals that should ensure the achievement of these objectives in order for the EU to be competitive and to fit within the global context of today's international taxation. This project still aspires mainly to the harmonization of the Corporate Income tax (CIT) systems within the internal market, after some unfruitful attempts.[32]

Second, the new political agenda of the EU has been set following the Letta report[33] and the Draghi report.[34] There is an urgent need for the EU to improve its competitivity and to strengthen its internal market to face the current global issues.[35] Tax fragmentation has been identified as one of the issues that must be solved in order to improve the efficiency of the internal market and so to improve the EU's competitivity.[36] This means that the field of direct taxation of businesses needs further harmonization within the internal market. Two elements can be identified from the Draghi report as obstacles in this field:

- 'First, Europe is lacking focus. We articulate common objectives, but we do not back them by setting clear priorities of following up with joined-up policy actions.'[37] According to Draghi, the governance of the EU must be strengthened. The EU's decision-making rules are based on a valid internal logic but there is little coordination across policy areas.[38]
- One of the major obstacles that prevents better coordination within the EU would be the fact that 'multiple veto players can delay or dilute action'.[39] Unanimity voting would be a major obstacle for harmonization and so for competitivity. For Draghi, Treaty changes would be needed, but they are

31 ibid 1

32 See European Commission, 'Proposal for a Council Directive on a Common Consolidated Corporate Tax Base (CCCTB)' COM (2016) 683 final; European Commission, 'Proposal for a Council Directive on a Common Corporate Tax Base' COM (2016) 685 final; European Commission, 'Proposal for a Council Directive on Business in Europe: Framework for Income Taxation (BEFIT)' COM (2023) 532 final

33 E Letta, '"Much More Than a Market" – Speed, Security, Solidarity, Empowering the Single Market to Deliver a Sustainable Future and Prosperity for All EU Citizens' [2024]

34 M Draghi, 'The Future of European Competitiveness' [2024]

35 European Commission, 'A Competitiveness Compass for the EU' (Communication) COM (2025) 30 final, 2

36 European Parliament, 'Draft Report on the Role of Simple Tax Rules and Tax Fragmentation in European Competitiveness' [2024] 2024/2118(INI), para 15

37 M Draghi, 'The Future of European Competitiveness' [2024] pt A, 8

38 ibid pt A, 67

39 ibid

not a precondition for the achievement of the competitivity of the internal market.[40] Before reaching a consensus on Treaty changes, a consensus can be reached on targeted adjustments.[41]

The Commission,[42] the European Council,[43] the Council[44] and the European Parliament[45] all took note of this urge to improve the cohesion of the internal market. In the field of direct taxation of businesses, it means simplification and decluttering. The institutions of the EU, and especially the Commission and the European Parliament, put in place an agenda with several concrete initiatives such as new directive proposals for the upcoming years.[46] Such proposals are supposed to simplify the cross-border application of the tax systems within the internal market, with the objective of improving its competitivity and so strengthening the cohesion between the Member States.

Thus, to attain such objectives, the different communications underline the importance of the people[47] and so of having a democratic backing.[48] As such, the Commission wants to improve the dialogue with the Member States and its people (more specifically the stakeholders here). This means improving the way the rules are made at the EU level. This could be done through a stronger sector focus, impact assessments to reduce the costs related to delegated and

40 ibid

41 ibid

42 European Commission, 'A Simpler and Faster Europe: Communication on Implementation and Simplification' [2024-2029]; European Commission, 'Moving Forward Together: A Bolder, Simpler, Faster Union' (Communication) COM (2025) 45 final

43 European Council, 'Budapest Declaration on the New European Competitiveness Deal' [2024]

44 'Council Conclusions on a Tax Decluttering and Simplification Agenda which Contributes to the EU's Competitiveness' [2025] 6748/25

45 European Parliament, 'Draft Report on the Role of Simple Tax Rules and Tax Fragmentation in European Competitiveness' [2024] 2024/2118(INI)

46 European Commission, 'Commission Work Programme 2026: Europe's Independence Moment' COM (2025) 870 final; European Parliament, 'Draft Report on the Role of Simple Tax Rules and Tax Fragmentation in European Competitiveness' [2024] 2024/2118(INI)

47 European Commission, 'A Competitiveness Compass for the EU' (Communication) COM (2025) 30 final, 22

48 M Draghi, 'Presentation of the Report on the Future of European Competitiveness' [2024] 10

implementing acts and other similar impact assessments in relation to significant amendments and digital innovation.[49]

Such reports and such declarations are welcome. They seem to understand what obstructs the evolution of the EU and the competitiveness of the internal market and of the Member States, from a policy point of view and from a technical point of view. Still, the different proposals that are made and the general agenda that is presented by the EU do not seem to consider the lessons of the history of the EU. First, in the field of direct taxation of businesses, most propositions are technical propositions in the form of directive proposals. There are many of them.[50] Already at the beginning of the European Communities, political discourse and reports insisted on the necessity of harmonization of direct taxation in the internal market without success.[51] There were also too many proposals at that time, drowning the step-by-step approach. Second, the technical requirement of unanimity voting is still seen as one of the major – if not the major – obstacles to harmonization in the internal market.[52] There were political and policy arguments at the beginning of the European Communities for keeping the direct competence to tax in the field of direct taxation with the Member States but the EU has evolved since then and the truth of that time is not the truth of today.[53] The Draghi report and the Letta report underline those aspects of the global change on the international scene. Thus, nowadays, debates on tax policies, and so on the distribution of the competence to tax, should not be limited to a persisting technical requirement. This is why a theory such as the theory of shared sovereignty is needed if the EU wants to overcome such technical obstacles. Policies, and here tax policies, should be based on a logic of system, not on a technical attribution of competences. In the logic of the latter, policies follow competences while competences should follow a policy organization for the coherence and the integrity of the political and legal system.

Thus, before applying the theory of shared sovereignty to the field of direct taxation of businesses in the EU, it must also be concretely analysed why the debate should not be strictly focused on the unanimity voting requirement as

---

49 European Commission, 'A Simpler and Faster Europe: Communication on Implementation and Simplification' [2024-2029] 8-10

50 See European Commission, 'Commission Work Programme 2026: Europe's Independence Moment' COM (2025) 870 final: the annexes show the number of new proposals and withdrawals from the Commission in general, with the field of direct taxation not being forgotten.

51 See in this chapter, section 7.2.1.1

52 M Draghi, 'The Future of European Competitiveness' [2024] pt B, 308

53 See eg the period of the Compromise of Luxembourg (January 1966) where the level of integration what less important and the European institutions different.

enshrined in material dispositions of the EU treaties for positive integration, and especially article 115 TFEU.

7.2.2 The Unsolvable Limits of the Current System to Solve Tax Fragmentation for an Enhanced Competitive Market

7.2.2.1 Positive integration in the field of direct taxation: about Article 115 TFEU

Concretely, article 115 TFEU is the disposition that allows positive tax integration in the EU by enacting directives. As such, it is through article 115 TFEU that the political agenda of the EU can become effective in the field of direct taxation of businesses. However, this article has two conditions which can be seen as limits for the EU to concretely attain its competence to tax. The first is unanimity voting, which can be understood as a veto right for the Member States. The second is that this article should only be used for the approximation of the laws[54] of the Member States to preserve or establish the internal market. Unanimity voting is a requirement dating back from the context of the beginning of the European Communities, and such technical requirement should be overcome by establishing the current context of the EU.[55] The true concern here is about the condition of 'approximation of laws'. Such condition can be understood as being vague and a synonym for the general word, that is, harmonization. However, it asks an important underlying question within the context of the legitimate shared competence to tax between the EU and the Member States under the shared competence for the internal market. This question asks about the legitimate interplay between the EU and the Member States. In other words, concerning a shared competence, in terms of legitimacy, how can it be determined what should depend on the competence of the EU and what should depend on the competence of the Member States? Here is a true policy and technical debate to attribute the underlying fields of competence within the general competence to tax in the field of direct taxation of businesses.

Such concrete issue can be illustrated by the enactment of the first Anti-Tax Avoidance Directive (ATAD)[56] in 2016. This directive is inspired by the

---

[54] This article is in: TFEU, title VII, ch 3. See G Kofler, 'EU Power to Tax: Competences in the Area of Direct Taxation' in CHJI Panayi, W Haslehner and E Traversa (eds) *Research Handbook on European Union Taxation Law* (Edward Elgar Publishing 2020) 21

[55] As the EU is a dynamic order.

[56] Council Directive (EU) 2016/1164 Laying Down Rules Against Tax Avoidance Practices that Directly Affect the Functioning of the Internal Market [2016] OJ L 193/1

Organization for Economic Co-operation and Development's (OECD) work on tax avoidance and base erosion.[57] In the directive, there are different anti-avoidance rules that had to be implemented by the Member States to protect their own tax bases. Thus, what must be emphasized is the criticisms of this directive in terms of EU law, and especially about the European objective of countering tax avoidance that can be understood as going beyond the approximation of laws.

- The first main issue concerns tax avoidance and the definition of abuse. The title of the directive mentions 'tax avoidance practices'[58] and the aim is to tackle aggressive tax planning. According to different scholars, the directive does not respect the concept of abuse as defined by the Court of Justice of the European Union (CJEU) case law.[59] On one side, it provokes an issue of respect of the fundamental freedoms by the directive;[60] on the other side, by not respecting the same definition, it creates inadequacies within EU law itself.[61] Indeed, the literature has highlighted that the Commission followed the OECD developments in order to implement the ATAD and that its concept of 'aggressive tax planning' goes beyond the notion of abuse as defined by the CJEU case law.[62] For the CJEU, there is a subjective criterion that does not exist for the OECD and the Commission.[63] It means that there are some non-artificial arrangements that could be struck by the directive but not under the fundamental freedoms.[64] There is an inadequacy. Furthermore, it has been argued that abuse

---

57 See eg L Cerioni, 'Corporate Tax Harmonization – Stage II' in CHJI Panayi, W Haslehner and E Traversa (eds) *Research Handbook on European Union Taxation Law* (Edward Elgar Publishing 2020) 303

58 Council Directive (EU) 2016/1164 Laying Down Rules Against Tax Avoidance Practices that Directly Affect the Functioning of the Internal Market [2016] OJ L 193/1

59 MC Barreiro Carril, 'Does the Anti-Tax Avoidance Directive Involve a Positive Step towards the Completion of the Internal Market? Some Reflections in the Light of Linking Rules Addressing Hybrid Mismatches' in P Pistone (ed), *European Tax Integration: Law, Policy and Politics* (IBFD 2018) 641

60 ibid

61 ibid 640-641

62 L Cerioni, 'Corporate Tax Harmonization – Stage II' in CHJI Panayi, W Haslehner and E Traversa (eds) *Research Handbook on European Union Taxation Law* (Edward Elgar Publishing 2020) 305

63 ibid

64 MC Barreiro Carril, 'Does the Anti-Tax Avoidance Directive Involve a Positive Step towards the Completion of the Internal Market? Some Reflections

is a justification in the non-discrimination test and not an EU objective.[65] It means that, with this new objective, there would be two contradictory interests: one at the EU level and one at the Member State level.[66] In this regard, it must be emphasized that the objective of countering abuse or tax avoidance is a policy objective that depends more on politics first, and that is then translated into legal means.

- Second, the actual main issue that must be mentioned is the use of article 115 TFEU as the legal basis for the ATAD. Indeed, the objective of article 115 TFEU is the approximation of laws and so, strictly speaking, harmonization. However, the main objective of the ATAD is to counter double non-taxation. The rules that the Member States had to implement have the purpose of avoiding the erosion of the national tax bases. Such rules, under such concept of tax avoidance, can restrict the fundamental freedoms and so the achievement of the single market as they can create barriers for free movements because of this objective.[67] This would not be in line with the notion of harmonization under article 115 TFEU, which is a direct reference to article 26 TFEU and so the fundamental freedoms. It is one of the main limits of the current state of positive integration. Still, in the same vein as the ATAD, Szudoczky notes that, with the *Tobacco Advertising* case law saga,[68] public health measures that restrict the exercise of the fundamental freedoms could still be implemented under a general provision (article 114 TFEU in this case, also in the section on approximation of laws).[69] This would be the expression of public interest objectives that go beyond the economic freedoms.[70]
- Third, another criticism is that tax avoidance practices do not directly affect the functioning of the internal market.[71] According to Barreiro:

---

in the Light of Linking Rules Addressing Hybrid Mismatches' in P Pistone (ed), *European Tax Integration: Law, Policy and Politics* (IBFD 2018) 641

65 ibid

66 ibid 640

67 ibid 633

68 Case C-376/98 *Germany v Council and Parliament (Tobacco Advertising)* [2000] ECR I-08419

69 R Szudoczky, 'The Relationship between Primary, Secondary and National Law' in CHJI Panayi, W Haslehner and E Traversa (eds) *Research Handbook on European Union Taxation Law* (Edward Elgar Publishing 2020) 100

70 ibid

71 MC Barreiro Carril, 'Does the Anti-Tax Avoidance Directive Involve a Positive Step towards the Completion of the Internal Market? Some Reflections in the Light of Linking Rules Addressing Hybrid Mismatches' in P Pistone (ed), *European Tax Integration: Law, Policy and Politics* (IBFD 2018) 641

> 'with the internal market being conceived as a place where taxpayers are entitled to enjoy fundamental freedoms, it seems that tax avoidance practices may affect the way it functions, but in a more indirect way.'[72] This indirect effect seems to be seen in the sense that the ATAD does not avoid double taxation, as the first objective of harmonization, or remove disparities. In contrast, it could create situations of double taxation and so restrictions. The ATAD's objective would not be the primary interest of the internal market under the fundamental freedoms. Furthermore, concerning tax practices it aims at eliminating, the ATAD targets the effects and not the causes of these practices, having only an indirect effect in this situation too for solving issues, and possibly to the detriment of the internal market.[73] For Barreiro, double non-taxation should be countered through a tool other than a directive under article 115 TFEU.[74] Such disposition has its own legal limits and is not just a political tool for the interest of the EU.

Such critics of the ATAD illustrate first the fact that article 115 TFEU remains a legal disposition with conditions. It is not a political tool where, when unanimity is reached, the Commission can do whatever it wants as long as it is through a directive. The real underlying limit is the objective of article 26 TFEU, which delimits the general field of competence of the EU as sovereign. Second, shared sovereignty needs coherence and so a dialogue between the two levels, being the EU level and the Member State level. This is why, when it comes to concretely acting and putting in action a political agenda in the field of direct taxation of businesses, a concrete repartition of competences must be made. Here, this means to attribute underlying fields within the general field of direct taxation of businesses between the EU and the Member States according to the legitimate objective of preserving and achieving the internal market and according to the legitimate individual objectives of the Member States. This aspect depends on the concrete application of the theory of shared sovereignty through the notion of tax policy. However, before deepening into the application of the theory of shared sovereignty, it must be demonstrated through other dispositions of the EU treaties than article 115 TFEU that the unanimity voting requirement should not be considered as a major obstacle for achieving the internal market in the field of direct taxation of businesses. Indeed, unanimity has been obtained for the ATAD and this directive still illustrates potential incoherences between the objectives of article 26 TFEU and article 115 TFEU, as a consequence of the policy objective of the directive.

---

72 ibid 642
73 ibid 647
74 ibid 644

7.2.2.2 The deadlock of unanimity voting in the field of direct taxation of businesses: a consequence of the material concept of tax sovereignty

When it comes to direct taxation in the EU, unanimity voting is often seen as the major obstacle for harmonization to achieve the internal market. This issue is understood as a substantive law[75] and a sovereignty[76] issue because unanimity voting confers a veto right to each Member State, which is a way to retain their sovereignty. Furthermore, under the concept of tax sovereignty, it can be thought that moving to Qualified Majority Voting (QMV) would extend the EU powers, so its field of competence, and can pose democratic issues.[77] In this sense, there is a working document of the European Parliament on overcoming the deadlock of unanimity voting from 2021[78] that follows previous propositions from the Commission.[79] It recommends different ways to overcome unanimity issues for the internal market. The main ideas are, first, to use enhanced cooperation and the passerelle clause of article 48(7) TEU and, second, to amend the EU Treaties.[80] Democratically, issues would be mainly linked to the role of the national Parliaments when it comes to deciding on the taxes to put in place ('no taxation without representation').[81] Thus, the European Parliament, in order to switch to QMV, argues for democratic

---

[75] A Maitrot de la Motte, *Souveraineté Fiscale et Construction Communautaire: Recherche sur les Impôts Directs* (Bibliothèque de Science Financière, tome 44, LGDJ 2005) 316–20

[76] ibid 316

[77] See AP Dourado, 'The Commission Proposal to Replace Unanimity with a Qualified Majority in the Case of Tax Matters' (2019) 47 [4] Intertax 341–44

[78] European Parliament, 'Working Document on Overcoming the Deadlock of Unanimity Voting' [2021] Committee on Constitutional Affairs <www.europarl.europa.eu/cmsdata/233740/AFCO%20Working%20Document%20on%20Overcoming%20the%20Deadlock%20of%20Unanimity%20Voting.pdf> accessed 25 November 2025

[79] See European Commission, 'Towards a more Efficient and Democratic Decision Making in EU Tax Policy' COM (2019) 8 final

[80] European Parliament, 'Working Document on Overcoming the Deadlock of Unanimity Voting' [2021] Committee on Constitutional Affairs, 5 <www.europarl.europa.eu/cmsdata/233740/AFCO%20Working%20Document%20on%20Overcoming%20the%20Deadlock%20of%20Unanimity%20Voting.pdf> accessed 25 November 2025

[81] On such democratic issue, see ch 6, section 6.3

accountability at the EU level according to the notion of consensus as, politically, even when QMV is in place in a field of competence, a consensus is often observed.[82]

Yet, in the light of the concept of sovereignty, it must be proven that the EU has the legitimacy to use QMV in tax matters and so to use article 48(7) TEU without regard to the other solutions proposed by the European Parliament. Similar to what Maitrot de la Motte[83] says but with slightly different argumentation, switching to QMV is only a question of procedure and would not change the EU competences or provoke further democratic issues. Indeed, the main issue is that the Member States have a veto right, which can be understood as a way to retain sovereignty. However, the Member States do not have this legitimacy to have this veto right as long as the field concerned is a European competence and so depends on the sovereignty of the EU, giving to it the power to decide in terms of tax policy. In this sense, it is legitimate to use QMV in the tax field when the market-based competence of the EU applies. This competence remains limited by the general limits of the general competences of the EU (the shared competence for the internal market). Furthermore, there is no democratic issue at this level because the competence to tax (right to enact the tax law) of the EU is limited by its general competence (for the internal market) and because the EU does not have a right to a power to tax (right to levy taxes). As such, applying QMV in EU's fields of competence, even in the tax field, is only legitimate and should rightly be applied. Nonetheless, there is a prior requirement of unanimity voting even for the application of article 48(7) TEU and so for the application of QMV in a specific field of competence.[84] The political and policy issue remains. It is similar to article 115 TFEU. This article remains substantially limited by its wording depending on its interpretation but, procedurally, there is a political deadlock due to the understanding of the initial attribution of competences between the EU and the Member States. A solution should be found not by answering how to overcome unanimity voting but by answering how legitimate fields of competence should be attributed between the EU and the Member States for the functioning of the internal market to the benefit of both levels.

---

[82] European Parliament, 'Working Document on Overcoming the Deadlock of Unanimity Voting' [2021] Committee on Constitutional Affairs, 2 <www.europarl.europa.eu/cmsdata/233740/AFCO%20Working%20Document%20on%20Overcoming%20the%20Deadlock%20of%20Unanimity%20Voting.pdf> accessed 25 November 2025

[83] A Maitrot de la Motte, *Souveraineté Fiscale et Construction Communautaire: Recherche sur les Impôts Directs* (Bibliothèque de Science Financière, tome 44, LGDJ 2005) 316–20

[84] See TEU, art 48 para 7

On the facts, the use of article 48(7) TEU as a palliative for the impossible use of article 115 TFEU in tax matters can be compared to a potential application of article 352 TFEU. Known as the flexibility clause, article 352 TFEU allows the EU to exercise a competence which is not one of its own. To do that, this exercise must be necessary in order to attain an EU objective. Furthermore, it must not extend the EU's powers beyond those contained in the Treaties and there must not be any already existing provision to apply this competence. As such, the EU's competence to tax in the field of direct taxation of businesses has been proved as necessary and as having legitimacy (as being in its field of competence) for the EU to attain its objectives. In addition, none of the current treaty provisions which are currently used are perfectly adequate, as has also been demonstrated. In this sense, the flexibility clause could be used for the EU to exercise its competence to tax in the field of direct taxation of businesses. However, similar to article 115 TFEU and article 48(7) TEU, unanimity voting is required. Thus, the current European context demonstrates the political importance and the political weight of the voice of the Member States on some aspects of the EU's competences and objectives, through the inflated importance of unanimity voting. This is why demonstrating the sovereignty of the EU and its legitimacy in terms of competence in such a field is necessary, from a legal point of view, to change the political position as being a question of institutional coherence and so of coherence of the system, involving as such a need for a policy coherence.

Thus, coming back to the solutions proposed by the European Parliament, it must also be underlined that enhanced cooperation should not be understood as a solution as it would not include the entire internal market;[85] it would still create inadequacies. It is the same with the idea of the political compact also evoked at the end of the working paper of the European Parliament on the matter,[86] even if the latter still deserves mention in relation to the application of the theory of shared sovereignty and so the need for a policy consensus. Finally, treaty amendment, in the light of the legitimacy of the EU's powers, should be understood as the very last solution.

---

[85] For a similar opinion, see R de La Feria, 'Pillar 2, Fiat, and the EU Unanimity Rule on Tax Matters' (2023) [1] EC Tax Review 7

[86] European Parliament, 'Working Document on Overcoming the Deadlock of Unanimity Voting' [2021] Committee on Constitutional Affairs, 12 <www.europarl.europa.eu/cmsdata/233740/AFCO%20Working%20Document%20on%20Overcoming%20the%20Deadlock%20of%20Unanimity%20Voting.pdf> accessed 25 November 2025

7.3 THE APPLICATION OF THE THEORY OF SHARED SOVEREIGNTY FOR A CONCRETE APPLICATION OF THE LEGITIMATE EUROPEAN UNION COMPETENCE TO TAX

7.3.1 The Application of the Theory of Shared Sovereignty to Unlock Tax Fragmentation

7.3.1.1 More than a political consensus, a policy consensus

Through the theory of shared sovereignty between the EU and the Member States, the attribution of competences between the EU and the Member States must be understood as being the last rung of the organization of the system that encompasses both levels. There is a logic of system where the EU has been created in order to have a common market for the Member States. Under this logic, the EU must get the necessary competences in order to achieve its sovereign objective, which is expressed in article 26 TFEU. Yet, as demonstrated, the EU cannot currently apply the necessary competences to attain its sovereign objective in the field of direct taxation of businesses. There is a strong political opposition from the Member States that is legally translated into the use of the veto right through article 115 TFEU. Thus, in the logic of system under the theory of shared sovereignty, tax policy must be separated, as far as possible, from politics. The technical competence does not define the policy and politics should be integrated in the logic of system that encompasses both the EU and the Member States for their common purpose of having an internal market integrated within the individual systems of each Member State. As such, as the tax policy must depend on sovereign objectives, which are dynamic in the context of the EU, and not on long-established competences, which can become technical jails by not following the evolution of the EU, the question that needs an answer is not how to get a political consensus but how to get a policy consensus. Here, what is important is to determine, in terms of legitimacy, which elements within the (shared) competence to tax must depend on the (shared) sovereignty of the Member States and which elements are crucial for the functioning of the internal market, and so which elements should depend on the (shared) sovereignty of the EU, under the logic of the system that encompasses both the EU and the Member States.

Therefore, it must first be observed what currently exists to get such a tax policy consensus at the EU level in the field of direct taxation of businesses. Political consensus is almost always sought in the decision-making process of the EU as indicated by the European Parliament,[87] even when it comes

[87] ibid 2

to QMV. Indeed, cohesion remains important, partly because of unanimity voting in some areas but mainly because of the logic of system of the EU as a common project. Still, not all the Member States have the same weight and small Member States can have different priorities than bigger Member States.[88] Consensus in the EU is a challenge. The main indication of this aspect is the proliferation of intermediate bodies for all the kinds of competences of the EU. According to Del Federico, intermediate bodies are 'stakeholders that are different from the EU and Member States' political institutions, located between the citizens and the institutions, such as the European Economic and Social Committee (EESC), the expert groups, the working groups with independent experts, the lobbies, etc'.[89] The view taken here is that these informal bodies, having only soft power through their opinions (soft law), are widely used within the EU decision-making process in order to reach political consensus and reconcile the Member States' views with the European view for the moment of the vote (the moment of the hard decision). For instance, the European Economic and Social Committee (EESC) self-declared as being 'a bridge between Europe and organized civil society'.[90] Such declaration seems to address the democratic gap between the EU and the European citizens but, consequently, also concerns the gaps that can exist between the EU institutions and the Member States' representatives. Still, as said by Advocate General Kokott on the VAT Committee, if such bodies can be an important 'aid to interpretation',[91] their role 'should not, however, be overestimated'.[92]

In the field of business taxation, the main instrument and the main body of such kind are the Code of Conduct and the Code of Conduct Group.[93] The Code has been created in 1997 and it is not a legally binding instrument.[94] It has only political force and it is an intergovernmental instrument. Its goal is 'primarily

---

[88] See C O'Brien, 'Smaller versus Bigger Member States: Applying the Political Science Research in the Tax Agenda' in P Pistone (ed), *European Tax Integration: Law, Policy and Politics* (IBFD 2018) 194

[89] L Del Federico, 'Monitoring Decision-Making, Enforcement and Application of EU Tax Law: The Role of Intermediate Bodies and Lobbies' in P Pistone (ed), *European Tax Integration: Law, Policy and Politics* (IBFD 2018) 195

[90] The EESC: A Bridge between European and Organized Civil Society [2003]

[91] Case C-155/12 *Minister Finansow v RR Donnelley Global Turnkey Solutions Poland Sp. Zoo* [2013] ECLI:EU:C:2013:434, Opinion of AG Kokott, para 50

[92] ibid

[93] Conclusions of the ECOFIN Council Meeting 98/C concerning Taxation Policy [1998] OJ 2/01

[94] See L Del Federico, 'Monitoring Decision-Making, Enforcement and Application of EU Tax Law: The Role of Intermediate Bodies and Lobbies' in P Pistone (ed), *European Tax Integration: Law, Policy and Politics* (IBFD 2018) 196

to identify and assess preferential tax measures (i.e. measures that provide for a lower level of taxation than the level which is applicable in general) that are possibly harmful'.[95] The Code restrains the introduction of harmful tax measures (standstill) and helps to amend already existing harmful domestic provisions (rollback).[96] Moreover, the Code was revised on 8 November 2022 in order to broaden its field of application.[97] Now, it is not only about preferential tax measures but also about tax features of general application.[98] The Code became an instrument 'which promotes fair tax competition',[99] which targets also 'opportunities for double non-taxation or that can lead to the double or multiple use of tax benefits'.[100] Then, generally speaking, the application of the Code can be considered as successful[101] even if limited as being a soft law instrument. Nonetheless, the Member States seem to respect the work of the Code of Conduct Group, which must analyse which measures are harmful to the internal market.

Thus, for the application of the Code, there is a general gateway criterion, which is whether the measure affects or potentially affects the place of business activities concerned by the Code.[102] Then, for preferential tax measures, in addition to a specific second gateway criterion which is an 'effective level of taxation significantly lower than the general level of taxation',[103] there are four criteria:

---

95 See European Union, 'Code of Conduct Group (Business Taxation)' <www .consilium.europa.eu/en/council-eu/preparatory-bodies/code-conduct-group/> accessed 25 November 2025

96 L Del Federico, 'Monitoring Decision-Making, Enforcement and Application of EU Tax Law: The Role of Intermediate Bodies and Lobbies' in P Pistone (ed), *European Tax Integration: Law, Policy and Politics* (IBFD 2018) 196

97 'Council Conclusions on the Reform of the Code of Conduct for Business Taxation' [2022] 14452/22

98 ibid 2

99 See European Union, 'Code of Conduct Group (Business Taxation)' <www .consilium.europa.eu/en/council-eu/preparatory-bodies/code-conduct-group/> accessed 25 November 2025. Thus, in the internal market, tax competition is understood as a legitimate aim, which requires harmonization but not unification.

100 'Council Conclusions on the Reform of the Code of Conduct for Business Taxation' [2022] 14452/22, 6

101 M Nouwen, 'The Market Distortion Provisions of Articles 116–117 TFEU: an Alternative Route to Qualified Majority Voting in Tax Matters?' (2021) 49 [1] Intertax 26

102 See European Union, 'Code of Conduct Group (Business Taxation)' <www .consilium.europa.eu/en/council-eu/preparatory-bodies/code-conduct-group/> accessed 25 November 2025

103 ibid

- Are the advantages 'ring-fenced' from the domestic market? Are they for example granted only to non-residents or for transactions with non-residents, or do they leave the national tax base unaffected?
- Are the advantages granted even without any real economic activity and substantial economic presence within the member state offering these tax advantages?
- Do the rules for determining profits of multinational groups deviate from internationally accepted principles, in particular the rules agreed within the OECD?
- Do the tax measures lack transparency? This could mean situations where legal provisions are relaxed at administrative level in a non-transparent way.[104]

Similarly, for the tax features of general application, there is a specific second gateway criterion, which is that the measure must 'lead to a lower tax liability than the nominal tax rate (or no tax liability at all), or to deferred taxation as a feature of a distribution tax system'.[105] Then, there are two connected criteria:

- Does the tax feature of general application lead to double non-taxation or does it allow the double or multiple use of tax benefits in connection with the same expenses, amount of income or chain of transactions, because it is not accompanied by appropriate anti-abuse provisions or other adequate safeguards?
- Does this affect in a significant way the place of business activity in the Union?[106]

On a political basis, the Code can help to eliminate market distortions similarly to State aid rules, fundamental freedoms or already existing tax directives as a useful complement. However, by targeting specific measures, it does not seem to be helpful to implement harmonized tax measures in the entire internal market to eradicate generic market distortions. Such generic distortions are the distortions that would need to fall under the EU's competence to tax in order to achieve its sovereign objectives. In a logic of system, coherence, and so harmonization in this context, needs general measures of general application that anticipate the organization of the system and not specific measures that react to already existing distortions. It is the idea of policy here. The EU's power to decide in the field of direct taxation of businesses needs to

---

104 ibid

105 ibid

106 ibid

be sufficiently efficient and stable to sustain its legal system. Parallel to this, it is also only through such sustainability of its power to decide and so through the enactment of general measures that the EU can improve its social legitimacy towards the taxpayer-citizen.[107] Similarly, a tax policy dialogue beyond politics between the EU and the Member States may be utopian but, imposed by the logic of system under the theory of shared sovereignty, would improve competitivity at both levels by solving tax fragmentation. In this sense, it must be remembered that there is unity between the EU and the Member States. Opposition against one level is opposition against oneself. Thus, to get such a coherence between the two levels, clarity is necessary. To help to reach it, the Code of Conduct Group, as a place that reached a political consensus between the Member States, could be the place to propose technical answers to the question of which elements within the competence to tax must depend on the Member States or on the EU to get the tax policy consensus. In terms of legitimacy, the EU should be able to primarily legislate in the fields that are directly linked to the internal market while other fields should be within the competence of the Member States. The fields that are directly linked to the internal market concern the general border of the EU that encompasses and concerns all of the Member States, and the internal borders between the Member States. The general border is more a question of customs, even if aspects such as competitivity of the whole internal market to attract external investments from third countries are also European concerns impacted by direct taxation. Still, in the field of direct taxation of businesses, it is distortions linked to internal borders that need to be eliminated first so that the Member States can speak with one voice in this matter. Here, experts within the Code of Conduct Group could determine what level of harmonization is needed to eliminate distortions. Such determination must derive from the sphere of competences of each level under the theory of shared sovereignty. Here, the policy consensus must not be the result of negotiations, like a political consensus, but the result of the technical understanding of the logic of system between the EU and the Member States in the field of direct taxation of businesses. Once such technical fields are legitimately defined, the policy consensus should impose itself as the logical consequence of the theory of shared sovereignty. Then, the dialogue between the EU and the Member States serves to keep the coherence under the logic of system and to realign the attribution of powers (the power to decide and the exercise of the competence to tax) when needed and due to the dynamic evolution of the EU.

Finally, a word must be said on the notion of political compact. It has been evoked in the European Parliament working paper as an aggressive way to

107 On social legitimacy and the taxpayer-citizen, see ch 6, section 6.3.1.2

overcome the deadlock of unanimity voting within the EU; 'political compact' being the term used for this procedure.[108] Actually, there is already a study on this solution from the European Parliament from 2020 in order to improve European integration.[109] In this study, the political compact is envisaged as a real possibility.[110] It is an international agreement that would be functionally and institutionally connected to the EU.[111] Its role would be to overcome the current issues of governance in the EU and especially unanimity voting in some areas.[112] Such kind of agreement was already adopted during the euro crisis, creating the European Monetary Union (EMU).[113] However, this time, the international agreement would concern the system of governance of the EU and, 'at the substantive level, the Political Compact could increase the EU powers and enforcement mechanisms'.[114] New competences could be given by the participating Member States to the EU[115] and the report includes 'the power to introduce direct taxes, which are crucial for a fiscal capacity'.[116] This agreement would be adopted by a super-majority and would be non-binding for non-ratifying Member States.[117] However, the pressuring effect on these non-ratifying Member States for a more integrated effect should not be neglected.[118] It could force these Member States to join but it could also end in a new Brexit for some of them. According to this last solution for overcoming the deadlock of unanimity voting, the EU is, crucially, at a crossroads. A policy consensus seems to be a better solution than political pressure and consent through politics. Still, for the EU to get a policy consensus, legitimacy must be respected down to the last detail, meaning when the competence to tax is exercised by the EU in its underlying legitimate fields of competence.

---

108 European Parliament, 'Working Document on Overcoming the Deadlock of Unanimity Voting' [2021] Committee on Constitutional Affairs, 12 <www.europarl.europa.eu/cmsdata/233740/AFCO%20Working%20Document%20on%20Overcoming%20the%20Deadlock%20of%20Unanimity%20Voting.pdf> accessed 25 November 2025: 'a solution of last resort' if 'political will is exhausted'.

109 European Parliament, 'Possible Avenues for Further Political Integration in Europe – A Political Compact for a More Democratic and Effective Union?' [2020]

110 See ibid

111 ibid 40

112 ibid 39

113 ibid

114 ibid 40

115 ibid

116 ibid

117 ibid 41

118 ibid 42

7.3.1.2 A policy consensus for a fair and legitimate application of the competences to tax between the EU and the Member States

It has been established that the EU must get its legitimate shared competence to tax in the field of direct taxation of businesses. However, in terms of legitimacy, the EU cannot attract such competence by indirect means and without respecting the policy dialogue, and so the coherence of the logic of the system between the EU and the Member States. This concern has already been clearly expressed by some Member States, for example when the EU proposed a regulation on an emergency intervention to address high energy prices on the basis of article 122 TFEU.[119] This emergency article gave the EU the possibility to put in place a windfall profit tax on the energy sector, avoiding unanimity voting. The required qualified majority was reached, even if the Slovakian and Polish delegations voted against.[120] Estonia said: 'in relation to future tax matters, Estonia continues to insist on the proper legal basis (Article 115 of the Treaty on the Functioning of the European Union) and the requirement of unanimity it prescribes.'[121] And Hungary said also: 'the Hungarian delegation expresses its reservation on the choice of the legal basis of this Regulation, as article 122 of the TFEU cannot be the sole legal basis for the solidarity contribution, which includes provisions of a fiscal nature, that should be discussed and adopted accordingly with unanimity.'[122] Only two Member States voted against the regulation but other countries also indicated their doubts about the use of this TFEU provision in order to adopt a tax measure.

In the current state of play, some other examples can be given:

- Concerning the ATAD, as one of its effects can be the creation of restrictions, it can be doubtful whether it was appropriate to implement such measures at the EU level or whether another approach should have been taken;[123]
- Concerning the Pillar 2 directive,[124] it has been enacted following the OECD's work on Pillar 2 in order to ensure a global minimum level of

---

119 Council Regulation (EU) 2022/1854 on an Emergency Intervention to Address High Energy Prices [2022] OJ LI 261/1, art 14-18

120 European Council, 'Proposal for a Council Regulation on an Emergency Intervention to Address High Energy Prices' (Communication) [2022] CM 4715/22, 1

121 ibid 3

122 ibid 6

123 See in this chapter, section 7.2.2.1

124 Council Directive (EU) 2022/2523 on Ensuring a Global Minimum Level of Taxation for Multinational Enterprise Groups and Large-Scale Domestic Groups in the Union [2022] OJ L 328/1

taxation of 15 per cent in a majority of jurisdictions (members of the Inclusive Framework).[125] The United States (US) finally decided not to implement Pillar 2.[126] This will impact the level playing field between the jurisdictions that are implementing Pillar 2. As such, if the best decision to preserve the competitivity of the EU is to give up on Pillar 2, the EU must act in order to preserve its objectives to the interest of the Member States. It means that the EU must not retain in force the Pillar 2 directive because it can act on a harmonized level of direct taxation within the Member States, and so have a power of decision in terms of tax policy, through such directive. Attracting a power of decision in terms of tax policy in the field of direct taxation of businesses in this way, via a political consensus first reached at the OECD level and not at the EU level, so not initially through a policy dialogue within the EU and according to the sovereign objectives of the EU, could damage the legitimacy of the EU's competence to tax from the Member States' point of view.

- Concerning the UN Framework Convention on International Tax Coordination,[127] there are discussions at the UN in order to propose, among other things,[128] a new Model Convention that would bring more equality between the source country and the residence country. The EU and the Member States are both participating in the discussions.[129] Thus, the UN Framework Convention concerns a broad range of topics that should impact the relations between the Member States and third countries and even the relations between the Member States. As such, here, the policy

---

[125] See Organization for Economic Co-operation and Development, 'Global Anti-Base Erosion Model Rules (Pillar Two)' <www.oecd.org/en/topics/sub-issues/global-minimum-tax/global-anti-base-erosion-model-rules-pillar-two.html> accessed 25 November 2025

[126] White House, 'Global Tax Deal' [2025] <www.whitehouse.gov/presidential-actions/2025/01/the-organization-for-economic-co-operation-and-development-oecd-global-tax-deal-global-tax-deal/> accessed 25 November 2025

[127] See B Obuoforibo, 'Negotiating the UN Framework Convention – What Next for the European Union?' [2025] IBFD <www.ibfd.org/sites/default/files/2025-03/Negotiating%20the%20UN%20Framework%20Convention.pdf> accessed 25 November 2025; X Garcia, 'UN Framework Convention: An Update from the European Perspective' [2025] IBFD <www.ibfd.org/sites/default/files/2025-09/un-framework-convention-an-update-from-the-european-perspective.pdf> accessed 25 November 2025

[128] ibid

[129] See B Obuoforibo, 'Negotiating the UN Framework Convention – What Next for the European Union?' [2025] IBFD <www.ibfd.org/sites/default/files/2025-03/Negotiating%20the%20UN%20Framework%20Convention.pdf> accessed 25 November 2025

dialogue is especially important between the EU and the Member States, so they can speak with one voice for the competitivity of both levels. A balance between individual and general interests should be found between the Member States. This is where the necessity to define which technical aspects of the competence to tax for the field of direct taxation of businesses must depend on the EU or on the Member States arises.

- Also, concerning the Corporate Resource for Europe (CORE) proposal, it is already established that, for the moment, the EU does not have a power to tax.[130]

On the other side, the Member States must also respect policy dialogue within the logic of system. An example is gold-plating in EU law, where the Member States do not limit themselves to the minimum requirements of a directive when they transpose it.[131] By going beyond such minimal requirements for harmonization within the internal market, they can create unexpected outcomes which could result in new restrictions within the EU.[132] The result would be contrary to the initial objective of the directive.

Thus, for a fair and legitimate application of the theory of shared sovereignty within the EU in order to improve the relations between both levels and so the competitivity of the internal market and of the individual Member States, it is important to respect a principle of coherence in terms of policy (through the policy dialogue, and by respecting a principle of legitimate expectations, for example) as well as in terms of legality (by respecting the scope of treaty dispositions). Therefore, some possibilities in EU law are proposed to reestablish the coherence between the sovereignty of the EU and its right to a shared competence to tax.

130 European Commission, 'Proposal for a Council Decision on the System of Own Resources of the European Union and Repealing Decision (EU, Euratom) 2020/2053' COM (2025) 574 final 2

131 M Draghi, 'The Future of European Competitiveness' [2024] pt B, 320

132 ibid

7.3.2 Finding a Treaty Solution

7.3.2.1 The Use of Article 116 TFEU in the field of direct taxation of businesses: about an interpretation under the application of the principle of proportionality

Article 116 TFEU (coupled with article 117 TFEU) is a passerelle clause that could be envisaged to overcome the unanimity deadlock. This possibility is a recurrent topic at the EU level.[133]

Article 116 TFEU is in the same legal block as articles 114 and 115 TFEU. It is considered as a lex specialis with respect to the other two.[134] To date, even if procedures were engaged at the beginning of the Communities, it has never been applied.[135] The purpose of this article is to address distortions of competition resulting from existing differences between national legislation.[136] Article 117 TFEU, on its side, targets future possible distortions that a Member State could put in place.[137] It is of less importance here as article 117 TFEU acts in a similar manner to the State aid rules through a consultation procedure on specific distortions, while article 116 TFEU brings a real possibility of positive integration across the entire single market. Article 116 TFEU applies to a specific kind of distortion which is initially different from the distortions targeted by State aid rules. Thus, according to Englisch, State aid rules keep primarily their field of application (industry-tax benefits would be a selective State aid and so article 108 TFEU would apply).[138]

Article 116 TFEU provides for a two-step procedure. First, there is a consultation of the Member States by the Commission, according to which there could be a distortion of competition by the application of their domestic laws,

---

[133] See eg M Nouwen, 'The Market Distortion Provisions of Articles 116–117 TFEU: an Alternative Route to Qualified Majority Voting in Tax Matters?' (2021) 49 [1] Intertax 14

[134] M Nouwen, 'The Market Distortion Provisions of Articles 116–117 TFEU: an Alternative Route to Qualified Majority Voting in Tax Matters?' (2021) 49 [1] Intertax 15

[135] M Kellerbauer, 'Commentary on Article 116 TFEU' in M Kellerbauer, M Klamert and J Tomkin (eds), *The EU Treaties and the Charter of Fundamental Rights: A Commentary* (Oxford University Press 2019) 1258; M Nouwen, 'The Market Distortion Provisions of Articles 116–117 TFEU: an Alternative Route to Qualified Majority Voting in Tax Matters?' (2021) 49 [1] Intertax s 4

[136] M Kellerbauer, 'Commentary on Article 116 TFEU' in M Kellerbauer, M Klamert and J Tomkin (eds), *The EU Treaties and the Charter of Fundamental Rights: A Commentary* (Oxford University Press 2019) 1258

[137] ibid 1259

[138] J Englisch, 'Article 116 TFEU – The Nuclear Option for Qualified Majority Tax Harmonization?' (2020) [2] EC Tax Review 61

regulations or administrative provisions.[139] Second, if the consultation does not give anything, a directive can be adopted following the ordinary legislative procedure (QMV) in order to eradicate the distortion.[140] However, this provision has never been applied.[141] It is 'among the most obscure of the Treaty, because neither their subject matter nor possible courses of action by institutions are clearly defined'.[142] Furthermore, the use of the legal basis must take into account the other possible legal bases that can contain the Treaties.

Thus, the conditions to apply the article are a difference between the Member States' legislations,[143] which can be understood as a disparity, and a distortion of competition,[144] so a harmful disparity. The latter has been interpreted restrictively by the Commission[145] and, according to Kellerbauer, article 116 TFEU can be used only for specific distortions[146] that occur where:

- an industry or part of an industry bears an additional burden – or enjoys an extra advantage – as compared with the burden carried by the remainder of the economy of the state to which it belongs; or
- no similar burden or advantage occurs in a similar industry or part of an industry in one or more of the other Member States.[147]

However, even if according to some scholars, such as Kellenbauer, such definition cannot include the tax field,[148] the Commission defined these specific

---

139 M Kellerbauer, 'Commentary on Article 116 TFEU' in M Kellerbauer, M Klamert and J Tomkin (eds), *The EU Treaties and the Charter of Fundamental Rights: A Commentary* (Oxford University Press 2019) 1259

140 ibid 1260

141 ibid 1258

142 P Pescatore, 'Public and Private Aspects of European Community Competition Law' (1986) 10 [1] Fordham International Law Journal 402

143 M Kellerbauer, 'Commentary on Article 116 TFEU' in M Kellerbauer, M Klamert and J Tomkin (eds), *The EU Treaties and the Charter of Fundamental Rights: A Commentary* (Oxford University Press 2019) 1259

144 ibid

145 ibid

146 ibid

147 European Commission, 'Supplementary Answer Given in Response to Written Question N 2226/80 by Mr. Hemmo Muntingh' [1983] OJ C257/1; see M Kellerbauer, 'Commentary on Article 116 TFEU' in M Kellerbauer, M Klamert and J Tomkin (eds), *The EU Treaties and the Charter of Fundamental Rights: A Commentary* (Oxford University Press 2019) 1259

148 In his own words: 'In contrast, in order to address distortions of competition resulting from an unequal burden to which national economies are exposed, e.g. due to a higher level of taxation or consumer protection, Articles 114 and 115

distortions before the new challenges of the 21st century and before the wide application of primary EU law to tax matters. The CJEU itself considered that article 116 TFEU is not limited to specific policy areas.[149] In consequence, Englisch and de la Feria both consider that the tax field could be concerned.[150]

Thus, to understand whether article 116 TFEU could be used in tax matters, the notion of market distortion as it is understood nowadays must be analysed. Considering the restrictive approach initiated by the Commission and knowing that article 116 TFEU is the lex specialis of article 115 TFEU, but also of article 114 TFEU, which does not require unanimity voting, the qualification of this provision by Englisch as a 'nuclear option'[151] seems right in the sense that the wording 'needs to be eliminated' in article 116 TFEU goes further than a general approximation of laws and so a general harmonization. Article 116 TFEU must not be a way to purely circumvent article 115 TFEU but whether it could be proportionally applied when it is possible and, even more, required must be analysed.

For Nouwen, the activation of this 'safety valve' requires more than a mere de minimis distortion of competition.[152] He underlines the fact that State aid rules and free movement rights already target distortions of competition.[153] In these cases, article 116 TFEU would not be needed and there would be a priority of application of these rules.[154] It is understandable as article 116 TFEU must remain a lex specialis of article 115 TFEU and so in its scope of application as a subsidiary measure. Consequently, to understand which kind of distortion could be within the scope of this article, Nouwen makes a distinction between the different kinds of distortions:

TFEU are the pertinent legal bases': M Kellerbauer, 'Commentary on Article 116 TFEU' in M Kellerbauer, M Klamert and J Tomkin (eds), *The EU Treaties and the Charter of Fundamental Rights: A Commentary* (Oxford University Press 2019) 1259

149 C-174/02 *Streekgewest* [2005] ECR I-00085, para 24

150 J Englisch, 'Article 116 TFEU – The Nuclear Option for Qualified Majority Tax Harmonization?' (2020) [2] EC Tax Review 58; R de La Feria, 'Pillar 2, Fiat, and the EU Unanimity Rule on Tax Matters' (2023) [1] EC Tax Review 7

151 J Englisch, 'Article 116 TFEU – The Nuclear Option for Qualified Majority Tax Harmonization?' (2020) [2] EC Tax Review 58-61

152 M Nouwen, 'The Market Distortion Provisions of Articles 116–117 TFEU: an Alternative Route to Qualified Majority Voting in Tax Matters?' (2021) 49 [1] Intertax 17

153 ibid

154 ibid

- *Global* distortions occur at macro level and manifest themselves, for example, in high labour costs and prices, leading to a structural current account deficit and rising unemployment, [...]
- *Generic* distortions occur at intermediate or sectoral level, mostly traceable to disparities in (systems of) legislation, [...]
- *Specific* market distortions may occur in specific parts of industry or in specific regions.[155]

In light of this distinction, at the beginning of the EU, the Commission restricted the application of article 116 TFEU to specific market distortions. For Englisch and Nouwen, the internal derogation criterion should be abandoned as it corresponds to unlawful State aid that should be addressed under article 107 TFEU, knowing that tax disparities fall outside the scope of the latter.[156] Furthermore, they underline that the Commission actually makes a distinction only between global and specific distortions.[157] Consequently, several scholars[158] argue that the Commission should reform its appreciation in order to include generic distortions within the scope of article 116 TFEU so it can target 'generic national measures affecting sectorally, regionally or categorically certain groups of companies'.[159] In the same direction, the CJEU, as early as 1974 and giving very little weight to the Spaak Report which initiated the Commission's criteria on market distortion for article 116 TFEU,[160] said: 'moreover, Article 92 to 102 of the Treaty provide for detailed rules for the abolition of generic distortions resulting from differences between the tax and social security systems of the different Member States whilst taking account of structural difficulties in certain sectors of industry.'[161]

Following this interpretation and the case law of the CJEU, it would be adequate to advocate for the use of article 116 TFEU when there is a generic

---

155 ibid

156 ibid 18

157 ibid

158 See J Englisch, 'Article 116 TFEU – The Nuclear Option for Qualified Majority Tax Harmonization?' (2020) [2] EC Tax Review 61; M Nouwen, 'The Market Distortion Provisions of Articles 116-117 TFEU: an Alternative Route to Qualified Majority Voting in Tax Matters?' (2021) 49 [1] Intertax 18, the latter quoting also: PJG Kapteyn, P VerLoren van Themaat, *Inleiding tot her Recht van de Europese Gemeenschappen* (5th edn, Deventer ed, Kluwer 1995) 469

159 M Nouwen, 'The Market Distortion Provisions of Articles 116–117 TFEU: an Alternative Route to Qualified Majority Voting in Tax Matters?' (2021) 49 [1] Intertax 19

160 ibid

161 Case 173/73 *Italy v Commission* [1974] ECR 709, para 17

market distortion. Still, some legal distinctions need to be made. Article 115 TFEU is about the approximation of laws while article 116 TFEU is about market distortions that need to be eliminated. Indeed, the wording of article 116 TFEU makes it similar to the State aid rules. Nonetheless, this article is in the chapter on approximation of laws and enacting a directive remains different than the application of the State aid rules. Furthermore, article 107 TFEU begins with the notion of aid that distorts the internal market while article 116 TFEU begins with the notion of disparity that distorts the internal market. In this sense, both provisions are different and do not target the exact same issues. They should not have the same initial starting point to define a market distortion (concerning the definition of the latter and because they are different by definition). Broadening article 116 TFEU to generic market distortions would be adequate as disparities are not limited to the notion of aid, the latter being more in line with the definition of specific market distortion. Then, still in the chapter on approximation of laws, unanimity voting and QMV are rules of procedure that must follow the prior legitimate repartition of competences. In this sense, article 116 TFEU must remain a lex specialis in comparison to article 115 TFEU, as a market distortion is a more severe attack on the internal market than a disparity that would need to be solved under article 115 TFEU. There is a hierarchy between both. However, it can still be considered also that the veto right in article 115 TFEU can be used as a political way to block further tax integration even when the application of the veto right is illegitimate (meaning when the tax issue depends on a legitimate competence of the EU). Still, legally and technically speaking, if article 116 TFEU is applied one day in the tax field, not only the notion of distortion that can be targeted should be explained, but also the hierarchy between article 115 TFEU and 116 TFEU. As already said, QMV and unanimity voting must be understood as a matter of procedure. However, article 115 TFEU is already an exception to article 114 TFEU, and using article 116 TFEU as a further measure needs a strict understanding of the objectives of the different articles and of their hierarchy.

Thus, this is where the principle of proportionality comes into play. This European principle is already applied by the CJEU in the discrimination test to authorize a legitimate violation of the fundamental freedoms. The same process would apply here. Article 116 TFEU is dependent from article 115 TFEU and it would be applied under the new proposed interpretation of the notion of distortion, at least to generic market distortions. It would be its scope of application. Hence, when in this framework article 115 TFEU is blocked by the veto right of one or several Member States, it could proportionally be decided to use article 116 TFEU to protect the internal market. Also, article 116 TFEU could be directly used when the targeted distortion is in its framework but not in the framework of article 115 TFEU under the application of the notion of approximation of laws as contained in article 115 TFEU itself. Thus, similarly to the application of the principle of proportionality in the discrimination test in favour of the Member States, this principle would be applied for the use of article 116 TFEU when article 115 TFEU cannot be used, but under the condition that the proposed tax directive proposes measures to solve disparities creating market distortions within the framework of article 116 TFEU. In this sense, article 116 TFEU can be legitimately used in tax matters. Also, some public interest issues could be proportionally solved through article 116 TFEU.[162] Not every disparity can be solved through this passerelle clause[163] and the application of the principle of proportionality will have to be clarified by the CJEU in the procedural application of article 116 TFEU in a strict way, but it could be one of the intermediate solutions in order to realign the legitimate competences between the EU and the Member States. Still, such legal possibility does not solve the policy consensus issue as article 116 TFEU overcomes the veto right of the Member States. To preserve the dialogue between the EU and the Member States, other solutions exist in the current decision-making process of the EU.

7.3.2.2 Shared sovereignty and comitology

The comitology procedure comes into play when the Commission, as part of the executive power of the EU, receives powers to enact a directive, a regulation or a decision as an executive act or even as a legislative act.[164] In this sense, a distinction must be made between articles 290 and 291 TFEU. The comitology committees are used to monitor the use of these powers by the Commission when it enacts such acts. Thus, the topic here is the margin that is given to the EU to use its competence to tax under articles 290 or 291 TFEU.[165] The

---

162 It would be similar to the application of the discrimination test: see pt 3, ch 6, para 6.2.1.2

163 English especially underlines the importance of the political dimension when such article is used and, as explained in the paragraph, the scope of application remains strictly framed and limited: 'its use needs to be carefully pondered, both legally and politically': J Englisch, 'Article 116 TFEU – The Nuclear Option for Qualified Majority Tax Harmonization?' (2020) [2] EC Tax Review 61

164 R Szudoczky, *The Sources of EU Law and Their Relationships: Lessons for the Field of Taxation* (IBFD Doctoral Series 32, IBFD 2014) s 4.2.1

165 There is a democratic issue with comitology, which is that it is a rather obscure procedure. The Commission adopted a proposal in 2017 (European Commission, 'Proposal for a Regulation of the Parliament and of the Council amending Regulation (EU) No 182/2011 laying down the Rules and General Principles concerning Mechanisms for Control by Member States of the Commission's Exercise of Implementing Powers' COM (2017) 85 final) to provide for more accountability and transparency but no progress has been made anymore since some reports have been published on it in 2020 and it has now been withdrawn: European

procedure that is at stake is the procedure as defined since the Lisbon treaty as, here, a solution for the future is proposed.[166]

Hence, delegated powers under article 290 TFEU and implementing powers under article 291 TFEU are often used due to the limited capacity of the legislative bodies and due to the need for experts to address all issues that need to be regulated.[167] However, the impact of such procedures remains limited in the field of direct taxation. Thus, it must be seen how its use could be increased to provide for a way for the EU to apply its competence to tax in the field of direct taxation of businesses while improving the policy consensus between the Member States.

Acts enacted according to articles 290 and 291 TFEU are secondary legislation as being acts based on an already existing act which is itself based on primary EU law.[168] First, when the Commission enacts an act under article 290 paragraph 1 TFEU, it exercises legislative powers because there is a delegation of powers. However, when the Commission must exercise implementing powers under article 291 paragraph 2 TFEU, it exercises executive powers to implement legislative acts of a general nature. The main difference is that delegated acts can only be general acts while implementing acts can be individual acts or acts with specific addressees.[169] However, with delegated acts, the Commission can supplement or amend non-essential elements, while non-legislative acts are by nature made for the concrete execution of the initial legislative act giving the implementing powers to the Commission. Thus, the CJEU underlined that, by supplementing, 'the purpose of granting a delegated power is to achieve the adoption of rules coming with the regulatory

---

Parliament, 'Revision of the Comitology Regulation' [2023] Legislative Train; European Commission, 'Report from the Commission to the European Parliament and the Council on the Working of Committees in 2021' COM (2022) 443 final, 2

166 It exists the regulatory procedure with scrutiny as from article 5a of the Comitology Decision of 1999 (Council Decision 1999/468/EC laying down the Procedures for the Exercise of Implementing Powers conferred on the Commission [1999] OJ L 184). However, this decision has been replaced by the Lisbon treaty and this procedure still exists for old acts containing it, but it cannot be used for new acts: European Commission, 'Report from the Commission to the European Parliament and the Council on the Working of Committees in 2021' COM (2022) 443 final, 1–2

167 AH Türk, 'Legislative, Delegated Acts, Comitology and Interinstitutional Conundrum in EU Law – Configuring EU Normative Spaces' (2020) 26 [5–6] European Law Journal 416–17

168 R Szudoczky, *The Sources of EU Law and Their Relationships: Lessons for the Field of Taxation* (IBFD Doctoral Series 32, IBFD 2014) s 4.2.1

169 ibid

framework as defined by the basic legislative act'[170] while, by implementing, it must be provided for 'further detail in relation to the content of legislative acts, in order to ensure it is implemented under uniform conditions in all Member States'.[171] It is the essential distinction between the two powers even if there is no meaningful criterion.[172] However, article 290 paragraph 1 TFEU still provides for a delegation and not for a habilitation. In this sense, the Commission (or the Council in special cases) must remain within the framework of the delegation and does not have any latitude in this sense, similarly to the implementing powers of article 291 TFEU. The only flexibility in article 290 TFEU is the distinction between essential and non-essential elements, knowing that 'the objective, content, scope and duration of delegation'[173] are essential elements of the delegation itself. Finally, there is no hierarchy between the acts enacted according to article 290 TFEU or to article 291 TFEU.[174] There is a hierarchy only with the act authorizing the delegation or the implementation.[175]

Then, comitology committees are different from intermediate bodies as they are legally regulated in EU law as part of the institutional system.[176] 'Comitology is a set of procedures under which the Commission adopts measures of an executive nature working "in tandem with a committee of representatives of national governments whose role is to oversee it"'.[177][178] However, with time, the procedure evolved in order to become a 'deliberative problem-solving'[179] system. The procedures are network structures characterized by

---

170 Case C-427/12 *Commission v European Parliament and Council* [2014] ECLI:EU:C:2014:170, para 38

171 ibid para 39

172 AH Türk, 'Legislative, Delegated Acts, Comitology and Interinstitutional Conundrum in EU Law – Configuring EU Normative Spaces' (2020) 26 [5–6] European Law Journal 421

173 R Szudoczky, *The Sources of EU Law and Their Relationships: Lessons for the Field of Taxation* (IBFD Doctoral Series 32, IBFD 2014) s 4.2.1

174 ibid

175 ibid

176 L Del Federico, 'Monitoring Decision-Making, Enforcement and Application of EU Tax Law: The Role of Intermediate Bodies and Lobbies' in P Pistone (ed), *European Tax Integration: Law, Policy and Politics* (IBFD 2018) 194

177 D Chalmers, G Davis, G Monti, *European Union Law* (2nd edn, Cambridge University Press 2010) 117

178 R Szudoczky, *The Sources of EU Law and Their Relationships: Lessons for the Field of Taxation* (IBFD Doctoral Series 32, IBFD 2014) s 4.2.2

179 P Adriaansen, 'Comitology: An Alternative Route towards European Direct Tax Integration' in D Weber (ed), *Traditional and Alternative Routes to European Tax Integration* (IBFD 2010) 136

administrative cooperation.[180] Thus, comitology applies when the Commission has received the power to enact an implementing act to execute a previous general act.[181] Consequently, as stated, comitology currently only applies on subsequent acts through implementing powers under article 291 paragraph 3 TFEU. Delegated acts of article 290 TFEU are not formally concerned by the comitology procedure. Instead, article 290 paragraph 2 TFEU provides for a power of supervision of the Council and of the European Parliament. However, due to the role of comitology committees (experts in their fields), it is argued that the Commission should still consult them under this procedure,[182] and it intends to do so but only on a consultative basis.[183]

Furthermore, a comitology committee is not mandatory and so they do not exist for all implementing acts.[184] Their use is a discretionary power at the EU level.[185] The comitology committees are set up by the legislator (Council and European Parliament or Council alone) and they include one representative of each Member State.[186] Then, when the Commission adopts an implementing act, if there is a comitology committee, two general procedures are possible (with a third one, which is an appeal procedure).

First, there is the examination procedure[187] for measures with general scope and measures with a potentially significant impact (including the taxation area). If a qualified majority is attained in the committee, the Commission must adopt the act. However, if the qualified majority votes against the act, the

[180] R Szudoczky, *The Sources of EU Law and Their Relationships: Lessons for the Field of Taxation* (IBFD Doctoral Series 32, IBFD 2014) s 4.2.2

[181] Regulation n 182/2011 of the European Parliament and of the Council laying down the Rules and General Principles concerning Mechanisms for Control by the Member States of the Commission's Exercise of Implementing Powers [2011] OJ L 55/13, art 1

[182] See R Szudoczky, *The Sources of EU Law and Their Relationships: Lessons for the Field of Taxation* (IBFD Doctoral Series 32, IBFD 2014) s 4.2.2

[183] European Commission, 'Implementation of Article 290 of the Treaty on the Functioning of the European Union' (Communication) COM (2009) 673 final

[184] See eg L Del Federico, 'Monitoring Decision-Making, Enforcement and Application of EU Tax Law: The Role of Intermediate Bodies and Lobbies' in P Pistone (ed), *European Tax Integration: Law, Policy and Politics* (IBFD 2018) 193

[185] AH Türk, 'Legislative, Delegated Acts, Comitology and Interinstitutional Conundrum in EU Law – Configuring EU Normative Spaces' (2020) 26 [5-6] European Law Journal 421

[186] Regulation n 182/2011 of the European Parliament and of the Council laying down the Rules and General Principles concerning Mechanisms for Control by the Member States of the Commission's Exercise of Implementing Powers [2011] OJ L 55/13

[187] ibid art 5

Commission may not adopt it. Then, if no qualified majority is attained, the Commission can either adopt the act (but not in specific fields such as taxation where an appeal for the implementation is necessary) or submit a new version. Second, there is the advisory procedure[188] that is generally used for all other implementing acts. The Commission keeps its power to decide but should 'take the utmost account'[189] of the committee's opinion. Third, there is an appeal procedure[190] in front of an appeal committee when the first committee voted against an implementing act in the examination procedure. If the appeal committee also votes against the act, then it cannot be implemented at all.

Thus, formally, QMV through comitology only exists under article 291 TFEU. However, the line is very fine between article 290 TFEU and article 291 TFEU. Szudoczky underlines the lack of distinction between the two categories with the example of the Common Consolidated Corporate Tax Base (CCCTB) directive proposal.[191] Some aspects of the proposal were subject to article 290 TFEU while other aspects were subject to article 291 TFEU without any consistent repartition. She explains that the lack of clear dividing line is problematic as the procedure is different.[192] The Commission enjoys a broader scope of discretion under the comitology procedure of article 291 TFEU, where the role of the committees is restricted, than under article 290 TFEU, where it is strictly supervised by the Council or the European Parliament or both. Yet, as there is no defined dividing line between the two, they must be envisaged together. Furthermore, in the field of direct taxation, they are both limited by the first act authorizing the delegation or the implementation: there is still the unanimity requirement. Still, supplementing through delegation can provide for interesting perspectives. Yet, it is article 291 TFEU which is the most interesting because of the importance of the political consensus, which must become a policy consensus under the theory of shared sovereignty. As Del Federico states, comitology can bring more flexibility in the decision-making process while considering the different Member States' interests.[193] Indeed,

---

[188] ibid art 4

[189] ibid

[190] ibid art 6

[191] R Szudoczky, *The Sources of EU Law and Their Relationships: Lessons for the Field of Taxation* (IBFD Doctoral Series 32, IBFD 2014) s 4.2.2

[192] ibid

[193] L Del Federico, 'Monitoring Decision-Making, Enforcement and Application of EU Tax Law: The Role of Intermediate Bodies and Lobbies' in P Pistone (ed), *European Tax Integration: Law, Policy and Politics* (IBFD 2018) 193. However, he also underlines the risk of excessive politicization and abuse of the system by different actors that still exists. It is the risk of sherpacracy for instance: sherpas are informal representatives of the heads of States and governments, they negotiate

the Council, even if it is an EU institution, is under the banner of the Member States when unanimity voting applies. It is a political matter that can be balanced by political consensus if they accept to apply the QMV. Such political consensus can be reached and become a policy consensus through the comitology procedure, where a technical dialogue can take place. In effect, comitology committees have already been used in the field of taxation and especially in the field of direct taxation, with the CCCTB directive proposal or the mutual assistance directive on administrative cooperation.[194] The use of comitology, even as a new phenomenon,[195] is not alien to the tax field.

Hence, the theory of shared sovereignty can find application through comitology. The distinction between the EU and the Member States operates at the level of their competences. However, there is one sovereignty that should be expressed through common interests. Member States are reluctant to accept QMV in the field of direct taxation of businesses because they want to protect their own private interests, even if some areas of the field of direct taxation of businesses depend on an EU competence. Thus, the protection of their veto right by the Member States is not legitimate and blocks the process of the European integration process. As such, the comitology process is a perfect expression of a dialogue between the EU and the Member States to reach the policy consensus.

There are two options. The first is the preservation of unanimity voting concerning the act authorizing the implementing act. The change is only political. The Member States, knowing that the comitology procedure applies, can agree to give a broad implementing power to the Commission and then can engage a dialogue. This option remains limited for the same reasons as the deadlock of unanimity voting. The comitology procedure remains obscure and essentially a discretionary power of the Commission. As such, a comitology committee could be either put in place or not under the examination procedure. There would be no legal safeguard for the Member States. This means that the Member States and the EU remain in a political tension due to the Member States' fear of losing out on their individual interests, instead of

now very often on behalf of them and they can define by themselves positions on key issues in the process of decision-making: European Parliament, 'Working Document on Overcoming the Deadlock of Unanimity Voting' [2021] Committee on Constitutional Affairs, 8 <www.europarl.europa.eu/cmsdata/233740/AFCO%20Working%20Document%20on%20Overcoming%20the%20Deadlock%20of%20Unanimity%20Voting.pdf> accessed 25 November 2025

194 L Del Federico, 'Monitoring Decision-Making, Enforcement and Application of EU Tax Law: The Role of Intermediate Bodies and Lobbies' in P Pistone (ed), *European Tax Integration: Law, Policy and Politics* (IBFD 2018) 193

195 ibid

working together as part of the same system. This is why the theory of shared sovereignty is necessary to restore trust between the two levels by explaining, through legitimacy, the logic of system that must apply to the benefit of both the EU and the Member States. Therefore, the second option is the application of QMV for the act authorizing the implementing act. It can be through an existing article of the EU treaties[196] or through a treaty revision. Then, comitology committees would be mandatory in the tax field under the examination procedure to decide on the implementing acts. The Member States would still be involved in the procedure, with a two-step possibility to refuse an act that they do not want in the field of direct taxation. The first step would be in the Council, with QMV and the adoption of the general act. The second step would be through the role of representatives through the mandatory examination procedure. In this sense, even if QMV applies instead of unanimity voting, the Member States can give their opinions and assert their interests twice. By having the possibility to do it twice, there would be a safety valve for them. In the end, if the general act and the implementing act are adopted, it can be considered that a policy consensus has been reached. This could be a way to balance the interests between the Member State level and the EU level. Such procedure would be a concrete expression of the shared sovereignty between the EU and the Member States: through QMV, the EU can access its legitimate competence to tax in legitimate fields of application, and through comitology, there is a true policy dialogue for the expression of the Member States' interests. In a way, this would legalize the policy consensus into a formal procedure.

7.4 CONCLUSION

The legitimacy of the EU's competence to tax in the field of direct taxation of businesses as a market-based competence under its general shared competence for the internal market has been demonstrated. This means a shared competence to tax with the Member States by integration within the shared competence of the EU for the internal market. Then the current limits of positive integration through article 115 TFEU in the field of direct taxation of businesses, especially through the material understanding of unanimity voting, was also demonstrated. This illustrates the mismatch between the European legitimacy for a competence in the field of direct taxation of businesses under the theory of shared sovereignty and the means the EU has to exercise it.

Yet, the EU knows, as illustrated by its political agenda, that it must achieve its sovereign objectives for the benefit of the competitiveness of both the

196 For instance, through article 116 TFEU

internal market and the individual Member States. Here, the theory of shared sovereignty becomes necessary to justify the logic of system that must apply between the EU and the Member States. In practice, for the EU and the Member States to legitimately share the competence to tax in the field of direct taxation of businesses, they must overcome the political tension that can exist between both levels due to individual interests and establish a policy dialogue. Through a policy consensus, technical fields of application within the competence to tax in the field of direct taxation of businesses could be legitimately attributed between the EU and the Member States. A logic of system would be respected from the established shared sovereignty of both the EU and the Member States until the practical application of the competence to tax to the interest of both levels. A principle of coherence between both levels would be in place for a fair and legitimate application of the shared competence to tax at each level. This principle of coherence is the legal application of the theory of shared sovereignty. It is inherent to the logic of system and it must provide for the respect of the policy consensus between the EU and the Member States. Technical legal dispositions such as unanimity voting would no longer be a means to prevent the EU from achieving its sovereign objectives. Consequently, as a call to action, through respect for the theory of shared sovereignty, and so for the legal principle of coherence, in order to have legitimacy in the application of the competence to tax within the internal market, the Member States should step back to let the EU apply the competence to tax in its legitimate fields of application.

Thus, within its specific framework, article 116 TFEU can be considered as a solution to apply the legitimate competence to tax of the EU under strict conditions. However, as the policy consensus must not be neglected, the comitology process is also proposed as a solution to balance the Member States' interests and the EU interests to maintain a policy dialogue between both levels. Treaty revision remains the last solution. Overall, the legal provisions should be exercised in adequation with the theory of shared sovereignty, according to which direct tax policy in the field of business taxation should be shared between the EU and the Member States under the logic of system.

8. Conclusion to *EU Sovereignty and Direct Taxation of Businesses*

In the field of direct taxation of businesses, it seems necessary to solve the distortions that prevent the achievement of the internal market to the benefit of both the EU and the Member States as being a common project, and so objective. To do so, empirical observation of the relations between both levels permits two assertions. The first is that the concept of sovereignty is an abstract concept that remains necessary for the organization of legal systems. As such, it obeys a specific methodology where appearance and recognition are central elements. Also, the new legal organization in which the European Union (EU) and the Member States are intertwined is not alien to the concept of sovereignty, as the latter is deemed necessary. Therefore, a theory of shared sovereignty has been proposed in order to explain that both levels, the European level and the Member State level, form only one legal system where the concept of sovereignty self-manifests as in every other kind of legal system. Still, according to Leibniz's theory of the monad, even if the term 'shared sovereignty' is used to explain the specific situation of the EU and of the Member States, it is the concept of sovereignty as a concept of unity that manifests itself through the European order and the Member States' orders. What is specifically provided through the theory of shared sovereignty, according to the monad of Leibniz, is that there is a principle of coherence that must regulate the relations between the EU and the Member States, putting the emphasis on the policy dialogue.

Once the relation between the EU and the Member States is explained according to the concept of sovereignty, there are logical concrete consequences. There must be coherence between the two levels. This is demonstrated concretely through the field of direct taxation of businesses according to the concept of legitimacy. There are inadequacies between the European objectives, as sovereign objectives, and its means to achieve them, as its competences. The consequence is that there exist harmful disparities (distortions) to the detriment of the internal market that cannot be adequately solved. Such distortions in the field of direct taxation of businesses are impeding the evolution of the European integration process. In this sense, they put into question the existence of the internal market, and this is why the theory of shared sovereignty is proposed in order to solve such inadequacies. As such, the second assertion is that the EU has the legitimacy to get a shared competence to tax (power to enact the tax law), as a direct competence, in the field of direct taxation of businesses in order to coherently achieve and preserve the internal market to the benefit of both the EU and the Member States as forming one legal system. Indeed, the value pattern of the EU, which is symbolized by its sovereign objectives and the interpretation work of the Court of Justice of the European Union (CJEU), must adequately correspond to its governmental outputs, which are adequate competences for a neutral and competitive internal market.

In order to do so, by getting a shared competence to tax, the EU must also get a shared power to decide in terms of direct tax policy. The Member States should accept that the EU has the legitimate competence in specific fields of direct taxation of businesses. As such, a policy dialogue should be envisaged between the two levels according to the theory of shared sovereignty, and so according to the principle of coherence that should regulate the relations between both levels, in order to reach a policy consensus to share the competence to tax. This means that the Member States should agree to give up, for example, on the technical requirement of unanimity voting of article 115 of the treaty on the functioning of the European Union (TFEU) in specific fields of direct taxation of businesses that legitimately depend on the EU. There are treaty solutions to do so, such as article 116 TFEU (respecting the provision's requirements), where Qualified Majority Voting (QMV) applies instead of unanimity voting. Comitology committees could also be a place where the policy consensus could be reached. Treaty revision should be envisaged as the last solution. The most important matter remains to respect the policy dialogue and the principle of coherence that must apply between the European level and the Member State level according to the theory of shared sovereignty. This theory must provide for a strong theoretical background for the European integration process. Such background should bring coherence and rationale in the political agenda of the EU. It should help to restore the legitimacy of the EU. Indeed, as said by Brinkhorst, 'the future of Europe is either becoming irrelevant or becoming more relevant with more European sovereignty and autonomy'.[1] The European objectives must be assumed, and a choice must be made to accept the EU as such or to step back.

---

1 LJ Brinkhorst, 'Common Market Law Review – A Journal for All Seasons' [2023] International Law Talk, A Wolters Kluwer Podcast <www.wolterskluwer.com/en/expert-insights/common-market-law-review-a-journal-for-all-seasons> accessed 27 November 2025

Finally, it is considered that the EU does not yet have the democratic legitimacy in order to have a power to tax (power to levy taxes) and so to get tax-based own resources. There are constitutional requirements, such as the motto 'no taxation without representation', that must be respected. This situation may change depending on the evolution of the European integration progress.

Index